Advance Praise for *Hang Tough*

"Stunning! This thoroughly researched and intimate work by Erik Dorr and Jared Frederick, complete with many never-before-published photos and color plates featuring personal artifacts, is a must read for anyone interested in the life, character, and leadership abilities of Band of Brothers hero Major Dick Winters."

—Larry Alexander, bestselling author of *Biggest Brother: The Life of Major Dick Winters, the Man Who Led the Band of Brothers*

"Ever since the public became aware of Dick Winters's exceptional leadership, there has been endless curiosity to learn what made him great. Winters left us a legacy of thoughtful and eloquent writings, in both his diary and correspondence. Erik Dorr and Jared Frederick have edited those words into this informative compilation. The book demonstrates that equal parts of courage and intelligence defined Major Winters as a warrior and an exemplary leader of paratroopers. This presentation is enhanced with color photos of Winters memorabilia, currently displayed at the Gettysburg Museum of History. Perhaps we have not seen the last of books on Dick Winters, but it is unlikely that this one will ever be surpassed."

—Mark A. Bando, author of six books on the 101st Airborne Division in World War II

"*Hang Tough* provides powerful insight into Dick Winters's military career, meaningfully integrating World War II artifacts now on display at the Gettysburg Museum of History. Following his exciting epic through Europe, from Normandy to Germany, the book skillfully shares the stories of Major Winters that have inspired so many."

—Michel de Trez, founder of the D-Day Experience Museum in Normandy

"What a compelling and absorbing book. Dick Winters's letters shed fascinating light on his character and motivations, greatly enhancing our understandings of one of America's most iconic World War II heroes. Expertly edited and framed with a highly knowledgeable contextual narrative, *Hang Tough* offers perspective and detail of one soldier's extraordinary wartime career."

—James Holland, bestselling author of *Normandy '44: D-Day and the Epic 77-Day Battle for France*

HANG TOUGH

THE WWII LETTERS AND ARTIFACTS OF MAJOR DICK WINTERS

ERIK DORR AND JARED FREDERICK

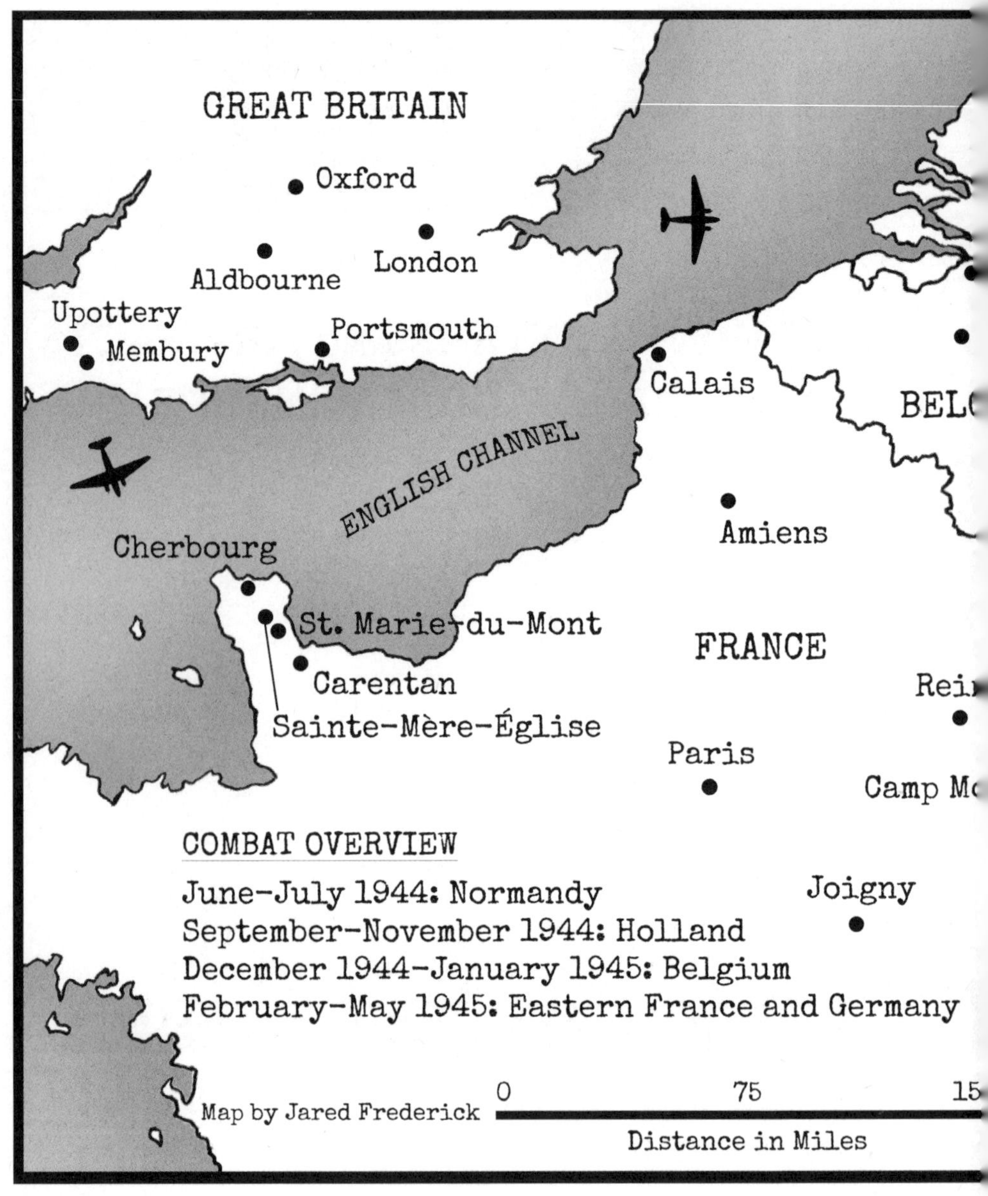
GREAT BRITAIN
Oxford
London
Aldbourne
Upottery
Membury
Portsmouth
Calais
ENGLISH CHANNEL
Amiens
Cherbourg
St. Marie-du-Mont
FRANCE
Carentan
Sainte-Mère-Église
Paris
COMBAT OVERVIEW
June-July 1944: Normandy
September-November 1944: Holland
December 1944-January 1945: Belgium
February-May 1945: Eastern France and Germany
Joigny
Map by Jared Frederick
0
75
Distance in Miles

HOLLAND
EUROPEAN THEATER
of OPERATIONS
...
DICK WINTERS and the
506th PARACHUTE INFANTRY REGIMENT
101st AIRBORNE DIVISION
SPRING 1944 - FALL 1945
AIRBORNE
Berlin
Nuenen
Eindhoven
Cologne
LUXEMBOURG
GERMANY
Drulingen
Haguenau
Hochstett
Stuttgart
Ulm
Munich
Landsberg am Lech
Berchtesgaden
N
Zürich
AUSTRIA
Zell am See
Kaprun
SWITZERLAND

A PERMUTED PRESS BOOK

ISBN: 978-1-68261-917-9
ISBN (eBook): 978-1-68261-918-6

Hang Tough:
The WWII Letters and Artifacts of Major Dick Winters

The authors are grateful to Major Dick Winters for granting approval for broad use of his letters before his passing. Winters wanted future generations to know the details of what he and his comrades endured in defense of their country. The Gettysburg Museum of History, from which a copy of these letters resides, disclaims ownership, but rather retains non-exclusive use of the letters for the purposes of ensuring the historical record is accurately conveyed.

Permuted Press, LLC
New York • Nashville
permutedpress.com

Published in the United States of America

"Wars do not make men great, but wars sometimes bring out the greatness in good men."

For DeEtta

TABLE OF CONTENTS

A NOTE FROM THE EDITORS

Sixteen million Americans served in uniform during the Second World War—one out of every eight citizens. Scores of veterans meticulously documented, preserved, and revisited their wartime journeys for the benefit of posterity. One such figure was Major Richard Davis Winters of the 101st Airborne's 506th Parachute Infantry Regiment. Born January 21, 1918, in the rich agricultural belt of southeastern Pennsylvania, his placid upbringing did not portend the destiny of distinguished soldier.

In certain respects, Dick Winters bears similarities to American Civil War legend Joshua Chamberlain. As the firstborn sons of pacifist mothers, they were imparted the virtues of self-reliance, introspection, and education. Introverts in their youths, they overcame certain insecurities via higher learning. They were driven by an undying motivation to grow and surpass expectations. When the United States confronted its greatest challenges, both eagerly sought to lead men in battle. Neither possessed formal military education, but both committed themselves to self-study and advancement. The two officers conducted themselves with great poise in the iconic clashes of their ages. Like thousands of fellow field officers, they contributed to morally driven causes of liberation. Both rest eternally under surprisingly modest headstones adorned with tokens of appreciation.

The greatest commonalities are indicated by postwar legacies. Although Chamberlain and Winters followed different career paths (academic and agricultural, respectively), the years in uniform served as the definitive episodes of their lives. Seemingly reserved in dispositions, the Mainer and Pennsylvanian energetically maintained ties to their wartime associations. Their fascinating tales of courage under fire captured the imagination of accomplished writers whose works, in turn, were adapted into wildly successful Hollywood productions. Chamberlain and Winters transcended the status of historical figures and entered the pantheon of popular imagination. The actions of each came to symbolize the struggles of a generation.

Band of Brothers, the far-reaching HBO miniseries that cemented Winters's fame, debuted a mere two days before the September 11 attacks. Parallels were inevitably drawn between past and present. According to the *Los Angeles Times*, "The series, while thanking the generation before, helped settle and inspire the one ahead."[1]

The film depicted troops who "were resilient and stuck together. It was a powerful message to a nation trying to overcome something like 9/11," observed Col. Eric Kail, a combat veteran and West Point professor. "Great strength is not from ourselves but from each other," he added. "That's a message soldiers have been trying to get out for a long time." Winters was an evocative conveyer of that message.[2]

Among those embodying the major's example was Pfc. Andrew Collins, who completed basic training at Fort Jackson in the spring of 2007. Collins, who repetitively absorbed lessons from *Band of Brothers* in his high school years, actualized such insights. "Being able to think on your feet and remain collected garners a certain amount of respect. But it's not always your first instinct," Collins admitted. "When a certain moment called for action, I sometimes wondered, 'What would Dick Winters do?' That philosophy served me well. Before I knew it, I was a confidant for comrades seeking advice. It seemed strange at age twenty-one to have soldiers younger and older than me seeking my guidance. As I reflect, I recognize Dick Winters as one whose attitudes I tried so hard to emulate." Collins maintained that mindset as a sergeant during a tour of duty in Iraq. The miniseries that inspired him remains a popular go-to for service members at home and overseas.[3]

One phrase exemplifies the Winters mantra more than any other: "Hang tough." The simple expression, with which he often concluded correspondence, epitomized his chief ethic. "That means you do your best every day," he claimed. If one abides by this philosophy, no day will be squandered. Though not commonly used during the war itself, the encouraging motto became Winters's byline later in life.[4]

When one delves deeper into the major's story, characters omitted in books and films emerge. Perhaps most notable among these personalities is a young lady from the mountains of North Carolina named DeEtta Almon. DeEtta was not an object of lust but rather an affectionate counselor, a pen pal who engaged in spirited intellectual discussion. The importance of her letters to the war-weary paratrooper is irrefutable. Throughout World War II, she composed over one hundred letters, and Dick responded in kind. While the whereabouts of the letters written by DeEtta are uncertain, those penned by Winters were returned to and transcribed by him and his wife in the 1990s. Those revealing glimpses into the 1940s serve as the basis for this book.

Our project does not claim to be the definitive biography of Dick Winters. Nor should it be considered a comprehensive history of his lionized unit. We seek to present Winters as a man of his times, adding context to his own words. How were his motivations, principles, and worldview representative of Americans at war? How did his experiences in barracks and on battlefields align with those in comparable circumstances? To answer these questions we have employed a wide array of primary and secondary sources to present broader perspective. Throughout the text, each of his letters is bridged with supporting commentary to offer a coherent historical timeline. With the exception of minor punctuation, bracketed points of clarification, and the occasional deletion of vague commentary, the text remains as Winters recorded it. Most letter headlines shown were added by Winters during his 1996 edits.

Several works were of particular value in our efforts to fully comprehend Dick Winters. *Biggest Brother* by Larry Alexander offers a richly detailed account of the major's life through 2004. Published shortly thereafter was Dick's own memoir, *Beyond Band of Brothers*, cowritten by his close friend, Col. Cole Kingseed. The engaging personal recollection ranks as one of the finer reminiscences of the frontlines. Following Winters's passing in 2011, Kingseed authored the equally compelling *Conversations with Major Dick Winters*. Kingseed shares an intimate, thematic perspective on the factors that made Winters a unique leader. Meanwhile, filmmaker Tim Gray's 2012 documentary, entitled *Dick Winters: Hang Tough*, offers helpful visualization of Winters's legacy. Dick's letters to DeEtta are sprinkled throughout many of these works but are rarely exhibited in full detail. There is inherent academic value in these wartime testimonies. Like newspapers of the era, the correspondence offers readers immersive opportunities. The letters plunge us into iconic places and moments of the historical record. Such perspectives, as one historian remarked, are "intellectual windows" that open to the past.[5]

Infusing additional layers of history into the narrative, we have incorporated a host of compelling World War II artifacts, documents, and photos into the book. Scores of these relics were used by Dick Winters himself. Other showcased items pertain to people and places Winters encountered throughout his journeys. We cordially invite you to view many of these noteworthy mementos in person at the Gettysburg Museum of History in Pennsylvania. Gettysburg is a fitting landmark to reflect upon World War II history. As the postwar home of Dwight Eisenhower, the final resting place of 1,600 GIs and the sister city of Sainte-Mère-Église, the area was also home for Dick Winters when he started a family.

This project would not have been possible without the steadfast support and assistance of key individuals. Our ever-dependable agent, Greg Johnson of WordServe Literary, found a worthy home for our project. We extend appreciation to Kathy Frederick and Cheryl Reichling, who have guided us in many realms of our lives, including this task. Recognition is due to Dan Jenkins, who skillfully photographed many of the artifacts highlighted within these pages. We express gratitude to Bill and Patrick Shea, who have graciously loaned select Dick Winters artifacts to the Gettysburg Museum of History. We likewise thank Bob Hoffman, one of Dick Winters's most trusted friends, who was supportive of our endeavor from the outset and offered invaluable perspective. Mark Bando, through his impressive writings and research, has offered crucial insight on the airborne experience during World War II. Similarly, Michel de Trez is an inspiration to any collector or museum that wishes to tell stories with artifacts. Immense appreciation is due to Maj. Kyle Hatzinger of the United States Army, who took great time and effort to review this text and offer suggestions. Heather King, Daniel Schuette, Travis Atria, and the entire Permuted Press team professionally helped us craft a stronger, beautifully designed book. To all of these people we are sincerely grateful.

We earnestly hope readers gain fresh insights on Dick Winters and his times. The distant wartime relationship of Dick and DeEtta reminds one never to underestimate the value of quiet dignity and friendship. There is much we can learn from this story.

World War II veteran paratrooper Bradford Freeman, a gentle Mississippian we know as "Mr. B," followed Dick Winters throughout much of the war in Europe. Quiet and noble, he still resides on the humble farmstead where he and Winters once swapped war stories. Winters referred to him as the "Salt of the Earth." Our friend Chris Langlois (grandson of Easy Company medic Eugene "Doc" Roe) likewise noted, "The world could use more Brad Freemans." When asked if he would write the foreword for this book, Freeman simply replied, "I would like that." We are honored to share his words. At age ninety-four, Freeman returned to Normandy for the campaign's seventy-fifth anniversary. "I think about them all the time," he said of his fallen comrades. "They are still back there. I haven't forgot it." Nor should we forget.[6]

Hang Tough,

Erik Dorr and Jared Frederick

February 29, 2020

FOREWORD

I am from Caledonia, Mississippi, and I served with Mr. Winters during World War II. You all call him "Major Winters," but I think of him as "Mr. Winters." You see, I was a friend with him more so as a civilian than as a soldier. I came in to "Easy" (Easy Company, 506th Parachute Infantry Regiment, 101st Airborne Division) in England. I was not trained in Toccoa, Georgia, like most of the other fellows. I did, though, fight with "Easy" through the whole war, except when I was wounded in the leg by a "Screamin' Mimi" near Neuville during the Battle of the Bulge. I was hit along with Ed Joint. The wound I got took me out for a few months, but I later joined back up with the fellows in Germany.

I first met Mr. Winters when I arrived in England. He picked me and a few other boys up in a Jeep and took us yonder to south England near Aldbourne. I was assigned to 2nd Platoon's Mortar Squad. "Wild Bill" Guarnere was my sergeant, and Don Malarkey was my mortar man. (Mortars were manned and carried by two men. They worked in teams.)

Around that time, Winters had a talk with me and even asked if I wanted to go to officer-candidate school. I replied, "No, I like being a private."

I would say I became pretty good friends with Mr. Winters, about as much as an enlisted man could be with an officer. I remember during one inspection, I handed him my M-1 Garand Rifle with the bolt open. Mr. Winters looked at it, closed the bolt, and tried to give it back to me. I just stood there and wouldn't take it. You know you are not supposed to take a rifle with the bolt closed. Winters stood there and looked at me. Then he smiled, opened the bolt, and gave the rifle back. This time I took it. He knew I was doing the right thing.

I have many good memories of Mr. Winters during the war. To sum it up, I always thought he really cared about the boys. I can only describe him as a really good teacher you could look up to. He would never let you down. I am most proud of my friendship with him after the war.

Mr. Winters and me didn't go to all the reunions like some of the fellows. We both started going a bit later. Mr. Winters would always have a private party when he did go with a select few of his friends. He and his wife, Miss Ethel, would always invite Willie (my wife) and me.

I am glad Erik and Jared are sharing Mr. Winters's letters. I think they will help people better understand the man I knew and respected so much. Folks should know what we all went through during the war. Every time I am asked to speak about my service, questions come up about *Band of Brothers*, Easy Company, or Mr. Winters.

He was a very good commander and a very good friend. I miss him very much.

Bradford C. Freeman
February 2020

Left: Bradford Freeman during the war. Right, top to bottom: Winters and Freeman at a reunion, Freeman and Erik Dorr, Freeman and Jared Frederick.

Introduction to the Letters By Richard D. Winters 1996

After graduating from Franklin and Marshall College in June 1941, I could start life in the real world in one of two ways:

1) Find a Job

   The Great Depression was just beginning to take a turn for the better, but jobs were still very hard to find.

2) Volunteer for the Army

   The compulsory draft for all young men was in effect. When your number was called you were obliged to spend one year in the service.

I decided to volunteer for the army at this time and not wait until my draft number was pulled. I would fulfill that obligation and then be free of a commitment to the army.

After volunteering and being sent to Camp Croft, South Carolina, in September 1941 for basic training, a friend of mine, also from Lancaster, Pennsylvania, and I decided to spend a weekend in Asheville, North Carolina. Having limited funds ($21 a month), we checked into the YMCA, where for a nominal price you could get a bunk in one of their dormitories. After checking in I found myself chatting with Mr. Hazard, the director of the Y.

Sunday morning Trent (my buddy) and I had plans of getting a few extra hours sleep. However, my plans were changed when Mr. Hazard came into the bunk room, gave me a shake, and announced that I was going to church with him. We went to his church, a Christian Scientist church. To attend a church of this denomination was a first for me. Trent, being a good Catholic, was spared all this and left to get that extra sack time.

After church one of the good families demonstrated the truth and goodness of the fabled phrase, "Southern hospitality." They invited Mr. Hazard and me to come to their home for a nice Sunday dinner.

The next week two Asheville girls approached Mr. Hazard for the names and addresses of some soldiers who might be appreciative of a package of brownies and fudge. As it turned out Trent and I were the two lucky soldiers who received benefit of the girls' goodwill toward the soldiers in the armed services.

We immediately sent a letter of thanks to the girls and mentioned that we would like to come back to that lovely "city in the sky" and thank them personally.

What followed for me was that I found a wonderful friend in DeEtta Almon. Between November 1941 and January 1946, when I was discharged from the army, she was my best friend and pen pal. She replied to every letter I wrote, and if I did not write, she continued to send letters. She kept me on the ball and helped me keep my head up.

I met her once after the war ended. We said goodbye and each went our separate ways with no further meetings or letters.

Fifty years later, in December 1995, I received a telephone call one evening. The voice on the other end of the line was one of a young lady.

"Mr. Winters?"

"Yes."

"Band of Brothers?"

"Yes."

"Do you remember a girl by the name of DeEtta Almon from Asheville, North Carolina?"

"Oh, my goodness, yes! I have many good memories of DeEtta!"

"I am her daughter, Hazel."

After establishing once again this long contact with DeEtta, we exchanged a few telephone calls and letters.

HANG TOUGH

In January 1996 DeEtta sent me two big scrapbooks that contained 117 letters that I, my father, and my sister Ann had written to her during World War II. She had saved almost every one, put them in scrapbooks and now, after all these years, she returned them all to me.

My wife Ethel and I read every letter. We found them interesting; in fact, for me they were fascinating. We decided to put each letter and its accompanying envelope in a special file, then make five copies of the original letter and five copies of the letter that Ethel would type. In the typewritten copy Ethel would correct the spelling and add a little punctuation to help make it a pleasure and not a hardship to read. However, care would be taken not to change the structure, the wording, or the meaning of the original in any way. The first copy was for DeEtta, which we plan to personally deliver to her on her birthday, May 14, 1996. Tim and Jill (our children), Ethel, and I would each have our personal copy.

I invite you to share my letters to DeEtta. Between the lines you will know exactly what DeEtta's letters to me had to say. You will find, from time to time, a 1996 P.S. that I have added to a letter, an untold story, sometimes a sudden memory that a letter has jolted to life.

[...] Following the letter of June 2, 1944, there is a summary of the previous three letters describing my feelings on the eve of D-Day.[1]

CHAPTER ONE
THAT LUCKY YANKEE

Beginnings to December 1941

He was a quiet boy. Reserved and hesitant to associate with schoolmates, the blond-haired, blue-eyed youth faded into the background of his classrooms. Spurning attention, he favored the solitude of books and exercise. The young man perceived himself as helplessly awkward, a still wallflower. Years later, despite his status as a decorated combat leader, he confessed, "As for social activities, I am a Class A flop." The boy's mother, a traditional woman of old Mennonite stock, instilled in him the durable moral fiber fundamental to his personal growth. His shyness and tranquil lifestyle in verdant Amish country offered little indication of a prominent future. He adored Babe Ruth, admired Milton Hershey, and enjoyed passing a football on fall afternoons. Dick Winters was little more than a normal kid.[1]

Born during the Great War, Winters was raised among one of the highest concentrations of German-Americans in the nation. Whereas anti-German sentiment flowed rampant in the age of World War I, the communities of Dick's upbringing—New Holland, Ephrata, and Lancaster—deeply bore the traditions of the Pennsylvania Dutch. Winters expressed an affinity for animals and likewise exhibited fondness for the agrarian diligence of his rural neighbors. Their "work ethic rubs off and it counts for the fact that each day, you strive to do your best," he recalled of the Anabaptists. The surroundings nurtured Dick's lifelong characteristics of simplicity, autonomy, and a heartfelt connection to the land.[2]

Dick graduated from a class of 247 at the Stevens and Boys' High School in 1937, where his two primary interests were athletics and chemistry. His senior yearbook photo revealed a pupil already sporting a square jaw. The image caption fittingly attested, "Powerful muscles—powerful mind! No better combination!" Although Winters's genial father thought him an academic underachiever, classmates believed Dick possessed abundant amounts of brawn and brains. Parents Richard and Edith worked respectively as an electrical foreman and a homemaker. In addition to caring for Dick and his sister, Ann, Edith produced corsets for supplemental income. Richard the elder, meanwhile, warned his son of the dangers of alcohol and tobacco—sincere cautions stemming from personal experiences. "[M]y grandfather was a confirmed alcoholic," Dick confessed decades later to Cole Kingseed. "I saw what it did to his family. So I never took a drink."[3]

The mother and father labored tirelessly and never took income for granted. The same spring Dick graduated, the federal government estimated that seven million Americans were unemployed. Dick intended to earn his keep and help sustain the household on Lancaster's South West End Avenue. Senior procured employment for his son at the Pennsylvania Power and Light electric company. In that capacity, Dick painted sky-high utility towers for the generous wage of forty cents per hour. He later deemed the altitudinous hazards as "prophetic of my future with the paratroopers," ancillary pay for excess danger.[4]

Awaiting an end to the Great Depression, Winters concluded higher education would diminish financial strife and present vocational opportunities. He thus enrolled at Franklin & Marshall College—a local institution that marked its sesquicentennial the autumn Winters enrolled. War preparations were apparent in new curriculum at the college, including an aviation program introduced in 1939.

Though tuition was less than two hundred dollars, Dick was obliged to tighten his fiscal responsibility and sharpen his study regimen. He withdrew from his fraternity due to the added costs—never having been comfortable at the club's social gatherings to begin with. Winters buried himself in used books, resisting freshman tendencies of philandering and reckless spending. He resided at the family home. Maintaining relationships beyond kin was not a priority. While some perceived him as a loner, Winters was in fact experiencing an intellectual awakening. Although he ultimately majored in economics and science (with honors), Winters savored philosophical classes. Such courses stimulated critical thought and encouraged creativity. The collegiate experience fostered within him a desire to succeed in all things—a compelling drive that elevated him from a college grad to an Army major in less than five years.[5]

Upon graduation from Franklin & Marshall in the fateful year of 1941, Winters and his nation stood at a crossroads. War was on the horizon. Dick fervently hoped for the continuation of American neutrality. The year prior, however, President Franklin Roosevelt authorized the Selective Training and Service Act, the first peacetime draft in United States history. Despite the rebounding economy, Winters cared not to enter the workforce only to be later conscripted. He therefore opted to bypass the draft entirely, enlist on his own volition, and complete his single year of service. Winters greeted the prospect of Army life with a degree of apathy. One day at work, Winters blustered too loudly of his intentions "to just pass my time" in the military. He was promptly confronted by a hardnosed veteran colleague who firmly suggested otherwise. In hindsight, Winters was thankful for the stern reprimand.[6]

On August 25, 1941, Winters traveled the short distance from Lancaster to New Cumberland to formally enlist in the Army. Physicians weighed him at a stout 164 pounds—hardly an ounce of fat on his athletic physique. In no time, Winters was bound for the humid but scenic Camp Croft in northwest South Carolina. His irenic parents bade him a fond farewell at Lancaster's ornate Pennsylvania Railroad station. They did not begrudge him for enlisting. Rather, they expressed pride in his initiative.

Winters's 1941 graduation photo from Franklin & Marshall College. Yearbook photo courtesy of Franklin & Marshall College.

Dick embraced his parents and boarded the crowded passenger car, bound for Dixie and a momentous chapter of his life.[7]

The routine at Camp Croft was not all the recruitment posters suggested. While Dick excelled in the rigors of physical training (PT) and marksmanship, he abhorred monotony. Most frustrating of all was his paltry private's pay of twenty-one dollars per month—less than one-fifth of a typical month's wages with the electric company. Winters obstinately regressed to the penny-pinching tactics of his college days. Had the Army not supplied clothing and rations, he could not have made ends meet. Dissatisfaction persisted. He grew languid and felt unproductive. "If anything, my career was aimlessly drifting," Winters recalled in his memoir.[8]

One redeeming feature of an otherwise dull existence was Dick's stalwart friendship with fellow enlisted man Tresta Dominic Trenta. Born in West Virginia two months after Winters, "Trent" was the son of hardworking Italian immigrants who whisked their four children to America in the 1910s. Trent was the first of his family born in the United States. In civilian life, Trent and his wife, Dorothy, rolled cigars for a living. Likewise confronted with the draft, he enlisted alongside Winters at New Cumberland that August. Coincidentally, he and Dick lived only a thirty-minute walk from each other in Lancaster. The fact that the two men had to travel over 500 miles to become steadfast companions was an irony not lost on them.[9]

A sketch of Dick's Lancaster comrade, Tresta Trenta, as recreated from a wartime photo.

Dick and Trent embarked on sporadic adventures in the South when time permitted. A location of particular appeal was the picturesque mountain city of Asheville, North Carolina, located some eighty miles beyond the post gate. The community boasted culture, history, theaters, fine dining—and girls. Outgrowing his cloistered lifestyle, Winters delighted in Trent's zest for sightseeing. Limited by fixed incomes, the GIs typically bunked at Asheville's YMCA, a modestly priced yet comfortable venue for late night reprieves. Through his good-natured acquaintance with a Mr. Hazard of the YMCA, Dick was informally introduced to a local belle named DeEtta Almon.

DeEtta Almon (front row, second from left) is shown at Asheville High School in 1928. Yearbook image courtesy of Asheville High School.

Born in Pyraton, Alabama, on May 14, 1912, DeEtta was the oldest of five siblings. The Almons lived in a cozy cottage on Asheville's Montana Avenue. The house was diligently maintained by her father, who was employed at a local sand company. DeEtta's warm demeanor evoked the best of Southern neighborliness. She attended Biltmore Junior College, participated in the drama club, and worked at a local department store. Generous, artistic, and dutiful, her tender spirit graced letters to Winters amid forthcoming strife and success. In recognition of the desserts DeEtta and friend Frances Johnson left for Dick and Trent, the soldiers planned to personally thank the kindly bakers. The following is the first letter Almon received from the Pennsylvania infantryman. The humble exchange marked the beginning of a meaningful friendship through the best and worst of times.[10]

Thursday Afternoon 2:30
November 27, 1941

Dear Gals:

Received your letter this morning and let me say that it was very well written, being light, easy-to-read, interesting and to the point.

As things stand now we'll be able to make Asheville this Saturday (11/29). But when I say we, I really mean just myself and roommate, Trent (the name is Tresta Trenta), for the other boys are leaving for Panama Monday. As a matter of fact Trent and I were all packed to go ourselves this morning when we received word that we could stay here for another period and also be given the rating of corporal. Naturally we jumped at the chance, for who wants to go down Panama way and wear yourself out fighting mosquitoes when you can stay down south and enjoy the good old traditional hospitality?

So unless some "extra duty" turns up, Trent and I will be up Saturday and we'll give you a call. In case we can't make it, word to the same effect will be sent immediately.

So if you should get to see Mr. Hazard (which is it, Hazzard or Hazard?), tell him to reserve a couple of good rooms.

"Dick" Winters

P.S. Trent said he prefers blondes. Personally I like redheads, but it's not the color of the hair that counts so much as the personality.

R.D.W.[11]

By the third month of training, the superlative efforts of Dick and Trent were evident to superiors. "You men know your stuff," admitted one sergeant. When presented the opportunity to remain in South Carolina and prepare incoming recruits, the Lancaster duo enthusiastically embraced the offer. The disease-ridden tropics did not seem an appealing change of scenery.[12]

By contrast, life at Camp Croft was comfortable. The stone entrance resembled that of a country club. The local chamber of commerce described the base as "one of the beautiful camps of the Army in the South." A mobile post-exchange bus roamed the grounds selling sandwiches and pastries to famished recruits—"Delivered right to your door!" one recalled. Art classes were offered. A base theater showed matinees for those unable to arrange transportation to nearby Spartanburg. Family guest house rooms were available for fifty cents per night. In-ground swimming pools lessened burdens of the heat.[13]

Spartanburg was a moderate-sized city of 32,000 residents. The citizenry generally accommodated the soldierly influx. Troops were shuttled to regional churches and synagogues for weekend services by a civilian force of gracious carpoolers. Dick and Trent could hitchhike to town and catch a movie at the brand new Palmetto Theater on Main Street. Six United Service Organization (USO) centers and canteens were established for the benefit of Croft's growing population. One was set aside for segregated African-American troops.[14]

During the final weekend of November 1941, Dick and Trent set forth to Asheville for a much-anticipated double date with DeEtta and Frances. Winters sensed a distinctive kindness in DeEtta. Her simple gesture of preparing brownies and fudge for random servicemen bespoke genuine civic virtue. As their first social outing commenced, Dick was immediately charmed by her genteel persona. He squandered little time informing her of these sentiments in an exuberant follow-up letter.

Tuesday 8:00 A.M.
Dec. 2, 1941

Pardon me, but are you Miss Almon?

Well, Miss Almon, I am that lucky Yankee who joined the army to see the world. At first he was a little disappointed when they only sent him a little bit south of North Carolina. But now that he's seen North Carolina and all of its beauty, he's glad that they didn't ship him to Panama. In fact he's even content to stay in So. Carolina, if they let him see the better half of the Carolinas once in awhile.

Practically the whole battalion left for Panama yesterday morning and so there isn't a great deal of activity around here and all we have to do is attend a few classes each day for non-commissioned officers. But that doesn't mean that we can lie in bed all morning as [we] could when going to school. No sir, you're up at 5:15 A.M. just the same, but after going through the old and traditional army ritual of reveille and cleaning up, you're free to do as you want as long as you stay in the company area. Of course that's after classes. That's how it happens that I am writing a letter at this un-Godly hour of the morning, for I figured that I might as well let you know that we still plan on keeping our horseback riding [date] for next weekend. In fact that's about all we talk about. That and the swell time we had last weekend.

On Sunday I enjoyed meeting Mr. H. K. Caskey, having dinner, and taking a ride in and around Asheville and through the nearby mountains with him. But the atmosphere was just a little too stilted and aristocratic for me to relax and really enjoy the experience. However, it was something new and different which made up for it all. For that is the only way you can learn how the fellow on the other side of the railroad tracks lives and thinks.

Trent left [for] camp at 6:00 A.M. Sunday to make sure he would be back in time to take over his job of "charge of quarters." I left at 4:00 P.M. I was supposed to be back by 5:00 for the farewell party at which attendance was compulsory. But since I don't drink or smoke, the party didn't appeal to me, so I just skipped it all, only to catch a little H (with capital letters) as a consequence. My first ride was going to Greenville so I thought it would be interesting to see some new country and went along. And though it meant going thirty miles further, the scenery was worth it. The first car to come along in Greenville gave me a ride to the camp. So if I had a car of my own I couldn't have made better time.

Another thing about hitchhiking is that it's so interesting. For normally if you were driving through strange country you'd miss half of the interesting things, but when you're hitchhiking, in most cases, you catch a ride with a native of the country, who take it upon themselves to act as your tourist guide, pointing out and bragging about the interesting points of the land. So, by just asking a few questions you find out all about the country and are relieved of the strain of finding a conversation in which they are interested.

Monday morning (the "morning-after" for the boys), Trent was sick, so I took over his duty as charge of quarters (the second time in three days). It was a madhouse, everybody leaving for Panama, payday, and a million things to do. A comparison might be Kress & Co. on Xmas. Then last night I had the pleasure of being guard in the writing room from 6–11. So I hope my turn for extra duty is coming to an end for I am reaching the stage where I need sleep, and lots of it.

In regards to the coming weekend—would you care to see a show Saturday evening? Or, just what would you suggest we do and what schedule would be most convenient for you? I think it would be best if you would make out the schedule in view of the fact that you know what time would be most convenient for you and also what's going on in Asheville.

Thanks again for the lovely time and supplying the inspiration to tear into things around camp so that the week will fly by and another weekend and another good time will come around before you know it. That makes life more pleasant, for you get more out of your work and you enjoy those hours you dream of all week so much more.

Let's hear the lowdown about the "cookies" from Asheville.

Dick

P.S. Please enclose a snapshot of yourself. For we do a great deal of talking around here and it's much easier to convince the other fellow if you have some actual proof of your sales talk. Also, most important, it would be nice to look at something a little more easy on the eye than a bunch of fellows with G.I. (Government Issued) haircuts and blue denims.

> These buttons you want are going to be hard to get. They can't be bought in camp. I've tried. But there's still an army and navy store in town which I haven't tried as yet. So, "at ease, soldier, at ease."
>
> R.D.W.[15]

The highest peaks of the Blue Ridge Mountains are found in the Asheville area of western North Carolina. Winters, ever the outdoorsman, luxuriated in the crisp air of the alpine ambience. Throughout his life, Dick welcomed sojourns into nature. Prior to the war, he gained refreshing summer employment on a professor's Vermont farm. Horseback riding and mountain hikes in North Carolina afforded him the solitude he enjoyed most. Wanderings up the slopes were invigorating, if not spiritual. Dick's amenable disposition to hitchhiking similarly attested to his breezy, open-minded attitude regarding travel.

Odysseys into the beryl summits engulfing Asheville were not always lonely affairs. On occasion, Dick saddled up with a local gentleman named Herbert K. Caskey. A pillar of the community, Caskey was an unusually well traveled altruist and civic-minded idealist. Having completed work for the YMCA since the days of the First World War, Caskey also dedicated considerable time as a foreign missionary. Nearing eighty years old, the aged traveler expressed concerns of the world's future. His global adventures took him to prewar China, Japan, and Germany. Dick empathized with Caskey's apprehensions of war but remained true to his principle of isolationism. "You take care of your side of the ocean, and I'll take care of mine," Winters subjectively warned leaders of belligerent nations.[16]

The backdrop of the equestrian explorations served as timely distraction to the anxieties of overseas affairs. Among the many landmarks Dick explored was the baroque Biltmore Estate. The astoundingly grand Châteauesque-style mansion at the heart of the property remains the largest home in the United States. Wheatland, the otherwise impressive Lancaster dwelling of President James Buchanan, seemed a shanty by contrast. Dick thought the Biltmore too "stilted and aristocratic" for his own tastes.

Other forms of scenery were in mind. Dick's request of DeEtta for a snapshot attested to his growing affection for the seemly Asheville dame. The necessity of producing "actual proof" of her for "sales talk" suggested a curiosity on the part of bunkmates. So-called "pin-up" photos of girlfriends and starlets in barracks, ships, and hangars were ubiquitous characteristics of male military life. Dick's earlier jaunts on the Biltmore property served as trial runs for his next date with DeEtta. Their afternoon together on Sunday, December 7, 1941, was bound to be memorable.

Dick and DeEtta enjoy horseback riding on the Biltmore Estate in late 1941.

Tuesday Evening 10:00 P.M.
December 9, 1941

Dear DeEtta:

I certainly hated leaving Asheville Sunday evening and realizing that the end had come to my peaceful weekend—which must have been a dream. For you, Frances, your folks, and your place are the essence of all that a "home" ought to be. The result of this atmosphere is that I've been walking around in a fog.

At times we all dream, I imagine, of things we'd like to do, places we'd like to see, of our future and how we'd like to see it unfold successfully, of the ideal home, and of course the most important of all contributions to our happiness, the "happy ending."

While going to school, naturally I did a great deal of reading. The subjects ran from poetry and literature to philosophy, ethics, religion, sociology, psychology and all the other subjects that go to making up a liberal education. Studies, work, and the ever-present lack of funds didn't provide much opportunity for running around, but I did have a great deal of time to spend with my own thoughts and ideas that were stimulated by reading. And that took the place of the actual fun and experiences that I could have had if I could have run around. So, if I wanted to dream and walk around on my own little world, that was O.K. for when I snapped out of it, all I had to do was catch up in a few subjects. But since I am in the army I haven't been able to enjoy the luxury of dreaming. For they manage to take up a good portion of the twenty-four hours each day and by the end of the day your body's half dead and your brain stopped functioning along about retreat. So these ideas that used to pop out a few months ago are practically dormant now. My loose-leaf notebook diary (not my day by day diary) shows this too, for I used to have something to say each day. Now I am lucky if I have something to make a note of every week and that lonely thought usually comes about and is inspired in church on Sundays. The sermon doesn't usually have much to do with it but I imagine the peace, quiet, and the whole atmosphere is what stimulates thought.

Since last Saturday I've been walking around in a dream. In fact the whole weekend was just one of my idealistic dreams, for oftentimes when something would happen or I'd observe something, I wasn't surprised, for it just seemed to fit right into the picture. It was as if I'd gone through the whole thing before. In fact I've been going through it over and over again ever since. For the warm fireplace, soft music, a newspaper, odors and sounds of a good steak dinner in the making, a quiet peaceful dinner, a ride through the majestic mountains, and a hostess with a way of entertaining and making you feel at home—it was a dream, so don't pinch me.

As I read back over this letter it looks sort of "foggy" with all that dreaming, so I'll try and make it more off-hand and as you'd say "cut the line." Also, I'd better come out of the "fog" around here for I am supposed to be training these dopes from Chicago and they sure need training in everything but sleeping—you should hear the racket they make snoring. In all seriousness, however, I am getting a kick out of training these rookies (I am two weeks out of that classification), and I am working hard to do a good job with the idea in mind of sticking around here. Which reminds me of the war we have on hand, and the faster cadence things have taken about camp for we have a definite purpose now as we work. They're cracking down on us, claiming no Xmas furloughs, censored mail, and everything according to wartime law. It gives you a funny feeling in the bottom of your stomach at first, but when you look at it in another light, you don't feel so bad. For the sooner we sail into those little "brown men" and the rest of the motley crew the quicker it'll be over. We've got the stuff to do it and by gosh we will.

Trent and I have been doing a lot of wondering about those pictures and each mail call finds us standing around first on one foot and then on the other in anticipation.

Also we've decided those scarves are much too good to be worn around here, although they would be mighty warm, so we're saving them for special occasions, such as when we want some mark of distinction for meeting another party among a crowd of strangers.

[...] On Sat. night you asked me what the "D" stands for in my initials, well it wasn't "Davis." Nope, I was wrong, since Sunday I've decided it's capital "D" for "Dopey."

Under your spell just
Richard "Dopey" Winters[17]

The trajectory of Dick Winters's life changed in a heartbeat. When he and DeEtta rode back into town that Sunday afternoon, they discovered residents with ears glued to radios. The Japanese bombing of Pearl Harbor sparked demands for immediate retribution. At that moment, the United States ranked eighteenth among the militaries of the world—smaller than Portugal's. Winters promptly realized his term of service would surpass a single year. DeEtta, too, prepared for the struggle, joining the Home Nursing Defense Club, sewing garments for those overseas and fund-raising for a Save the Children campaign.[18]

Winters was angered by the war. He characterized the "empty feeling in the bottom of our stomachs that the country had been attacked without provocation." This quiet rage prompted his affirmation to plow into "those little 'brown men.'" Winters embraced the philosophy of William T. Sherman: "War is cruelty. There is no use trying to reform it; the crueler it is, the sooner it will be over." Winters possessed no illusions of that underlying truth.[19]

Camp Croft and Asheville underwent rapid transformations. Although the camp was only six months old when Winters first entered its gates, the installation was bound to become one of the largest in the South. Within five years, some 200,000 troops trained on the 20,000-acre site. French immigrant Bernard Dargols was among the multitudes who trained in the backcountry. "Camp Croft was huge," he recalled. "Discipline and schedules were very strict: we woke up very early and had to make our beds with hospital corners and without a single crease.... Even if my blonde stubble seemed imperceptible, the sergeant inspecting made sure daily we were well-shaved." Winters, for one, relished his daily shave—a pastime he maintained even in the combat zone.[20]

Dec. 16, 1941
Tuesday, 6:15 A.M.
(it's still pitch dark,
although I've been up an
hour already and
shivering all the while)

Dear DeEtta:

Don't call me Richard. "Dick" sounds more natural to me and personally I prefer it. For in my childhood I developed a dislike for the sound of the name after my aunts mauled it around. So just call me "Dick" and say what you have to say straight from the shoulder.

[...] In answer to your letter, I'd like to have a few hours to talk over your philosophy of life and, in particular, your idea of just what you mean by enjoying life. That's the kind of thing I like and then, too, it's a darn good way of getting to know the other guy.

[...] Pardon, but I must fall out for calisthenics.

9:15—Well, that's that. Exercises are over, we've had a class on the Garand rifle, and now they're having another on the gas mask. But, since I go on guard at 11:15, I am cutting this class (just like college), giving the excuse that I have to pick up a revolver and shine up.

Last evening I mailed my Xmas cards and presents home, so I guess we were doing the same thing on Sunday.

You ask me to give my autobiography. Well, that's OK only I'd rather if we talk about you. It'd be far more interesting I am sure. But, since I am on the talking end this time, I might as well tell my story.

I was born Jan. 21, 1918 in New Holland (small town close to Lancaster). Just a minute. On reading between the lines, what I think you'd really like to know is about all the girls in my home town and not so much about my school days. So I think I'll skip Chapter One, (School Days with Dick Winters), and turn to Chapter Two (title unknown), for as I've said it'll be more interesting, perhaps, to you, and I know it'll be shorter for me to write. Chapter One will be explained either in person, or by installments—via letter—in the future.

Chapter II

It wasn't until the year 1937 when our hero first entered college that he had his first date—and that was compulsory—by order of his fraternity brothers. As it turned out, the date was a nightmare because of a combination of circumstances. The party was a dance. I couldn't dance, didn't even know how to hold the girl. They told me to just go out there and walk to the music. So, I did, but most of the time it was on her feet. That was the first and last dance I went to, for soon afterward I dropped out of the fraternity—too much money for a guy working his way through college.

Later that year I took the same girl ice skating a couple of times. That was better for me, but she didn't do so well, with the result that the experience proved "painful." That was the end of that brunette.

Later on in the season I spotted a beautiful blonde. So I had a date with her—went to Hershey to see a hockey game, as I remember it. But she proved the law about women "beautiful but dumb." So that was that—one date.

Next gal to catch my eye was a little nurse—yep, you guessed it, a redhead at that. She was all right, in fact that was the first time I enjoyed going out with a girl. She had something between her ears and could carry on an interesting conversation. That all started at the beginning of my sophomore year and the conclusion came about the middle of my junior year. Reason for conclusion—just take it from me—it was my idea and I had my reasons.

After that, outside of a few dates with the first redhead's roommate, who also was a redhead, I didn't bother with girls the rest of my junior year. And in my senior year I didn't even take the time out to look at a girl. Then, last summer I had a few more dates with the second redhead before going to Vermont for a month to work on a prof's farm in the mountains. Then home to volunteer for the army instead of waiting for them to take me.

Since I am in the army, I had one date before meeting you. It was with a dizzy little sophomore from Converse College in Spartanburg. We met at a church party and she invited me to a concert.

So there you are—short and sweet, wasn't it? But that's my secret for enjoying life in the army. Outside of my family I don't care a whole lot if I go home over Xmas and I don't give a darn where they ship me—that was B.M.Y.

Perhaps you can better understand why I enjoyed the other weekend so much, and maybe you'll see that it wasn't just a line.

Well, I've got to go again, for it's time to get ready for the guard.

1:30 P.M. I am off until 4:00 now and then I am on until 10:00 P.M., then again tomorrow at 11:30. This job I have is a snap tho [*sic*], for I am an M.P. (military police) in the PX (post exchange) and all I have to do is sit around and look wise, telling them to button up that collar, fix that tie. Then, if anybody gets a little too much beer, out the door they go, if they want to or not.

However, a bad feature about the job is you spend too much money; sitting around looking at things you need just makes the money burn your pocket. I bought Dale Carnegie's book on *How to Win Friends and Influence People*, after looking it over. Also I picked up those hobby prints of those pictures. As I expected, the ones of you came out swell, and of me, as usual, no good. I'll enclose a set.

Trent's Charge of Quarters today and he just dropped in and asked if this is a book. I said "nope, it's a couple of letters." So if it's that bad, I'd better close. Your boss might not like it if you spend more than half an hour trying to figure this all out.

[...] Anyhow, let us know how things stand and include some more drawings; we enjoy them a lot.

As ever,
"Dick"

P.S. On second thought I am keeping the pictures.
R.D.W.[21]

Although socially timid, Winters exhibited pride in being a man of his own thoughts and convictions. Observant, deeply philosophical inclinations compelled him to gain understandings of those around him. Similarly, the wish to discover a friend who had "something between her ears and could carry on an interesting conversation" was no trivial matter. Winters's solitary school years and a lack of enthusiasm to visit acquaintances over the holidays underscored his struggles to meaningfully connect with those other than family. His purchasing of the popular *How to Win Friends and Influence People* (published in 1936) testified to an ambition of polishing personality skills.

Apart from inquisitiveness, understanding the "philosophy of life" was key to compatibility and instilling trust. Only through knowing subordinates can one truly lead them. Dick remembered his men's names, he recognized their strengths, and he assessed their weaknesses. Similarly, through years of letter writing, DeEtta Almon served as a sounding board and means of moral support. Dick and DeEtta imbued confidence in each other. Though he required little advice regarding calisthenics or weaponry, she revealed to him something else entirely—the value of someone who listened.

Thursday Evening 8:00 P.M.
Dec. 18, 1941

Dear DeEtta,

Today finds me playing Charge of Quarters–I think it's just a glorified name for an errand boy. The duties of a C.Q. are to turn out all the lights at nine, make a bed check at eleven to make sure everybody is present and accounted for. Then you clean up the orderly room (company quarters), after which you can go to bed. But you must sleep in the orderly room. This has only gone into effect since we've declared war, the reason being that in case of emergency you have a sentinel standing by all ready to arouse the company on a moment's notice. Tonight I am that guy, so I sleep fully dressed, even to the necktie. In the morning I am up at 4:45 A.M. to arouse the K.P.[Kitchen Police or Kitchen Patrol], then at 5:15 I roll the whole company out, after which I collect all mail and then run errands until noon when I am relieved. The afternoon is supposed to be mine, but really they catch you and put you to work. But here's one guy they're not going to catch tomorrow, no sir, for I am going to start packing and shining up, so that Saturday noon I can pull out of here so fast they won't see me for dust, for I'm heading for home–in a round about way. I just found out definitely tonight that I have my furlough which starts Monday morning, but I am going to get a weekend pass, or I am just going to take one, but one way or another, I am leaving.

Since Asheville lies in line, quite by accident, with my planned trip, I'll be going through your town in the afternoon, so I'll drop by and say hello sometime in the afternoon, and perhaps if it's around chow time, I'll stick around and we can have supper together, if you're agreeable. After that I think I'll have a chance on making Knoxville, even though it will be dark, although I don't know as yet if I want to do this for I'd be missing a lot of scenery, and that's the whole idea of this extended detour home.

Last evening, about nine, they sent up an order to collect and pack all gas masks for shipment immediately. Where they shipped them, I don't know, but the rumor is the Pacific coast and cities like San Francisco. It makes you realize that we are far from being adequately prepared for war in this country, especially when you think of the few insignificant gas masks sent out there and the quality of masks, for they were really only training masks.

They've warned us of censoring mail and of telling about such inside matters, but I think the information is safe in your hands.

The "old man" [captain] is hovering around like a lean old vulture, always trying to make up a new job. So I'll just close this letter to make him happy.

I was just interrupted for an hour at that point. So don't work too hard over this Xmas rush, and tell Frances to be on the lookout with the glasses on Saturday.

Dick[22]

Charge of Quarters (CQ) duties were often consumed by tedium and bothersome busywork. They were nonetheless elemental facets of post life. Those on Kitchen Patrol toiled in the mess halls, sometimes past the sounding of retreat. There was never a shortage of items to be scrubbed, baked, peeled, diced, washed, or boiled. During warmer months, the kitchen was oppressively hot. Flypaper was the seasonal décor of dining areas. On a rotating basis, corporals such as Winters served as glorified alarm clocks for sleep-deprived hash slingers. The work was expected of him, and he did it well. He cared not, however, to have his leisure time impeded upon. With the holidays approaching, Dick wisely opted to make use of his leave.[23]

Plans to visit family for Christmas culminated in one of his last great road trips before voyaging overseas. The incongruous route heightened Dick's ambition to experience the countryside. Following a respite in North Carolina, hitchhiking ushered him west through the mountains of Tennessee and into the bluegrass of Kentucky. He wrote from Louisville, Kentucky, on December 21:

> The ride up here was really interesting—first, those huge mountains, then the Tenn. shacks and mountaineers, next was Kentucky and its rich farm land and stock raising enterprises. It was something to see and it made you think. In fact, my mind's like the revolving door at S&W—it has thoughts popping into it, taking a turn or two and then going out.
>
> One thing that struck me was the wealth of the farm land and stock raising farms about Danville, Ky. I always thought that when it came to wealth and beautiful farm land and farms, nothing could beat Lancaster and Lanc. Co., but I saw better today, which just goes to show you that if you get out and look around a little, you'll find that you have lots of competition and while you might think you're the big cheese at home and that your home is the one and only, all you have to do is travel. Other things I noticed were the way they build their homes, farms, lay out their towns, light their stores, and a million and one other things.[24]

During the Great Depression, there was a peculiar art to the pastime of hitchhiking. This means of transportation was slow and rarely efficient but free and a fine alternative to walking. Small-town folk gauged outsiders with wariness. Farmers were generally cooperative but rarely traveled the long distances hitchhikers required. Four-way stops or Y intersections were the best locations to await a lift. Though plagued by inconsistencies and the unpredictability of weather, hitchhikers experienced a slice of Americana through the scenery they absorbed and the drivers they encountered.

Observant of motorists' color commentary, Winters enjoyed informal lessons in cultural geography. "Have you been through Kentucky? Around Lexington?" he asked DeEtta. "That's really a sight to see with its miles and miles of rolling green meadows, circled with white fences, and those big massive homes and stables. It was the most beautiful sight I've ever seen. Then came the coal mines of West Virginia and the oil wells. This, of course, wasn't so beautiful, but it was interesting."[25]

James R. Clark, a fellow wartime wanderer, relayed similar tactics employed by Winters to gain complimentary ridership: Look clean. Don't smell. Pack lightly. Smile at drivers. Stand under lampposts at night. Always point your thumb in the direction you are heading. If one abided by these courtesies, additional amenities such as meals, lodging, or employment could be rendered at the hospitable discretion of benefactors. Always clean cut and sporting a sharp mustard wool enlisted man's uniform, Dick experienced little trouble in winning the trust of drivers. On one occasion, however, the friendliness of a certain motorist surprised Winters beyond all expectations and prior experiences. In 1996, Dick explained why he was suddenly stranded atop a mountain near Spencer, West Virginia.[26]

My ride was with a good looking, well-spoken man with a very nice car. The conversation was pleasant and normal.

Suddenly the man reached over and put his hand on my leg and suggested when we reach Spencer that he would find a nice hotel, treat me to a nice dinner, and that he would make me feel "very happy."

This was a "first" in my life. I'd heard of guys like this but to my knowledge never met or talked to one.

Immediately, I told him, "Do you see that crossroads up ahead? Stop right there. I am getting out!" He stopped. I got out.

[...] I was lucky for it was dark and cold in the mountains and the next guy to come down the road was an old man in a logging truck. He had been cutting wood all day and as we slowly bumped into Spencer, I explained to him why I had been stranded on top of the mountain. He did not say much, he was a good listener. I never forgot him for he was a friend at the time I needed a friend.[27]

Following his protracted journey to Pennsylvania, Dick reached his homestead in the early morning hours of Christmas Eve. "I finally got home at 12 but I was dead tired, wet, disgusted with these damn Yankees, but glad to get home," he wrote DeEtta. "I couldn't sleep very well for I guess it was starting to get me, but today I am over it and I've been sleepy all day." Lancaster's weather was pleasantly mild, abnormally so for late December. Savoring the niceties of home and the quaint charms of the family's grandfather clock on Christmas Eve was a nostalgic reversal. Domestic cleanliness and motherly comforts were wistful amenities. Dick's demanding trek thus culminated with a sense of fatigued relief. The impressive hitchhiking journey swept him from the heart of Dixie to Dutch Country in three days. His visualizations of home as conveyed to DeEtta were reminiscent of tender Norman Rockwell scenes.[28]

Gaining fresh perspectives of each other's personalities, Dick and DeEtta admitted that neither was prolific in verbal discourse. Once more commending his Pennsylvania upbringing, Winters extolled the virtues of Quaker humility and meditation. One must strive to be a listener, not a loudmouth, he assured. Quiet contemplation and focus were effective means of comprehending people and their perspectives.

In contrast to Dick's holiday sojourn, many members of the Armed Services did not obtain Christmas leave. Offering a taste of home for heartsick GIs, the War Department ordered 1.5 million pounds of turkey for 12,000 mess halls. Meanwhile, resolute religious themes were intertwined in the broader patriotic fervor of the troubled Yuletide season. The *Washington Post* noted on December 25, "With firm reliance upon a merciful God, they [the American people] anticipate the happier Christmases yet to dawn." As he drifted into a deep slumber, Dick wondered where he would be one year from then. Considerable time passed before he celebrated another Christmas on South West End Avenue.[29]

Dec. 28, 1941
11:45 P.M.

Dear DeEtta:

Thanks a lot for the scratching paper with the "hen tracks" (as you call them) and the special delivery, which I received this morning. Both are greatly appreciated and needed.

Trent called me up yesterday and told me about receiving a box of writing paper too, he seemed quite pleased as well as surprised. Although I haven't been able to see him as yet, I plan to drop around tomorrow and meet the family. As a matter of fact that's just about all I have been doing since I am home, just visiting, and all the things you planned to do just fade away and you become a slave to social etiquette. But I have [had] just about all I can stand now and these last two days are going to be spent doing things I want to do. Such as taking a long hike in the country with my rifle, doing a little reading, taking a workout—that's about the only thing I've done every day that I really like to do and wanted to do. The rest has been to satisfy the curious bystanders, so to speak. In fact these folks at home have me about nuts. I'll be glad to get back to camp—and Asheville—where they don't worry so much about the war, and instead of talking, they do something. In fact, never remind me that I am a Yankee, for they seem less prepared for a war than the South and the whole reason is that they're soft, afraid they—oh nuts, I could go on for hours, but I'll let it go by saying I'll be glad to get back in action instead of this role of a Morris chair philosopher.

I intend to start south Wed. morning and hope to reach Winston-Salem by night. That'll put me in easy reach of camp for the last day.

I imagine you had a lovely Xmas, according to your letter, especially since your parents were on the feminine and impractical side. You mentioned about your brother calling home from Portland, which reminds me of your planned trip north in the early spring. Now, that's going to be one long trip, and it'll be especially tiresome by bus, so unless you have any other plans I'd like to have you stop over in Lancaster for a few days and take in the Lancaster County Dutch. My parents both thought it a good idea and would be delighted to have you. In all probability, I won't be able to be on hand to show you around myself, but I know they'll do their best. In fact they've been wondering if they can compare to the southern hospitality after I got done with my story about the glories of the South. So, don't forget my bid for a few days of your vacation, for as I said there's much to see around these parts and it's a great deal different than the South.

In answer to your query about my enjoying this ten day furlough, I guess after the start of this letter you think it's a flop. Well, in one sense it is, for I came home with the thought in mind of getting lots of rest, doing the things I like—athletics, hiking, shooting, reading, sleeping and enjoying a soft life and good food. But I find I haven't time to enjoy myself and I can't even enjoy the good and soft chairs, radio, etc. as I expected. It's just that I'd have to adjust myself to this life all over again. However, last evening I pulled a good one. First of all, I cancelled an invitation to a party saying I wanted to stay home. Then I thought I'd read a little, drop you a line, then listen to some music. In other words, just take it easy. Well I went upstairs to read in bed and, as you might expect, I fell asleep and I didn't wake up until nine this morning. So I had about fourteen hours sleep with the result that I haven't been nodding every time I sat down today.

It looks as if I won't get any ice skating [in] this year for the weather is too warm. They had a few days of it the other week but that was about all. I'd like to have you as a pupil in learning to ice skate and I'd bet you'd do all right, for you seem to be of the athletic type and then too, when you'd fall you wouldn't have so far to drop, which would be a decided advantage to you.

[...] As for the subject of dieting, there is much to be said. I have made a study of it for quite a few years (ahem!) and I have decided that each person does best by working out their own program. All it takes is a little common sense and lots and lots of willpower. I think you have both—plus. But, I'll be only too willing to give you my theory of the whole subject, only I'll save that one for our rendezvous or round-table discussion. (Which reminds me, when is Chapter I of your autobiography going to be released?) In connection with this dieting—don't call it a diet, anything but that. Whenever anybody I've ever heard of or seen goes on a diet it always starts out with a flurry and about one week later, it's all over, given up as a bad job. Now if you go in training, shall we say, that's different, for you start off a little slow, getting the feel of things, adjusting yourself to the new way of living, then you gradually cut down as you see the best, but always keeping on the job. After you've reached the desired goal, you don't give up, or quit, nope, you just ease up a bit perhaps, but you keep on training.

But speaking of training, reminds me I'd better get some sleep so that I'll be in shape to beat the "rising sun" on some future date in the battle for the championship of the world. After which, I am looking forward to retiring from battle, but not stopping training.

As ever,
Dick

It doesn't surprise me that you get these letters even if they're addressed to So. C. I'll bet I could just address this letter "Miss Asheville" and you'd get it. But being as you're so modest, I won't embarrass you by such a display.

R.D.W.[30]

"They don't know me," Winters later noted of acquaintances. "Nobody knows me. The neighbors, people whom I've lived with and worked for over the years, they have never known me." He was a man unto himself. To quote a phrase applied to Franklin Roosevelt's similarly enigmatic demeanor, Winters possessed a "thickly forested interior," a protective screen shielding his soul and innermost thoughts from those even closest to him. He categorized few individuals as lifelong friends. "I like to count my close friends on one hand," he later admitted. Winters maintained that standard his entire life. His desires to enjoy the outdoors and avoid houseguests were indicative of his yearnings for solitude.[31]

In addition to the annoyance of being "a slave to social etiquette," Winters experienced a boiling frustration felt by many service members: animus toward civilians. Resentment of those opting to remain stateside was expressed with varying levels of severity. Antipathy toward draft dodgers, slackers, strikers, those with deferments, and so-called "feather merchants" grew common in the ranks. Although Pennsylvanians comprised one out of every twelve Americans to serve in uniform during the Second World War, Dick was none too impressed with the commonwealth's initial response to mobilization. Southern "rebels" he encountered seemed more prone to combative eagerness.[32]

The topic of dieting frequently emerged in writings with DeEtta. She was curious about Dick's physical regimen and expressed a desire to condition herself as wartime opportunities for women expanded. Throughout his life, Winters interpreted physical stamina as a key component of broader intellectual fortitude. "I'm Pennsylvania Dutch," he once boasted. "I don't quit. I made a commitment. Moral courage is based on physical fitness. Courage is a combination of willpower and determination." Be strong in all things you do, he professed. Anything less was a detriment to one's abilities to grow and excel.[33]

CHAPTER TWO

RESPECT AND AUTHORITY

January 1942 to January 1943

"Oh, go write a letter to Asheville."

Tuesday Evening, 9:00 P.M.
Jan. 6, 1942

Dear DeEtta:

They always told me the South was warm the year round. Well, I am warm for the first time today and that's only because I've just had a good warm shower. All day, and yesterday too, we've been walking around through a stream of water up to my knees, so that my shoes were wet all day. Whenever I'd go to Trent for sympathy he'd say, "Oh, go write a letter to Asheville." But I have the last laugh now, for he has a sore ankle from too much hiking the last few days and now he's moaning.

[...] Trent and I are coming up to Asheville, unless circumstances beyond our control dictate otherwise, this coming weekend and we'd like to make it a point to see the show, *Sgt. York*. In fact as matters stand right now we have a bet as to who will pay for the show. The bet is that he'll pay if I can pin him in less than five minutes of wrestling. So we're going to settle that the first thing when we hit the Y at Asheville. In case you can reserve seats for that show, we'd appreciate it if you'd take care of that detail for a party of four (in Lancaster you can sometimes do that for an extraordinary picture).

[...] Out of our battalion (3 companies) they are going to take a company of cadremen and ship them to Ft. McClennan [McClellan], Ala. Trent and I aren't scheduled to go as yet, so I guess they must think a little bit of us. Otherwise we'd have been given a ticket.

How's the diet coming along? Don't bother to tell me, I know just how tough it is to go hungry. But don't cut down too hard at first for you don't have to take off much weight by a certain date. Besides, that kind of diet is hard on you and the first thing you know you give the whole idea up. The job of taking off weight is a slow and tedious task but don't forget Rome wasn't built in a day so you can't expect to burn it down in five minutes.

I intend to read a little more of *Dodsworth* this evening after giving away here at the table to Trent, but I just know that it'll end up with me either going to sleep (after being out in the wind all day), or Trent and I getting into one of our nightly bull sessions. Anyhow, I've got old "D" in America now and things are going right along.

Trent is lying here talking to me about how he loves the army, as he shivers. He hasn't gotten over the night problem we had tonight between 6:30 and 8:30, which was one of those affairs where you go stumbling through the woods in the dark, falling in holes, over rocks, etc., so to quiet his chatter I think I'll give way.

As ever,
Dick[1]

The Warner Brothers blockbuster *Sergeant York* prompted significant considerations for Americans in 1941 and 1942—issues Winters himself contemplated. Though actor Gary Cooper's titular character was embellished for the big screen, the film plucked the heartstrings of audiences teetering between war and peace. Depicting a famed Tennessee dove-turned-war-hero, *Sergeant York* presented a not-so-subtle lesson in foreign intervention. Prior to Pearl Harbor, moviegoers related to York's inner struggle of conscience. After December 7, Sergeant York symbolized the reluctant hero. The film permitted citizens to internally rebuke violence before embracing it as a means of promoting security and Christian morality. Although the real Alvin York was a talkative celebrity, Cooper's stoical portrayal was one with which Winters could readily identify. The representation of a shy, awkward country boy with pacifist origins who ascends to fame through battlefield heroics would mirror Winters's own future in unimaginable ways.[2]

"So cold—ink will freeze in the pen."

Noon
Wed. Jan. 7, 1942

Dear DeEtta:

Can you imagine what my Dad had to say to me when I received the enclosed letter from home? Well, it carried the idea of snapping out of it.

It's still cold as hell around here and Trent's really limping with his ankle. Last night we slept under all blankets, overcoats, and with our John L's on, and today we're wearing gloves to read our letters from home. The next thing you know the ink will freeze in the pen and then I'll have to use a pencil.

We're looking forward to the weekend with enthusiasm already. In fact, Trent was just counting off the days on his fingers as we crawled out for reveille this morning.

Dick[3]

Physical endurance and tolerance were key elements to the success of any recruit or non-commissioned officer at Camp Croft. In cases more often than not, freshly inducted troops were unprepared for the routine demands of military life. "It was hard not to feel sorry for those guys, especially when they didn't know the first things about the army," noted Richard M. Blackburn, a young second lieutenant on the base. "Most of them were good boys and did their best in whatever they were required to do. Plenty of patience was required on the drill field when teaching those boys how to march in step." Blackburn even handed one youth a stone to clutch so he could distinguish right from left.[4]

As Winters suggested, the power of reassurance carried weight in motivating a man to perform his duty. "I was right there in their shoes. I would never ask of them anything that I could not do myself," Blackburn likewise concluded. This distinguished sense of teamwork, whether highlighted by a platoon or an individual, marked a core component of unit cohesion and camaraderie. "Hardship and stress bring a family together," Winters observed of this basic unit dynamic. Despite the frigid Carolina nights and Trent's bum ankle, backcountry maneuvers at Croft sharpened Dick's skills and endurance for harsher days ahead.[5]

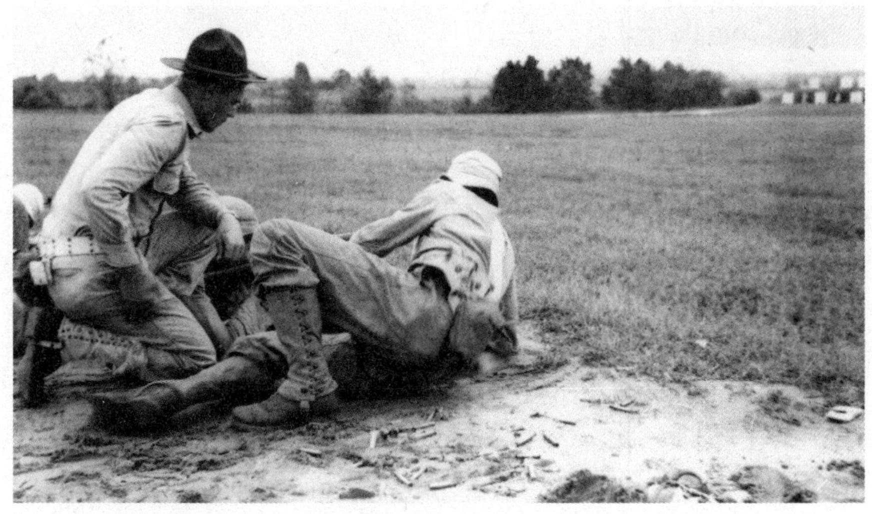

Winters (left) supervises a soldier on the firing range at Camp Croft in 1941.

Only on the occasional late night did Winters grow lenient on matters of barracks discipline. He was not above taking the human element into consideration. The pressures of training presented infrequent opportunities to decompress. Dick thus afforded green recruits "a little fun" now and again. Flexibility and compassion were acceptable when earned.

Daylight hours of garrison life required constant attention to spit-and-polish demands. Vigilant non-coms enforced uninterrupted policing of the grounds for garbage. As one sergeant barked, "We got to police up this here company yard and pick up everything that ain't red hot or nailed down." Recruits retrieved cigarette butts, poured out the tobacco from the paper, and then crunched the paper into small wads for disposal. Barracks were literally given the white glove treatment. As future paratrooper Zig Boroughs attested, "The original idea for barracks cleanliness and order, I am sure, related to efficiency in management and maintenance of good health among the troops." This standard shifted in its aims when competitive officers obsessed over orderliness for pure sport. "Praise and honor for good inspections, or severe reproof if deficiencies were reported, completely overshadowed the original purpose of regular inspections," Boroughs complained.[6]

Alongside Dale Carnegie's self-help manifesto, Sinclair Lewis's 1929 novel *Dodsworth* garnered frequent mention in Dick's correspondence. "Someday I'd like to reread it, when I can sit down and read uninterrupted for a few hours at a time, instead of by snatches of two and three pages, between interruptions and ten-minute breaks," he remarked. The romantic tale revolves around a retiring automobile designer whose vainglorious wife grows dissatisfied and seeks youthful revelry as the couple travels abroad. The book conveys a story of love, pain, morality, and quiet dignity Winters found captivating. Naturally, he equated DeEtta to the book's heroine, one who could "sweep the cobwebs from any man's heart."[7]

"Letter with a tomato soup flavor."

Tues. 5:30 P.M.
Jan. 13, 1942

Dear DeEtta:

Well, I am "at ease" as we say it in the army. Usually when you're expecting a letter or package from home, you walk around feeling ill at ease for something is bothering you sub-consciously and you can't seem to lay your finger on it. That's the way I was feeling the last few days, but yesterday a package from home arrived and today your letter, so I am "at ease" once again.

Trent just picked up the Sociology book I had sent down and by the way he's been interrupting me, evidently he likes it. Speaking of books, reminds me of your description of your favorite type of book—incidentally the letter was very good (and juicy)—it seems to me you have a natural tendency toward books of travel and stories concerning frontiers, as "China, Africa, and the South." I've found the South, especially, has frontiers to be conquered.

Nothing would please Trent and me more than if *Sgt. York* would be held over, for we'd like to bust out of camp this weekend and that'd be a good excuse.

Your speaking of going ice skating makes me feel homesick for the feel of a long smooth stroke and the swish of ice flakes as you come to a stop. When I was home a party wanted to take me to the Hershey Ice Palace the last night I was home. I would have gone along, but the combined—pardon me, we're called out on an alert call.

9:30 P.M. (Same day, or rather, night)

Oh boy! I sure hope that's the end of the schedule for today. Out of a clear sky we're ordered to fall out with rifles, belts, light packs, blankets, canteens, etc. and here we were all sitting around with shoes off and set to relax. We dashed down to a valley, without a vocal command, whisper, or light, jumped into a steam, and then stood there for half an hour. After that we sent out patrols. It wasn't so bad for us, for we (Trent and I) just stood around giving orders. Now I have some soup on our grid, and if we ever get caught it'll mean that we'll be broken.

A shower and I am all set to do a little reading on Dale Carnegie's book, *How to Win Friends and Influence People*, which is really good, being both interesting and educational. It brings out points we all have recognized before, but he proves the points in such a manner that you are completely won over and convinced and so inspired.

Now we just took a couple of pictures of this set-up: cooking, writing letters, the room. If it comes out OK we'll show them to you, but it'll be a very sloppy room.

To get back to this thing of reading—I am looking forward to that story you were glamorizing. I believe it was "French River."

Let's see, I was talking about going ice skating around 5:30 and never finished. Well, the combined factors of starting off early for camp the next day and that you must just skate around on a peanut shell, in a crowd that reminds you of a subway in N.Y. at five o'clock, were too much for me, so I turned it down. I'd rather not go at all than just enjoy an imitation of the real thing.

Is cheese fattening? What a question! What's cheese made out of? Well, is milk and butter fattening? Ok, then, stay away from the cheese, eat more proteins, like that steak, but no carbohydrates.

Trent just said to ask how you like this letter with the spilled tomato flavor. Quite a wit, this boy, Trent.

That sounds like a good idea about you bringing us back [from Asheville to Camp Croft], providing conditions are favorable. We'd get a kick out of showing you the way down, I dare say I know it better than you, and Camp Croft. There isn't a great deal to see here but it'll give you an idea of what the polished up side of the Camp looks like. By the way, this little book that they just got out down at the P.X. helps show highlights of our training here, but it forgets all about the misery of reveille, long hikes, and other work. It's just like college, everybody sees only the football games and other sporting events, but forgets all about the work in back of them and the studying.

Here's hoping that the military brain trusts can see their way clear without our services this weekend and that dear old mother nature allows us to pass through those mountains to a place a little bit closer to heaven. Until then I'll just be

As ever,
Dick[8]

Winters's eagerness to return to the systematic regimen of military life following a Christmastime interlude did not desensitize him from hometown allures. A fixture of Dick's teenage years was the venerable Ice Palace located in Hershey, Pennsylvania—about an hour's drive northwest of Lancaster. The former convention hall was converted into a massive ice rink, the popularity of which prompted the civic-minded Milton Hershey to construct an even more substantial sports arena. Dick even mustered the courage to take the rare date to a Hershey Bears hockey match. Dick whimsically yearned to share such a moment with DeEtta. But it was not to be.[9]

Other forms of sentimentality emerged as well. The market for souvenirs from Camp Croft arose as an overnight cottage industry in South Carolina's "newest city." Sent with these homebound military mementos were conventional messages of love, war, frustration, and desire. The base's Post Exchange offered everything from custom ash trays, folding frames, miniature footballs, child-size khaki caps, pillow cases, coin purses, bayonet-shaped letter openers, and earrings—all stamped "Camp Croft, S. C." The demand for charms was never in short supply for corralled recruits with little else to purchase. Among the tokens mailed to DeEtta was a pictorial guide of the base, entitled *A Camera Trip through Camp Croft*. The thirty-page publication was typical of wartime keepsake literature. The photo collages within revealed every facet of camp culture—from movies, to field maneuvers, to segregated swing dances. The book's introduction concluded, "Camp Croft carries on with every man resolved that the dawn of victory shall dispel the darkening shadows of aggression on the not too distant horizons."[10]

As Dick suggested, more arduous aspects were omitted from the booklet. A continuous plight during his maneuvers was mud. The never-ending clumps of murk plagued infantrymen at every turn. Richard Blackburn unhappily echoed Winters's complaints of the "darn muddy" conditions during night marches. "We had been wallowing around in the mud all week," he bickered, "and the rain continued to pour on our weary bodies. Each day, we began at 4:00 a.m. and came back at 1:00 a.m., shortly into the next day. The men managed to get a little sleep, but I got a lot less." They trained in the strenuous state of sleep deprivation—a merciless but necessary task.[11]

Mock campaigns through the South Carolina brush lasted days. Sweeps through phony villages, navigating minefields, crossing streams, and crawling through barbed wire under live fire was only a mild simulation of conditions to come. Aspiring leaders such as Winters and Blackburn endured the physical pains to prepare greenhorns for the impending challenges of combat. The discipline was a form of harsh affection. As Blackburn attested, "[I]t was my job to oversee some very valuable training that could very well save their lives one day."[12]

Jan. 17, 1942–third date.

Thursday, 8:30 P.M.
Jan. 22, 1942

Dear DeEtta:

Thanks for your remembrance, via telegram, of my twenty-fourth birthday. Also, I wish to express my appreciation for the thoughtfulness and effort both you and Frances put forward in making my birthday party such a success.

The thing I have been expecting, yet dreading, has happened, only in a different form in which I thought it would come. This dreaded thing is that starting Saturday we go on a six day week, which sort of squashes any kind of a weekend trip you might plan. Also, there are rumors that we'll be going on a seven day week before long. So from now on it looks like just about all work. A fellow wouldn't mind so much if this thing of fighting a war was like any other job, which would mean the harder you worked, the quicker the job would be done. Perhaps it is possible, after all. At any rate, that's one way of looking at the matter to console yourself.

Last Sunday Trent and I had no trouble at all in getting back to camp. In fact, you were no more than out of sight than we were on a non-stop ride to Spartanburg.

This week has been a "killer." Mon., Tues., and Wed. we were on the go from 4:45 until 7:00 P.M. After that, between inspecting rifles, we'd read a little then to bed, absolutely dead on our feet. Today was just as tough, but I guess you get toughened to being on the double all day for I am not so tired this evening. It's been lots of work but the fun of being on the range more than compensates for it. At least now we have some new experiences to talk about and we won't have to listen to the same old ones over and over again.

Trent's feet have had a nice rest now, for all week he's been goldbricking, riding out to the range and then just watching the ammunition all day. I am glad he got the break for he's much better for the rest. Both of us had bad colds at the beginning of the week, but we're coming around now.

Starting Monday I went to work on getting acquainted with the C.O. (Commanding Officer) and the officers. Before, I'd just been tending to my business and keeping out of the road—sort of sizing up the situation. Anyhow, to make a long story short, the C.O. asked me if I was interested in going to Officers Training School. Of course I answered in the affirmative, with the result that this evening they gave me an application to fill out. If anything ever comes of it or not, of course, remains to be seen.

But if they give me the chance, I'll show them I can work when I want to. That's something I want and, by gosh, I'll get it.

Now that it looks as if I might be going to [Fort] Benning, Trent's dug up that old desire of his to be a member of the Parachute Troops. I've been telling him he's nuts for that's a suicide outfit. But one nice thing, we'd both be in Benning together for three more months. That's just a dream. Lots of good fellows have flunked this chance, but lots of bozos have passed. So I'll just dig in from now on and hope for a break when I hit that board that gives you the final exam before going to Benning.

Just this evening I finished Dale Carnegie's famous book. It really was good. What I'll read now, I don't know. I have *One Foot in Heaven* and the books you gave me, and then, too, I could stand a lot of study on the technicalities of the mechanics of guns, and tactics, and other things that go into making a soldier.

How's the diet coming along? Also, is Frances getting to it or has she rebelled? Just remember "you must pay the price," for physical fitness doesn't just happen, it's created.

As ever,
Dick

P.S. I still think you write a good P.S.[13]

Winters's dismissive comments of the paratroops remain perhaps the most ironic words he penned to DeEtta. Little could he have conceived in January 1942 how profoundly instrumental a role the paratroops would play in his future. Before he was gripped by the aspirations of joining "a suicide outfit," Winters pondered a feasible course of action: methodically rise to officer status. Dick grew annoyed by the number of inept officers who misinformed recruits about weapons, tactics, and common-sense leadership. He became increasingly confident in his abilities to exceed their lackluster performances.

For any aspiring non-com, Officer Candidate School was the place to be. Over 100,000 OCS candidates enrolled in the program between 1941 and 1947. Two-thirds of those students graduated as freshly-minted second lieutenants. A pillar landmark of the initiative was the Infantry School at Fort Benning, Georgia—where some 14,000 candidates enrolled between September and December 1942 alone. The program became a cornerstone of the modernized Army. In hindsight, Gen. Omar Bradley admitted, "I considered the founding of the Fort Benning OCS my greatest contribution to the mobilization effort." Little wonder Trent and Dick desired to join its esteemed personnel.[14]

Colds and flu–15 out of 55 to the hospital

Tuesday Evening 7:45 P.M.
Feb. 10, 1942

Dear DeEtta:

Received your letter this morning and in view of the fact that you intend to leave this weekend, and I believe you look for an explanation for not hearing from me, I've just taken myself by the scuff of the neck, so to speak, and now we'll see what this old pen has to say.

I am glad to hear things are shaping up and taking definite form concerning your trip. As for the folks, I've told you before, just consider the whole thing as a reservation at a tourist home. Only in this case I hope you spend more than just the night for there is much to see about

Lancaster and I hope my dad has time to show it to you. I am quite sure they won't bite your ears off, but I've a precognition that the neighbors will do a little "blind lifting." Outside of the scrutiny I think it should be quite enjoyable, for in some respects, it's a quaint old place—that is the county itself.

As for not writing, last week I was one sick puppy just about all week. We were out on the range and it was so cold I just froze. Then I hadn't had enough rest with guard and everything so my resistance was low. I was just existing from one day to another. We had fifteen go to the hospital out of fifty-five in our barracks. I am feeling OK now, having shaken that cold and touch of flu. Last weekend our boys were moving out so there was plenty of work around here and no time off. Now, however, it isn't so bad, we just do a little bit each day in preparation for the new group. But yesterday Trent and I pulled K.P. for the first time in four months and for the third time since I've been in the army—and that wasn't so easy.

Speaking of Trent, reminds me to mention the fact that he's leaving this weekend or the beginning of next for Ft. McClellan, Ala. That's going to leave me without a roommate and he sure has been a good one.

[...] If I hit Asheville Sat., I'll give you a ring. However, in case I don't make it, let me wish you now a very pleasant vacation and may you find your brother enjoying life as a member of our country's first line of defenses.

As ever,
Dick[15]

Almon's invitation to Lancaster expressed the flourishing sense of kinship shared by Dick and DeEtta. Per Dick's recommendations, DeEtta and Frances planned to play tourist in central Pennsylvania. Prior to the war years, Dutch Country received little recognition from outsiders. Awareness of the region's traditional Amish culture surged in 1937 when the state attempted to eliminate the Amish's one-room schoolhouses. The effort gained national attention and spurred a defense of "old-fashioned American virtues." The debate shined a spotlight on what was previously perceived as a backward religious lifestyle. By the end of World War II, bus tours showcasing Amish life treated curious onlookers to a dreamy glimpse of the past. Accessibility to the pastoral attractions was expedited by the expanding Pennsylvania Turnpike. DeEtta's plans to savor the bucolic countryside were representative of a desire possessed by many tourists even today. After all, Winters referred to his home county as the "Garden Spot of the U. S."[16]

Far removed from the violence of war, the Winters homestead was nonetheless part of a community actively contributing to the national effort. Even before Pearl Harbor, the Lancaster Defense Council guarded surrounding hydroelectric plants, railroads, and bridges. The Army Air Forces later commandeered the municipal airport. By 1942, the Armstrong Cork Company manufactured ordnance casings, while the Pequea Works assembled fishing kits for life rafts. Housing for defense workers congested the city of 61,000 residents. Several German-Americans of the area, accused of being allegiant to their native land, were imprisoned.

DeEtta, Frances Johnson, and Richard Winters stand outside the Winters home in Lancaster in February 1942.

Edith Winters shows Frances and DeEtta the new Hersheypark Stadium in February 1942. Part of the Milton Hershey School can be seen in the far background. Dick introduced President George W. Bush at this stadium sixty-two years later.

No aspect of life was unchanged. Ann Winters participated in school-affiliated scrap drives. Her family abided by strict rationing regulations. Some 17,000 Lancastrians, including Dick, served in uniform. More than 500 sons of the city never returned home. Richard and Edith prayed their boy would not be among the lost.[17]

In the meantime, Winters "breezed through" physical examinations for OCS and successfully enrolled in a three-week preparation course for Fort Benning. He noted:

The competition is stiff and I'll certainly have to work to make the grade for just about everybody is at least a sergeant. I feel like a young innocent babe in the woods. Also, we live out in the barracks and are packed together like sardines. After living in one platoon for six months, and in one room for four, I feel rather homesick and lost. This is my first move since I came to camp. In fact I am writing this letter at home, so to speak, and later intend to do a little studying before going back to bed.

If things are as tough as they say, I think I'll stay right here in camp and put my nose to the grindstone for three weeks. But I plan to get up to see you about March 21. Last week I thought I'd be up but it was such a tough one that I stayed right here in camp all week.[18]

DeEtta fondly reminisced about her travels to Lancaster while Dick remained engrossed in his studies. Winters desired nothing more than to confirm his own tenacity. Later in the war, however, he affectionately reflected on times when he lacked certain responsibilities. Rank offered burdens as well as privileges. A degree of flexibility afforded him time for travel and leisure. His rise through the ranks later diminished those opportunities. "During the war I now had real responsibility….I was accountable for my men. I wore the bars," he recalled. "I no longer had time for fun."[19]

"Been in camp nigh unto two months."

Sun. March 8, 1942
3:00 P.M.-and raining

Dear DeEtta:

In answer to your P.S. which asked if I still was in S.C., yep, I am still here. But if it keeps snowing and raining, it's hard to tell how long I'll be able to hold on for it's getting darn muddy around here. In fact, for the past three weeks, it's been just about one long, continuous siege of mud vs. soap and water and shoe polish.

What's happening, I believe, is that we're having the spring rains now, rather than in April, as we do in Penna. At least, I hope that's right and I hope all the rain that we're due comes right now or within the next few days. Why? Because, about Wed. we're due to make another move. This one will be to "tent city," which is going to be mighty cold and damp and minus all the latest conveniences, I can see that right now.

This past week has been another trying week for I had to adjust myself to living in a barracks again. And then you'd think you were in West Point the way they keep going, shoes and clothes, just perfect, classes all day, study till late at night. It's a change in routine I wasn't used to any more. But I've adjusted myself and now I am fully acclimated so that I am enjoying this course and opportunity to get a little extra training.

In fact the training is very broad and comprehensive, when you think it over. For we have the head man from say, Intelligence, Communications, Heavy Weapons, come over and give us a summary in half a day of their whole course. They really tear into it for they know their subjects and you get a lot out of it. By the end of three weeks we'll have a summary like this on just about every phase of the army covered here in camp.

[...] This past week a new ruling came out that men being transferred to O.C.S. are not connected with their old companies, so Company A has put in for a corporal's rating for me. If it comes through this week, I'll be mighty happy for it means darn near a 50% raise in pay.

Being unfamiliar with the navy, their insignia denoting rank means nothing to me. So just what position corresponding to the army is a 2nd Class Petty Officer?

Did you receive those pictures from home as yet? I am anxious to see them. In fact, I might just forget the books next week and run up there to see them. This life is becoming monotonous. I haven't been away from Croft and Spartanburg for nigh unto two months now.

It's about time I find out what makes that Garand rifle tick, so I'll be seeing you in church.

As ever,
Dick[20]

Reconditioning himself to the communal standards of barracks life, Winters again recognized the broad array of personalities populating the bunks. Soldier Stevan Dedijer experienced a similar sensation at the camp. His comrades were predominantly blue-collar workers, many of whom possessed high school educations or less. Some were drafted and others enlisted voluntarily. "We lived together in barracks, ate together, trained together, and relaxed together, spent twenty-four hours in close proximity," recalled Dedijer. "I learned the names of everybody in my platoon but never tried to remember their last names. Of course, I learned the differences in their personalities. On some one could rely more than others. The language they used, the norms of behavior they practiced with each other, the country & western music they loved to listen to, all was a revelation to me. I can still hear their favorite plaintive song."[21]

A different manner of music resounded from the firing ranges. The .30 caliber M-1 Garand was Dick's primary weapon of choice throughout the war. Hefty and expensive (eighty-five dollars each), the rifle was the first standard-issue semiautomatic weapon in history. Some high-ranking officers foolhardily believed the rapid-fire weapon would compel soldiers to wastefully expend ammunition. Functioning in sharp contrast to Germany's standard, bolt action K-98 Mauser, the Garand fired its eight .30-06 rounds as fast as the operator could pull the trigger. Gen. George Patton referred to the rifle as "the greatest battle implement ever devised." Winters wielded the weapon with lethal effectiveness.[22]

Armored or Infantry?

Sunday, 3:30 P.M.
March 29, 1942

Dear Miss A:

Your letter left me quite confused, for while I never did profess to understand a woman's mind, nor to be abridge [*sic*] of all the rules of etiquette—and they sure do seem to differ somewhat in the various parts of the country—at least I thought that I knew the common definition of the term "gold-digging" when applied to women. However, it seems quite evident that I am wrong—at least around here—after your very positive letter. So please accept my humble apology and please apologize to Frances for my rudeness. But, it still beats me, just can't digest it as yet, but perhaps a few more days of studious thought will clear up the problem.

[...] The reason I didn't write last week was that I'd made up my mind to wait until I'd heard some definite news about my next move. On Wed. I had an offer to go to Ft. Knox, Ky., to the O.C.S. in the Armored Division. That was a chance to put an end to all suspense and to get going quickly for I'd have left Friday. After thinking it over and asking the advice of other officers, I decided against the common advice and decided to stick to the Infantry. I have seven months of background already and thirteen weeks at Benning should give me a background sturdy enough to enable me to carry my head up. In the Armored Division I'd be taking it cold and I'll be darned if I want to be an officer if I can't be a good one, so I'll be a good doughboy. Also, Benning is tops and I am not taking any substitute for my goal, not now. Just yesterday I had news I'll be leaving for Benning on the 6th of April to make the class that starts on the 7th.

Now my scheming mind has turned to how I can take a little vacation before starting that thirteen week marathon in the Georgia swamps. I've decided to ask for a three day pass (Fri., Sat., Sun.) on the grounds that I am almost due a furlough now but to the fact that I'll be going to Benning, I won't have more than a ten minute break for the next three and a half months. If it works, fine, I'll get out of here as quickly as possible—maybe Thursday night. If not, I'll gold-brick right here in camp. This next week is going to be my week, one time I am not going to "buck" from reveille till taps.

This last week my sister wrote and told me she received some bottles of perfume from you and that Dad received a very nice book of waltzes. They seem to appreciate their presents a lot. So thanks for your thoughtfulness as well as your kindness.

It's a typical Sun. afternoon for me. Play a little ball, write letters, and listen to the Philharmonic Orchestra until sleepy. I am sleepy now, so I'll let the music and sleep's drowsy breeze blow out the candles of thought.

As ever,
Dick

P.S. If I get that three day pass, I want to pick out the highest hilltop around and just park my carcass there for at least one whole day.[23]

Dick's preference of Infantry School at Fort Benning over armored training at Fort Knox was of little surprise. Not wishing to reinvent the wheel, Winters stuck to his guns and opted to "be a good doughboy." By 1942, Officer Candidate School was, as Dick surmised, one of the foremost military institutions in the country. Omar Bradley modeled the schooling on his educational experience at West Point. Candidates arose at 0600. After breakfast they attended courses and training for ten hours. Thirteen weeks of classes were taught within a "block system." Individual subjects were instructed over weeks-long periods rather than being taught concurrently. Following supper, two hours of evening study were granted. Lights were out by 2200. The school molded tens of thousands of company-level officers. Over time, an airborne training center emerged at the base comprising nearly 200,000 acres, which extended into neighboring Alabama.[24]

Winters thoroughly enjoyed the routines and scenery of Benning. On April 8, he noted, "There's lots of trees and grass, good streets, side-walks and in the brick barracks they have modern furniture and reading rooms. It's all so swell, you enjoy looking at it." His mess options were not bountiful, but were of high quality. "[I]t's as good as home cooking, and we even have table cloths and napkins," he observed. "Some class!" The candidates wore ties, their uniforms crisply pressed. Dick appreciated the meticulous attention to detail. But not all was pleasant—including his initial reception. "The trip down here, processing in, and cleaning a new M-1 rifle last night made it all a nightmare," he concluded to DeEtta. "We couldn't sleep Monday night and on the go, not knowing what the score was, left us worn out."[25]

Despite Benning's homey atmosphere, Officer Candidate School was unforgivingly strict. The cadre actively roamed the barracks with white gloves and rulers, seeking the most miniscule of errors and imperfections. Clothing, bedsheets, and shoes had to be spaced or folded at precise distances and lengths. Candidates were immediately dismissed if absent for formation. "They ran us ragged daily and we studied like fools each and every night," Dick remembered. Because transportation to any outside point of civilization was lacking, Winters buried his head in books. His idle hours on base consisted of movie matinees and ice cream treats.[26]

Less than two weeks after Dick's arrival at the fort, President Franklin Roosevelt conducted an inspection while en route to his retreat at Warm Springs. The preparations created circumstances even more rigid than usual. The effort was apparently worth the hassle, for Roosevelt and staff were duly impressed by infantry exercises and paratrooper demonstrations. In an assessment of the trip, one FDR staffer noted, "Fort Benning is such an immense post, and there was so much of interest happening here today, as to create within one the same feeling he would experience in attending his first five-ring circus." One could hardly decide which ring to watch. "Fort Benning's wooded, hilly and rolling terrain lends greatly to realistic training of our infantrymen and mechanized forces trained here," the aide added. "Many of the classes in these various schools are held in the open air here, and some begin as early as 3:00 A.M."[27]

Courses delved into a multitude of topics including map reading, logistics, offensive and defensive tactics, weapons, and leadership skills. The difficulty of each session intensified by the day.[28]

"You sent me flowers–God bless you!"

Sunday 10:00 P.M.
May 10, 1942

Dear DeEtta:

There's nothing like being original, doing the unexpected, to get the desired effect. If that's what you had in mind when you sent those flowers, it sure worked. It so happened that when we came in that day from the fields, we were hot, dirty and dead tired. Then when I received a box so light in weight, it stumped me as to what it could be. Upon examination, when I found some flowers, it struck me as rather funny.

A soldier receiving flowers! So whenever I think of it, it's still good for a laugh. One thing's certain, I won't forget the distinction between the two species.

Before I forget it, let me extend my best wishes for a happy birthday. If my memory serves me correctly, your birthday should be about this Thursday. I had thought of sending you a card, but I'll be darned if I can find a decent card even in Columbus. So the best I can do at this time is say happy birthday.

The weeks have just been flying by at school. Each week they tell us the [succeeding] one will be the toughest yet, and so far they've been right, in fact the last two were terrific. We've been on the machine gun and studying how to shoot over the heads of your own troops and hit the enemy. Also, how to aim at one target and hit another, the idea being that you could still score a hit if a smoke screen were laid down obscuring the target.

[...] My parents had planned on coming down here this weekend before gas rationing started, but that's all that came out of it. Dad wired me last Saturday of his plans and I was all excited. Then, Sunday he wrote that he'd changed his mind. I received the word Thursday. Need I say how I felt?

When I announced my plans to join the paratroops to my parents, I received a long veto, and since then many more from both my parents, friends and neighbors. I've always taken their advice so far, but this time I think I'll try my own judgment. They think it's the money and glamour that seems attractive to me. In a way it is, but the main thing is it looks like interesting work, something I'll enjoy. So I still think I'll take a try at it.

As ever,
Dick

P.S. This Georgia sun still feels plenty good and as per usual, I'm drinking it all in.[29]

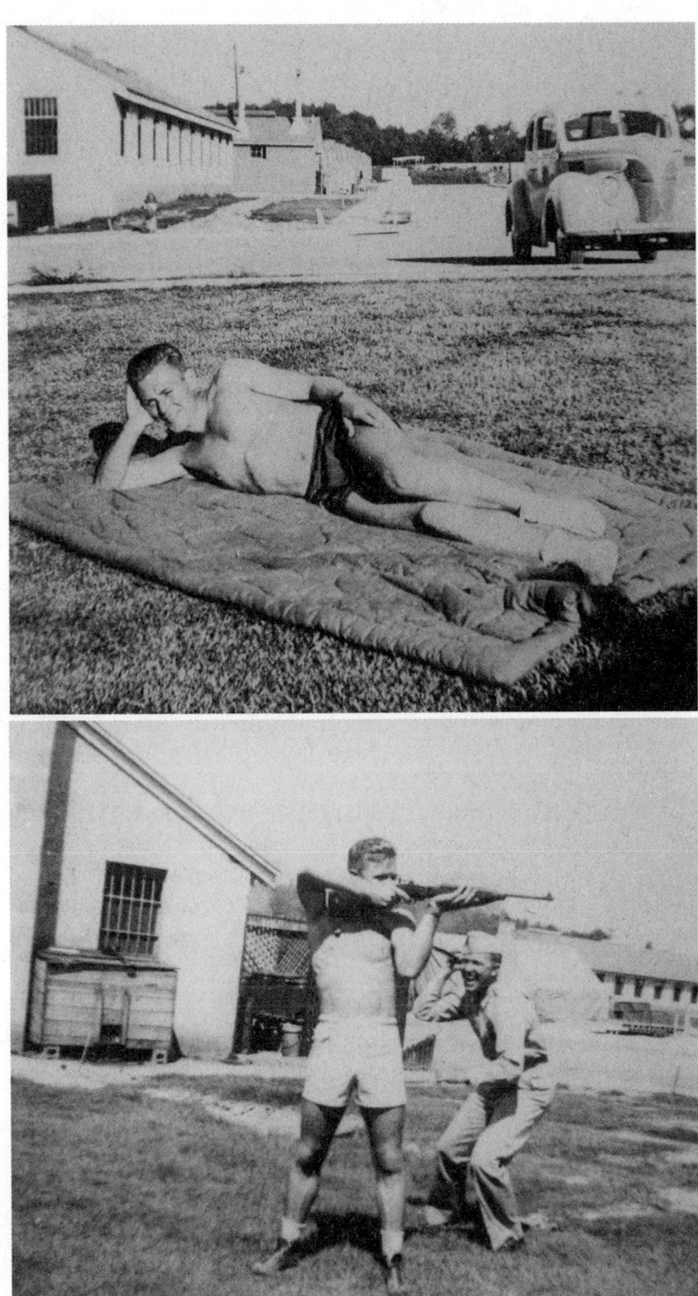

Strictness did not always get the best of Winters. Whether sunbathing or posing with his carbine, Dick welcomed brief moments of lightheartedness on base.

The Winters family was hesitant to bless Dick's ambition of joining the paratroops. They recognized an inherent danger to the trade, one far exceeding the perils of a typical infantryman. Yet, paratroopers possessed a distinct fellowship. "We paratroopers had an abundance of esprit de corps and rightly so," recalled Guy Whidden of the 502nd Parachute Infantry Regiment. "[W]e were generally recognized in those days to be an elite branch of the service—unmatched by any other military unit." An advertisement presenting the romanticized allure of the airborne was "a big factor in my decision to become a paratrooper," Whidden concluded.[30]

The risks were plentiful. Don Malarkey, a future non-commissioned officer under Winters, faced pushback from family members when he announced his intentions to become a paratrooper. Shortly after Malarkey received his draft notice, a friend on leave from Fort Lewis underscored the grim potentials of the paratroops. "Whatever you do, don't say yes, Malarkey," warned the buddy. "It's a death sentence. You're jumping out of a friggin' airplane going a couple hundred miles an hour—and right into enemy territory. The odds stink."

"But I'd made up my mind," Malarkey remembered. His heart was set.

"You're nuts," the friend retorted.

In Malarkey's view, there was a world of "difference between a paratrooper and a guy slinging hash in some back-of-the-lines mess hall." Like Winters and Whidden, Malarkey possessed a drive pushing himself to the limits of endurance. On May 24, Winters made his case clear to DeEtta. He planned "to be a paratrooper despite all advice to the negative." Nobody could convince him otherwise.[31]

Instruction on Marksmanship

Sunday 1:30 P.M.
May 31, 1942
Macon, Georgia

Dear DeEtta:

No, I haven't managed to see Florida yet, but the next Saturday we get off, I will. When that will be is hard to say. No, my parents never went through with their plans to come down–just got cold feet on the tires and gas [rationing] situation. I graduate July 4th. President Roosevelt is supposed to be here for the occasion (and that's no joke). Hope to sign up with the paratroops any week now. S.T.R. means Student Training Regiment and you leave me breathless with that kind of a firing line.

I've been hearing jokes about girls taking up marksmanship, but thought it only a joke. However, I see it's the truth and also it's a good idea. What kind of rifle are they using? Sure wish I'd be lucky once for a change and get that kind of a job. If they ever let you shoot the darn thing remember to squeeze the trigger; it's the all-important thing. And to avoid flinching, concentrate on the bull and as you squeeze, force your eye open as far as you can, concentrate on that eye and you'll never know when the gun goes off. Also, be sure your sling adjustment is tight; it's another key to success.

This last week we finished the weapons end of the course and I am not sorry for all I've been thinking about are lugs, cams, operating rods, gas-operated, recoil-operated, etc., etc. Now we go into tactics and I can use my own head once again. I like that. In fact, I like the whole course, which, incidentally, costs $3,500 per man. Yesterday we saw a battalion in attack at a river crossing as a company of engineers threw up a footbridge, a bridge, and a ferry under fire of guns, cover of smoke, and fire of airplanes. They had all kinds of trucks, guns, tanks, and everything else running around there.

I heard from Sgt. Trenta this last week and he's doing all right up at McClellan. Hope to get up there to see him sometime. I asked him to join up in the paratroops with me but he's afraid his flat feet would bother him. I agree. He had the idea of the paratroops first. I thought he was crazy. After seeing the life a doughboy will live, I think a doughboy is crazy. Fifty percent die of disease living in the filth up on the front lines, and that's the best it's ever been, not the highest.

My latest desire is to try and talk myself into a situation where I could instruct wrestling to the troops. That would be heaven to me. It's just an idea, and if it doesn't work out, I'll still be satisfied to be with the troops. My parents must think I've dropped the idea when I dropped the subject in my letters. Hope they aren't too shocked.

The big problem nowadays is buying clothes. They sure are high priced and it's hard to get just what you want. But, boy, it's fun, just like having a dream turn out to be true.

Think I'll take a "postman's holiday" now and run out to Camp Wheeler.

Did I tell you I've been moved into a double room? We had a rating the other week where everybody rates the other fellow on leadership, ability, personality, etc. Shortly afterward, I was moved into this room with a master sgt.—37 years old. In fact, that's who I came down here with. He went on to Augusta to his family and will pick me up this evening.

As ever,
Dick[32]

Like many civilians in wartime, DeEtta enrolled in a marksmanship program, perhaps as a primer for her forthcoming military service. Such courses grew in scale and frequency across the country, especially among females and young adults. "We've got a good many members who are thoroughly competent to give instruction," one gun-club official declared weeks after Pearl Harbor. "We're ready to help any of the watchmen or other individuals hired to protect our reservoirs and utilities in becoming more expert with sidearms...So long as we have cartridges, we'll hold our matches. It is good for defense preparation."[33]

Dick, too, actively ventured to firing ranges. Instructors demonstrated a variety of marksmanship techniques to make candidates effective riflemen. Winters enjoyed the process but was appreciative when it was done, for all he could think about were weaponry mechanisms.[34]

More pressing an issue for Winters was the shortage of suitable apparel representative of his upcoming lieutenant's rank. "One headache of becoming an officer is getting a uniform," he complained to DeEtta on June 23. "In fact, I've one good outfit, that's all. Can't find anything else to suit me so I'll wait until I go north when I'll go shopping in Philadelphia." Depending on the season, army officers frequently sported chocolate brown Class A dress jackets with pale khaki trousers. This sharp combination was often described as "pinks and greens," an aesthetic look that gained the attention of passersby. Dick aspired to look the role of a leader. Still pondering his immediate future, he added, "My ambition is still with the paratroops and the more I learn about the infantry, the more I am sold on the fact that I don't want any part of it."[35]

Although Dick and Trent were no longer together, they later fought in the same campaigns. Following training at Fort McClellan, Trent rose to the rank of staff sergeant and was wounded on January 23, 1945, during the Battle of the Bulge. After the war, he returned to Lancaster and worked at the Burnham Corporation boiler manufacturing plant for thirty-six years. He died unexpectedly at home on February 20, 1985. He was sixty-six years of age.[36]

"What is the next assignment?"

Tuesday, 8:30 P.M.
June 30, 1942

Dear DeEtta:

Thanks for the swell pictures. They are very nice and I do believe you are losing weight. Is it the rifle marksmanship, swimming, hard work, or combination of all three that is responsible?

Am I excited about graduation? No, in fact I've been a little despondent the last few days. It's the first time I've really been down since my last furlough. This time it's a combination of not knowing where or what my assignment will be and then, if I will get that leave or not. It sure is a strain for I've been counting on it for so darn long and so darn strong and the closer the time comes, it may be tomorrow, Thursday, or Friday A.M., the more certain I feel that I am not going to get my precious leave. What makes it so tough is that I feel sure I can't have my cake and eat it.

[...] We finish work tomorrow A.M. and then start physical exams and deprocessing [*sic*] with graduation Friday. A.M., lunch in the officer's club, and then we are free.

Uniforms have been arriving the past few days and it looks like a fashion show with the boys parading around, flashing bars and decorations and smiles. Here we are about to reach that charmed class, a distinct social class. We'll command respect and authority. It's the dream of every rookie from the day he comes into the army and we are just about to reach out and grasp it. Even the fact that Friday will find some of us heading for combat seems to make no difference. But that's the way to be, live and let live. However, at times it's hard to convince yourself that it's true.

As ever,
Dick[37]

In retrospect, Dick described OCS "as a thirteen-week marathon in the Georgia swamps." The experience was no picnic, but the program made him physically and intellectually stronger. Upon graduation on July 2, 1942 (which FDR did not attend), Dick accepted a new level of responsibility. During those months of rigorous training, Winters crossed paths with a smart, privileged, hard-drinking Ivy Leaguer named Lewis Nixon. At face value, Nixon was very unlike the mild-mannered Winters. However, Dick sensed they shared distinct, common outlooks. Their reciprocal ideals and ambitions ultimately carried them to a place where their destinies intertwined—Camp Toccoa.[38]

Lewis Nixon, Dick's most trusted compatriot.

506th P.I.R.–Camp Toombs, GA.

Mon. 7:45 P.M.
August 31, 1942

Dear DeEtta:

As an officer I didn't last long at Croft. About four or five weeks to be exact. Then, bingo, I received orders to the 506th Parachute Regiment, Camp Toombs, Ga.

While at Croft I was able to get away one weekend. All the rest I was getting the dirt as a junior officer, in the form of officer of the day for the company, regiment, or battalion.

At first I hated to leave Croft for I was well acquainted, both with my old outfit and the new company to which I was assigned. There I had four boys from home in my platoon. The one I went to college with and wrestled with while in school. So we continued to pal around for I didn't believe a little hardware should stand between us. Other officers frowned on it all, I know, but what did that mean to me—nothing. I worked darn hard on that platoon and just before I left they all qualified on the range but two, which is darn good, better than any other outfit ever did around here. How's that compare with your rifle team? Before I left they gave me a Shaffer pen and pencil set. I believe I could do better if I'd use it. Then I left, leaving a camp that held many fond memories.

Camp Toombs—changed to Toccoa—is located in the foothills of the Blue Mountains. We only have 800 men, who sleep in tents, officers in unfinished huts, no lights, mud galore when it rains, cool every night so that you need two blankets. Most of the day we run around in shorts taking exercises and pre-jump training. Then we go for a six mile run uphill, then down, and it's plenty stony and rough. In the evening you can write until dusk, then to bed. It sure is healthy, just like training for a football team and the camp, country, and men all seem to blend together to form the perfect picture.

In about three weeks I'll be going to Benning for a week of jumping. After five jumps, last on Thursday, I am a qualified paratrooper, wings, pay and all. Then I report back here Monday for further training of the unit for this is my combat outfit, unless I am transferred.

Best wishes to you and all the family.
Dick[39]

The 506th Parachute Infantry Regiment (PIR) was established on July 20, 1942. Creation of the unit was spearheaded by the thirty-seven-year-old West Pointer, Col. Robert Sink. A perceptive North Carolinian known as "the Fox," the colonel sported a dignified mustache and demanded the highest standards. At the outset, some 6,000 prospective paratroopers marched through the gates of Camp Toccoa in northern Georgia with the intention of earning wings. Over 80 percent of the men did not gain the distinction. The opening of the intense, thirteen-week

506th Parachute Infantry
Airborne Command
United States Army
Camp Toccoa, Ga.

This is to Certify That:

1st Lieut. RICHARD D. WINTERS, 0-1286582

has satisfactorily completed the prescribed course in Parachute Packing, Ground Training, and Jumping from a plane in flight. He is, therefore, entitled to be rated from this date, 9-30-42, as a qualified Parachutist.

Colonel, 506th Prcht. Inf.
Commanding

Left: Winters, a fresh lieutenant, looks the part for a photographer while posing at Toccoa. Dick's athleticism secured his place as the first man to jump from a plane at the camp. Right: Winters qualified as a paratrooper at Toccoa on September 30, 1942. His certificate was signed by Col. Robert Sink.

training program commenced with demanding rounds of calisthenics and forced marches of twenty miles. Sink supervised the creation of a devilish, zigzagging obstacle course featuring elements both natural and manmade. According to legend, Sink challenged Marines from Parris Island to complete the course. They could not.[40]

Largely composed of twelve rows of makeshift wooden huts, Toccoa lacked the postcard attributes of Fort Benning. Bill Guarnere, a streetwise kid from Philadelphia, was less than impressed by the facilities. "The place was a sloppy mess, all muddy, red clay. The barracks and buildings were under construction, dirt and mud everywhere. We slept in tents on cots and when it rained your cot floated away. But where do you think you're going, to a resort?" The experience was not for the faint of heart. "There were bugs, mosquitoes, rats, mice, everything. It's out in the woods. But the war was on. Times were hard." In Guarnere's opinion, Camp Toccoa served one primary purpose: "Weeding out the weaklings." On September 24, Dick penned an enthused letter detailing aspects of training, part of which noted:[41]

> The other week I won the weekly track meet, so to speak, then passed a two day course on chute packing, taken at night, and now, this week I live a normal life before leaving for Benning on Saturday to make my five jumps and qualify. Then I'll wear a pair of silver wings. Damn boy, will I be proud! Then I'll really strut!
>
> Last Sunday I had a couple of snapshots taken. Here's one of them. The rifle is a carbine, a just new rifle. Four months ago there were only four in existence, two at Benning. Here all officers have them. We rate A-1 in priority. It weighs 5 ½ lb., semi-automatic, gas-operated, 15 shots. You ought to have one for your marksmanship. It would be easy to handle. Now look closely at the right boot. That's a trench knife, with brass knuckles attached, a very effective weapon for the type of warfare we'll be doing—close in. The platform is used for jumping off of and then going into a tumble for landings. We do it by the hour. I love it for it comes easy with experience in wrestling.[42]

Earning accolades for his achievements, Winters was a subject of an article in Lancaster's *Sunday News* on October 4, 1942. The piece described the exploits of several Lancastrians, all while offering an exceptional description of paratrooper education:

New Technique for F-M Wrestler in Paratroops: Throwing Himself Down!
Cloudy Trail Is Long and Tough but—Anything to Jump on the Axis

"Hit the silk!"

That's the paratrooper's paraphrase for "Jump!"—and they do mean out of an airplane.

How do they get that way? Well, a couple of Lancaster soldiers are learning how the hardest possible way.

They're well along the cloudy trail to becoming parachute troopers, who have to be some of the world's toughest fighters to get by. Two of them took muscles, hardened on wrestling mats here, into the service, and one took along one of the finest intercollegiate wrestling records on the books.

Frankie Burgess is the varsity grappler, and in a recent letter he told Lancaster friends about his surprise meeting with three other Lancastrians during his preliminary training. Lieutenant Dick Winters, another F&M wrestler, was in charge of Burgess' platoon during preliminary training. Virgil Parmer, Manheim Township, and Earl Rice of Lancaster, were also in his outfit, and still are with him learning the radio specialist's business.

They've licked that first toughening-up period, and Winters has gone to the paratrooper's headquarters, Fort Benning, Ga., while the other three are busy learning the dashes and dots that a radio specialist must know.

These Men from Mars—and Lancaster—went through plenty to get this far, and there's a lot more ahead before they'll be graduated paratroopers. Burgess writes:

"I enlisted in the paratroopers for action and so far I haven't been close enough to a parachute to see one. It seems as if they really prepare you, even before you start your actual parachute training.

"Well, I spent six weeks here at Croft, being schooled in the art of how the Infantry soldier learns his stuff. We're taught the hard way.

"Our training was tough as hell, but looking back on it, it wasn't too bad.

"We learned every single little part of three rifles and also how to use them on the Japs and Germans. In addition to that, we were taught how to use a bayonet to the very best advantage. Map reading and compass reading were also included. The thing I liked best of all was our 2-mile run over a cross-country course every morning.

"They were a happy six weeks—now as I look back on them.

"At present I am attending a radio school for six more weeks. Cripes, I'll go crazy from hearing dits and dots (dots and dashes to you) all day. We also learn how to operate many different types of radio sets. I am classed as a radio specialist in the paratroopers.

"When I came into Camp Croft I had quite a surprise.

"The first time I fell out for a formation, who should I see before me but Lieutenant Dick Winters, who was in charge of my platoon.

"You remember Dick, he went to F&M and graduated in '41. He didn't wrestle varsity but came to practice nearly every day to work out for four years. He wrestled and took first place, I believe, in the Middle Atlantics at Philadelphia. That was the Diplomat outfit that won the Ray Fabiani Trophy, now in our trophy case.

"What I'm driving at is this. I think he deserves some recognition in the home town. He signed up a year ago and worked up the hard way. A finer officer and fellow you won't find anywhere.

"The boys in Croft all liked him, and at the end of six weeks training our platoon presented him with a pen and pencil set to show our appreciation for him.

"Last week he was shipped to Benning, Georgia, to be a parachute instructor and his silver bars (1st Lieut.) will soon be gotten if not already."

At the Georgia Camp he'll quite likely encounter Capt. Barney Oldfield, of Lincoln, Neb., first newspaperman to become a paratrooper. To Winters and Oldfield the thrill of that first jump is old stuff now, but a description of it might make good reading for Burgess and Rice and Parmer, and other Lancastrians for whom it's coming up.

Here's how Capt. Oldfield remembers it, anyhow, in a description he wrote for Wide World feature service:

"We were 1,500 feet above Lawson Field when the jumpmaster commanded: 'Stand in the door!'

"First up was Lt. Leonard Anglin, of Lumpkin, Ga. He planted his feet and let the prop blast roar into his face as he stuck his head out the door.

"We were all hooked up, our static lines fastened to the long cable in the roof of the transport. It was graduation day for paratroopers.

"Then the jumpmaster, swinging the flat of his hand hard up against the underside of Anglin's leg, yelled: 'Go!'

"As in an unfinished old-fashioned two-step, left foot in the lead, right coming up but never passing, we shuffled to the door. Pivot on the right foot, left to the ledge, a push and we hurled through space, turning a quarter turn left and dropping under the tail of the plane.

'1,000, 2,000, 3,000,' we said.

"That's three seconds.

"If that snap of the chute opening hadn't been felt by then, we were instructed to pull the reserve ripcord on '4,000.' Mine opened in the middle of '2,000.' I said it something like 'two-UMPH-thousand.'

"I looked up and the canopy was over me like a tent, suspension lines taut. Below me was the field, like a well-kept lawn. There was no feeling of falling or height, but I was swinging a little, so grabbed the right front and left rear risers, chinning myself to check the oscillation.

"We were about 800 feet up. Somebody yelled. It was Lt. Rodger Meadows, of Akron, OH.

'Nobody in Akron would believe I'd ever do this,' he said. Same goes for all of us in our hometowns, I guess.

"An air current hit me at 100 feet. I grabbed the risers, rocked them hard to keep oscillation from setting in again.

"Twenty feet up, I looked down, prayed I'd land lightly on that week-old sprained ankle, then suddenly realized I was coming in backwards.

"The ground...

"I spilled backward, did a complete roll, and never touched the ankle. The chute collapsed, and as I unsnapped the harness, I looked for the next groups already in descent.

"Meadows lit fairly easy. Lt. Henry Buchanan, late of Anderson, SC, came in on a slight knee bend and stood up without a roll. There was a puddle of water off to the right, and Lt. Robert Carison, Utica, NY, plowed it up like a motorboat.

"We started rolling up our chutes to get off the field.

"And that, with accompanying post mortems, covered the first of five jumps necessary to qualify as a parachute trooper. It took the Army four weeks to train us for this landing, which is about two percent of what a parachutist has to do. The other 98 percent is fighting the enemy tooth and nail, when encountered, and winning."[43]

Four sons of Lancaster at Camp Croft in 1942. Left to right are Winters, Virgil Parmer, Frankie Burgess, and Earl Rice.

By fall, Dick overcame intensified hurdles at Toccoa. Many officers, including Winters, completed jump school on site, while enlisted men generally did so at Fort Benning. Exercises on the scramble net tower, flight swings, and improvised gadgets were ritual. There was little rest to be had—even on Thanksgiving. The Second Battalion of the 506th PIR, commanded by disciplined taskmaster Maj. Robert Strayer, was bestowed a caustic holiday treat. During a two-day field exercise, Winters and company encountered the infamous "Hawg Innards Problem." The diabolical obstacle course consisted of barbed wire stretched eighteen inches above the ground, with .30 caliber machine guns firing overhead as men crawled below. The wide pit through which soldiers slithered was strewn with a bloody assortment of hog entrails. Dick was invited to Asheville for dinner that day but instead slushed through putrid pig intestines.[44]

Second Battalion confronted new challenges five days later. Its regiment received orders to report to Fort Benning in early December. First Battalion set forth by train but alternative plans were in store for Second Battalion. Col. Sink wished to outshine a marching record set by elite Japanese troops. With Sink's blessing, Strayer thus orchestrated a 118-mile march from Toccoa to Atlanta. Rain and snow plagued the sodden marchers on the first day of the trek, during which forty miles were covered. Mike Ranney of E Company long remembered that first, freezing night. "I'll never forget the morning agony of trying to cram my swollen feet into those GI shoes. Somehow I did, along with 600 other guys, and that day we covered another 40 miles, now with much attention on us." The journey was undertaken partially for public relations and, when the battalion finally reached Atlanta, the city hospitably welcomed it. The men were generally too battered to hit the town. Ranney, for one, was presented two bottles of bourbon by a stranger at a liquor store. He whisked the hooch back to grateful comrades.[45]

Even two weeks after the hike, Winters wrote of the pain he and the men still felt in their raw feet and strained muscles. "We're not over our three day maneuver yet," he explained on December 16. "Everybody is all washed out with colds and lack of vitamins."[46]

The competitive Third Battalion commander, Lt. Col. Robert Wolverton—not to be outperformed by Strayer—had his troops disembark their train in Atlanta to march the remaining 136 miles to Fort Benning. The men confronted equally dismal weather. Wolverton's feet became so blistered that he completed the march by walking bootless, wearing only three pairs of socks. The colonel exhibited an undeterred style mirroring Winters's own qualities. Sadly, Wolverton was brutally killed in the early moments of D-Day. Germans used his corpse for target practice.[47]

There was much to do in the year and a half prior to the invasion of France. The 506th Parachute Infantry Regiment commenced jump school at Fort Benning and had yet to find a home within a division. Dick removed himself from that concern as he happily made use of a ten-day pass for New Years. Back in Lancaster, Winters felt astray in his hometown. He noticed the troubling disconnect with civilians—a detachment that widened over time. "Home is still a wonderful place but nowadays I am a stranger among friends at home," he wrote to DeEtta on January 15, 1943. "Also, it's good to get away from there. They don't even know a war's going on."[48]

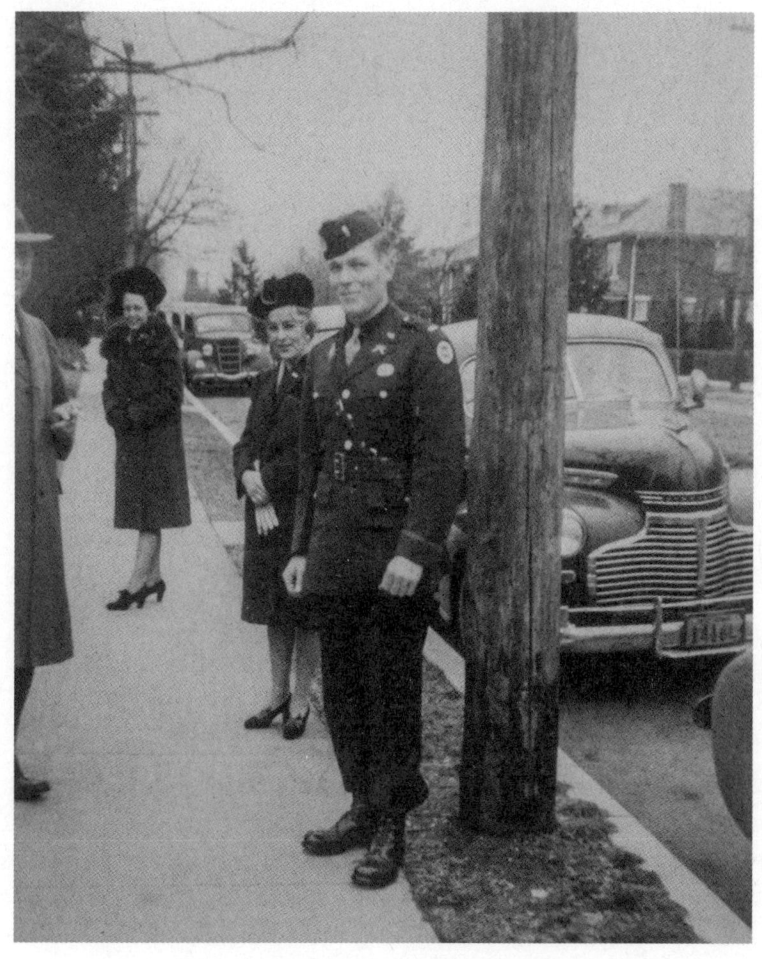

Dick mingles with family and friends in Lancaster, January 1943.

CHAPTER THREE

WORSE THAN BATTLE

February 1943 to May 1944

"Someday you will have a letter and a souvenir from each country."

Sunday evening
Feb. 7, 1943

Dear DeEtta:

The army has a way of changing its mind without explaining how and why, so all I know is that the 506th instead of moving to Hoffman, N.C. today, walks nine miles further into the country from Ga. to Ala. and takes up new quarters in the swamps of Alabama. That's life and so there goes a nice set-up and a lot of nice dreams. Now it'll take a three day pass to go to town for we're three miles from transportation now and we'll be twelve when we're settled in our new town. That too, is all right, you make a better outfit that way and we have a crack outfit.

Curahee [*sic*] is our motto, our battle cry. In Indian it means "stand alone." We have it mean "we stand alone." It's taken from the mountain Curahee at Toccoa, Ga., that one three miles high, rising 1,200 ft. that we used to run up. The record was 42 min. I made it in 44 one day. I am strictly no runner though, just did it by plugging along.

My picture, glad you like it, but as to where I'd like it, well I've never quite gotten over being bashful, even after a year and a half in the army, so I'd rather not be decorating the piano. Really, I need a haircut and I am slightly worn out. We'd just come in from three days of hell on a canteen of water and some biscuits, besides freezing to death.

Glad to hear you're taking it easy at the store. Perhaps you just learned to use your aides instead of doing it all yourself. Personally, I've been going pretty strong from 6:30 to 10 or 11 every day trying to get an athletic program going in the 2nd Bn. and teaching wrestling as well in the gym. As a result, I am grateful for Sundays, (this is the first one we've had off though for over a month), so rest up. With all the mat burns from teaching rookies, I look like a piece of hamburger. But I still love to wrestle—and the army—more all the time. Of course the latter had a good start for it started at zero.

Don't let your studies or lack of ambition—I should talk though—keep your letters so far apart.

When I hit Europe in my travels, you'll have a letter from each country the 506th takes and a souvenir, and that includes Berlin and Tokyo, if I must do it myself.

As ever,
Dick

P.S. I'll do it for I've made up my mind![1]

With Camp Toccoa behind them, the men of the 506th nonetheless retained a strong emotional attachment to the landmark. At the isolated, ramshackle post in the Georgia pines, strangers became brothers. The repetitive hardships they endured cemented their bonds. Most daunting of all were the grueling climbs up the mountain in whose shadow Toccoa stood. Ed Shames remembered the first time he was introduced to Currahee. An instructor stood before his formation and declared, "Gentleman, today we are going to put your fitness to the test....You see that lump of rock? It's called Currahee....Any of you who do not make the 6-mile round trip within 1 hour and 10 minutes will fail and be immediately reassigned to a non-airborne outfit."[2]

Among the officers pushing his men up the steep gravel slopes was Lt. Herbert Sobel, the obstinate commander of E Company. Sobel was deemed well-intentioned by some, hardnosed by others, but despised by most. Many of the men believed Sobel exacted the frustrations of his own shortcomings upon subordinates. In their various memoirs, Easy Company veterans described Sobel as awkward, susceptive, insecure, and vindictive. Bill Guarnere went so far as to call him "a mean son of a bitch." Sobel's antics and harsh protocols forged camaraderie among his enlisted men while physically preparing them for trials ahead. Yet his troops had no confidence in his abilities as a tactician. He froze under pressure and committed glaring errors during maneuvers. After one particularly grievous offense, Winters heard a soldier mutter, "Jesus Christ, I'm going into combat with this man? He'll get us all killed." Growing friction between Winters and Sobel would reach a boiling point after the division shipped to England that fall.[3]

The contrasting dispositions of Winters (left) and Sobel (right) are best exhibited in these portraits taken at Camp Mackall. Indicative of his displeasure with Sobel, Winters drew a mustache on the photo of his superior he mailed home.

The high demands hardly let up as the regiment relocated to Camp Mackall in early 1943. On March 28, Dick underscored his agitation over shifting from one base to another: "Speaking of going across [the Atlantic] is a subject that's very close to me for I'd sure like to go. As things stand now we (the 506th) aren't attached to any airborne division as yet and in fact we're the only qualified outfit that isn't. I have hopes that will mean maybe six more months over here training as a unit of a division. I want to get going myself." Temporarily serving as company commander that month, Winters embraced the learning opportunity. "The darndest part of it all is that we've had the hardest part of our training in those weeks," he observed. "That, plus the trials of a new job have been quite a strain, so when I came in from the field yesterday, I was just about out. I hadn't been to bed but four times in eleven days."[4]

Company Executive Officer.

April 15, 1943
Easter Sunday

Dear DeEtta—

Thanks for the Easter card and for the letters. You'll have to excuse my rate of correspondence for it's darn seldom I have the time and inclination to write. We're out in the field night and day for five days of the week. In a week's time, when you have a little sleep, you certainly can become tired.

[...] Nowadays I am holding the new title of executive officer for Co. E, 506th, a position I've been holding for three months without title. My job is to take charge of the company when the captain isn't around, and he never is, and do the paper work. Don't ask me what the captain does. Also, I now have six months seniority as a 1st Lt. so I am eligible for promotion, but that's out of the question for there are no openings.

What I am anxious to see is for this outfit to go across and see some action. Gosh, I am tired of suffering in N.C., S.C., Ga., and Ala. When this war's over I want to be able to say more than how much I suffered down south.

Camp Mackall is really a part of Bragg although we are about 50 miles apart. We're the airborne part of Bragg. That's all we have here, paratroopers. It's near Southern Pines and Pinehurst, two swanky winter resorts. What the hell people do there, I don't know. Also Rockingham is about 25 miles away. In about the center of there, Mackall is located.

Happy Easter.

As ever,
Dick[5]

Winters's subtle jab at the newly promoted Capt. Sobel was as antagonistic a description of his superior as he dared to write. After all, Sobel was known for searches and seizures of "contraband" in soldier footlockers. The captain possessed talent in molding men into athletic fighting machines. At the same time, his physical absence from clerical duties and his psychological absence during war games prompted Winters to warrant a vote of no confidence. "Any relationship between company commander and company officers that existed in Easy Company remained strictly professional," Dick recalled. "Sobel had no friends within the company and few within the regiment." The men played vengeful pranks on the captain, igniting his rage even further.[6]

Celebrated correspondent Ernie Pyle recognized such toxic leadership as highly volatile. "I've been around war long enough to know that nine-tenths of morale is pride in your outfit and confidence in your leaders and fellow fighters." Morale is essential to unit cohesion. Reporter Hanson Baldwin likewise contended that the ruthless elimination of the "unfit, inept, stuffed-shirt, and inefficient leaders" was a necessary measure in ensuring military efficiency. Members of untested American divisions required "good leadership" because they held "the future in their hands."[7]

In July 1943, Dick welcomed a final hiatus to Lancaster during a ten-day leave. He was happy to escape Sobel's wrath for even a short period of time. Winters was emphatic in his desires to fight overseas but also yearned for the innocence of bygone days. As he departed his hometown, Dick realized embarkation for England was on the horizon. "I may soon start sending those letters from different foreign countries," he informed DeEtta on July 3. In the back of his mind, a glimmer of concern compelled him to wonder if this would be his last time home.[8]

These July 1943 photos are from Dick's last visit home before voyaging overseas. At left, mother Edith and sister Ann greet him at the Lancaster Pennsylvania Railroad station. At right, Dick casually sports his Fort Benning t-shirt on his parents' front lawn.

Fort Bragg–Getting ready to ship out.

August 2, 1943

Dear DeEtta-

It just doesn't add up. You know when I graduated from college Kresge [department stores] offered me a job of some kind with chances to hit the sky and I was the only one out of my whole class that was interviewed. He promised me lots of hard work and years of it. Now you tell me you're the prospective manager. A comely girl, who looks so well in shorts, you certainly wouldn't think she had the brains or could be stern enough to run a business. But lots of funny things happen nowadays—girls running around army camps, driving trucks. It just doesn't make sense.

[...] So you think I'll be tired of the outdoors after this is over. No, after two months of not sleeping on a bed, clothes dirty, etc. etc. I was enjoying it more all the time. Just one thing bothers me and that's those emergency rations they claimed they designed for paratroopers. K ration and D ration, ugh. To read the list it sounds great, to eat it over a period of time, well it's more than a fellow can take. It's just too concentrated. In fact, I've sent word home to buy a farm after they get done paying off the house with the money I send home each month. I want a good investment and a place to go to after this war's over. I'd sure like to see what they pick out though, but I guess any place in Lancaster County would be O.K. by me.

We've been going slowly crazy around here in our haste and rush to get ready, all new equipment and everything in 1st class order. Boy, there are a million things going on at once. It's really worse than battle. Which reminds me, did you see what the paratroopers are doing over there? Well wait until I land. I'll take that company on a sight-seeing tour and the places we won't see and things we won't do just won't be worthwhile. I hope, yes, I sure hope, they give me just one good chance and then give us fifteen minutes to get set once we hit.

It'd be nice if Italy just said, "comrade," and we could walk in. But I've been counting on helping take that big old boot and trying it on for size.

Incidentally, among my various duties as E.O. of Co. E, I am now also postal officer. In other words, I censor all mail. That has possibilities of being very interesting and educational despite the added hours of work. Well, I don't have company but I sure am getting tired and sleepy so I think I'll close and catch a decent night's rest.

As ever
Dick[9]

The 506th Parachute Infantry Regiment shuffled from one military installation to another until finally, in September 1943, the regiment departed New York City for Europe. Pvt. David Webster of E Company, a literature student from Harvard, long dreamed of sailing to England. "I wanted to ride a big, black boat with white cabins and red funnels across the Atlantic and bicycle through the British Isles to the places that I had read about" in the classics. Though not as romantic as he originally envisioned, Webster was off to that ancient land. "I was a little boy no longer," he confessed in his excellent memoir. "The toy soldiers had come to life. Instead of a Black Watch cap with ribbons, I wore a steel helmet with a parachutist's chin strap. Jump boots were my leggings now, an M-1 rifle my steamer basket." The departure was not sent off with confetti but rather "a handful of bored stevedores." For many aboard, the embarkation marked the last time they saw America.[10]

Once in England, the regiment settled in for months of training, education, and assimilation. Pvt. Donald Burgett of Company A, a fresh enlisted man recently added to the ranks, felt at home. "The new men blended into the outfit as though they had always been there. For the rest of them, as for myself, we now had an outfit, a home, and a name, a feeling of pride, belonging, and brotherhood that all paratroopers hold for each other." Preparation now began in earnest. Maneuvers increased as personal time decreased. "Weapon inspections became daily routine until our equipment was in top condition, and night assembly practice after simulated jumps was pulled almost every night for a week," claimed Burgett. "We knew the field like the back of our hands."[11]

Winters further cemented his bonds with the men in this time. Amid a brief pause during maneuvers, Dick encountered the weary Pvt. Clarence "Shep" Howell gazing at a photo of his girlfriend. Winters initiated small talk and Howell confessed his desire to return safely to his sweetheart. "You will," Winters insisted. "Just keep your mind focused on your job. You're a good man, Shep. Hang tough."[12]

Efforts to maintain comradeship were not always painless. By late October, any hopes of Winters and Sobel mending their professional relationship had come to naught. Sobel reportedly fabricated a petty accusation claiming Winters failed to report on time for a latrine inspection.

The captain had changed the time without informing Dick. As punishment for this trivial transgression, Sobel presented Winters two options: disciplinary actions under Article of War 104 designated for "minor infractions," or the more serious court martial. Knowing he had done nothing wrong and Sobel was attempting to "gig" him, Winters sought to vindicate himself via court martial proceedings. There was scant evidence of this drama in letters to DeEtta that autumn.[13]

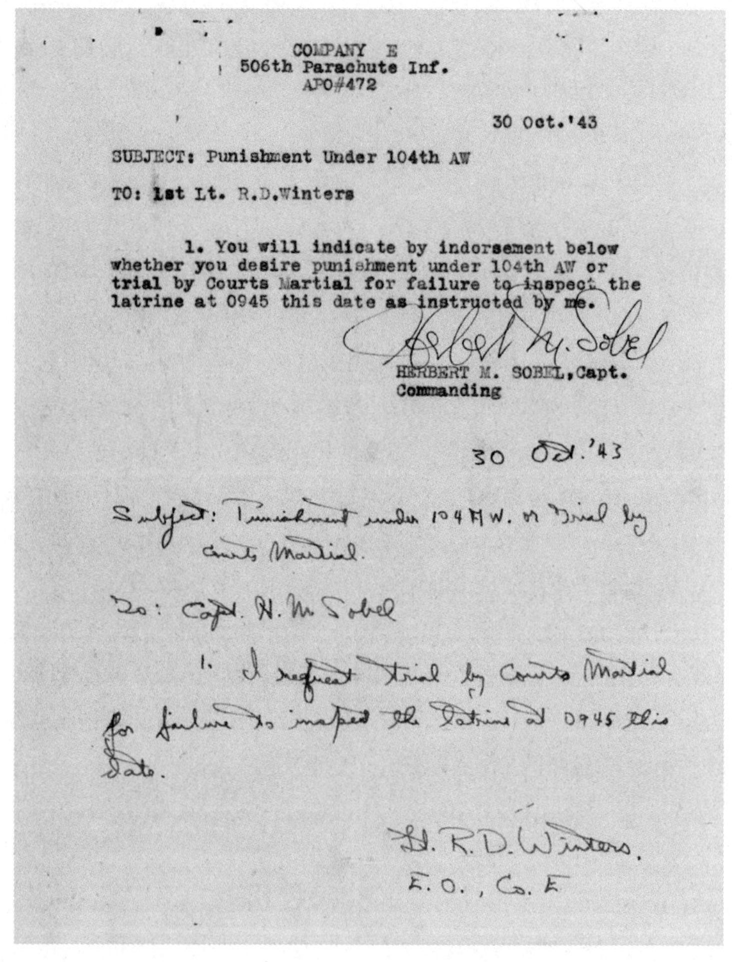

COMPANY E
506th Parachute Inf.
APO#472

30 Oct.'43

SUBJECT: Punishment Under 104th AW

TO: 1st Lt. R.D.Winters

1. You will indicate by indorsement below whether you desire punishment under 104th AW or trial by Courts Martial for failure to inspect the latrine at 0945 this date as instructed by me.

Herbert M. Sobel
HERBERT M. SOBEL, Capt.
Commanding

30 Oct.'43

Subject: Punishment under 104 AW. or Trial by Courts Martial.

To: Capt. H. M. Sobel

1. I request trial by Courts Martial for failure to inspect the latrine at 0945 this date.

Lt. R.D. Winters.
E.O., Co. E

Rather than falsely admitting wrongdoing, Winters requested a "trial by Courts Martial for failure to inspect the latrine at 0945 this date," October 30, 1943.

"Thanks for the Xmas package."
"The children of Aldbourne thank you."
"Two years since Dec. 7, 1941"

V-MAIL

December 11, 1943
1615 [Hours]

My Favorite Southern Belle–

Yes, you were, but now that you're going in the navy, you're just another member of the Ferry Boat Command. Just too lazy to walk so you make sure you never have to by joining the navy. But I'll overlook all that since it looks like you're going to be an officer. Good work! You shouldn't have too much trouble with your background in handling people. By the way just what does a Wave do beside take up time and space? And do they send any to the E.T.O.? If so, drop me a line when you arrive after the war.

Received your Xmas package and letter today. FDR changed Thanksgiving, so I thought I could change Xmas. It's always a pleasure to open your packages. A fellow never knows what it can be. There's always so much color. Those little candy canes and books you put in are going to be my gift to some of my younger friends about town. They've never seen the like, so when I receive their thanks and see their eyes shine, I know you'll be aware of the happy moment for you're the one they'll be thanking.

You know I never forgot that promise of a stamp from each country, and one day I'll do it. Incidentally, we've just passed another Dec. 7th. Never will I forget the one two years ago. Two years ago, in some ways it seems longer. I certainly feel more mature and a little harder due to wear and tear. This outfit leaves a man with many aches, pains, and memories.

From now on do a little less thinking about me and a little more writing to me, "Chicken—Southern Style."

Paratroops 14–Navy 0
Dick

[P.S. 1996 to DeEtta:]
We have known each other for two years.
We have had exactly five dates.
I have written 45 letters–you have sent me many packages.
In 1944 you are to become a very important friend in my life!
By Dec. 25, 1944, I will be surrounded at Bastogne.[14]

V-mail was an innovative method of the military diminishing postal weight at the height of the war. Service members could write abridged letters on stationary of a designated size that was thereafter censored, photographed, transported on microfilm to the States, reprinted, and finally delivered. The glossy paper was durable and compact, measuring approximately 4x5 inches. DeEtta received one such note two weeks before Christmas 1943.

Like the two previous Christmases, the holiday was somber for Americans at home and overseas. Bing Crosby's "I'll Be Home for Christmas" was released for the season, capturing the solemn yet sentimental mood of the citizenry. In England, the BBC opted not to play the tune over the air for fear of fostering melancholy. Winters likewise shared a gloomy state of mind as the holiday approached. Although he had been acquitted for his court martial offense, Strayer appointed Dick as battalion mess officer so as to keep him at arm's length from Sobel. Winters felt like a pariah, banished to the sidelines. Infuriated by the apparent demotion, he bided his time. One saving grace Dick welcomed was the meaningful relationship he formed with a gracious family in the quaint village of Aldbourne.[15]

Adopted by the Barnes family.

Thursday evening
Feb. 10, 1944

Dear DeEtta,

Well it looks like I might finally be able to put my conscience at ease and drop you a line and a word of thanks. I've received your V-mail letter, birthday card, and Valentine card. Your remembrance is greatly appreciated.

Writing isn't a task and it's not that a fellow doesn't want to write, it really comes down to the point that the available time isn't to be had. Paratroopers lead a pretty strenuous life and the training schedule, as usual, takes up most of my time and energy.

This evening I am our [battalion] Duty Officer, and between telephone calls, answering questions, and seeing things are done, I am trying to write a letter. Don't expect too much.

[...] About that point of writing from every country—as yet I've only been seeing England, but in a few weeks, if all goes well, I'll be getting leave and hope to see Scotland, and, if possible, Ireland, besides some more of England. Later on, in the spring, I'll drop you a note of remembrance from a few other European countries on the way to Berlin.

I've often wondered if you ever went through with that idea you had about joining the Waves? Remembering that you were to get a store by Xmas if you didn't join the services, I deduce you've stuck to the home front. Personally, it appears to me like that's the place you can do the most good. With your experience in that line of work and position, you're doing more than you would learning a new job and having somebody step into your position. Besides, that's a lot of glamour, the Waves, and you shouldn't let a uniform make your heart do things your head tells you is wrong.

Life in the E.T.O.-things are pretty good over here. I can truthfully say the food is darn good. Much better than they gave us in the States. Of course, when the food's good, a fellow has nothing to complain about, that's about everything. Back home you could go out and buy yourself a good meal or a worthwhile snack. Here the rationing makes all that just out of the question.

Just to prove my point, I started this note at 1900 on the above date and here it is now 0700 the following day. Which all goes to show you how it goes in the army.

To continue with life with a Yank in the E.T.O., I might say I've been very lucky. After a few weeks here I ran into a family that has more or less adopted me. They lost a son in the R.A.F. a year ago and by some coincidence, I seem to remind them of their boy. By working a few angles, I managed to get billet with them, so I am living a very comfortable and homey life when I get the chance.

Notes on the English—it's surprising how far behind America the English are in many things. For example: plumbing, electric light (wiring and use), furniture, homes, heating (all by fireplace), cooking, and many other things. Some little points are: they never heard or thought of butter or jam on toast, on bread, yes. Popcorn, marshmallows, hot dogs, and other eatables seem to be strictly Yank chow.

They've never heard of the stuff. Automobiles are far behind ours. They look like a full grown Austin. Dress is different, for both sexes, but not too sharp a difference. You know more about that angle than I do anyhow. Then of course speech and slang cause amusement and confusion. They don't possess the large and varied assortment of expressive adjectives that we do and often an expression of ours means something entirely different to them.

Your Valentine gave me a thrill. When I opened it the slight sense of perfume gave me an extremely delightful sensation.

Although I've many other things to say that are allowed by the censor, I must close now and start a new day rolling.

As ever,
Dick[16]

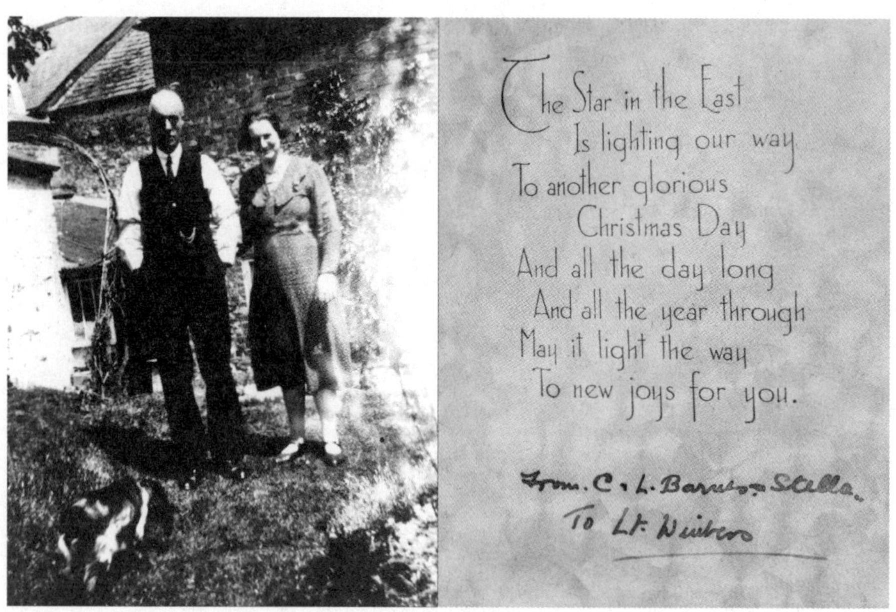

The Star in the East
Is lighting our way
To another glorious
Christmas Day
And all the day long
And all the year through
May it light the way
To new joys for you.

Dick established a loving relationship with Francis Charles Barnes and Louie May Barnes, his hosts in Aldbourne. The image at right shows the interior of the card they presented him for Christmas 1943.

Rationing, bombings, and a wide range of deprivations daily tormented the British. "London has been bombed and blitzed," one GI wrote home, "but night life goes on." If "in a theater and the alarm sounds they will flash alert on the screen, and continue with the picture. Perhaps a few of the older people will leave, but the majority never bothers to go underground or even to a shelter." Dick noticed this calmness when he traveled around England and Scotland in February 1944. He purchased a Glengarry bonnet for his sister, a silver necklace for his mother, and a stiletto knife to stow inside his jump boot. "Hope it isn't long until I can write you a letter from across the channel going east," he wrote to DeEtta from Glasgow. With invasion quickly approaching, civilians maintained their composure.[17]

Reporter Allan Morrison of *Stars and Stripes* perhaps best conveyed the cool demeanor of British civilians prior to the campaign. "Down in the pub, talk is not of the invasion," he observed. "There are no rumors. The center of interest is a 10-shilling note bearing the signature of Sgt. Joe Louis. The champ signed it for the proprietor, an ardent fan of the heavyweight king." The same pub owner resurrected a sign he hung during the Blitz that read, "When the siren goes, customers may have a drink on the house." That was "the one invasion touch," noted Morrison. When the momentous invasion day finally arrives, "the people in this frontline island will probably pause for a moment, slowly saying, 'Ave a good go, lads,' and continue with what they were doing."[18]

This tranquil bravado was noticeably demonstrated by the beloved Barnes family, who graciously billeted Dick and Lt. Harry Welsh in their Aldbourne home. Francis and Louie May Barnes fondly treated the two officers as their own. The couple even gifted Winters a British storybook. The Barnes's son, Cpl. Leonard John Barnes of the Royal Air Force Volunteer Reserve, was killed on June 12, 1942, at age twenty-six. No child can be replaced, but Winters did his utmost to fill a void in the household. "My association with the Barnes family was one of the most enjoyable experiences in my life," he recalled over sixty years later. The family's dignified comportment showed Dick how to cope with personal loss.[19]

Dick Winters and Harry Welsh. Winters later described Welsh as one of the few people who truly knew him.

Dick had other reasons to be grateful. A band of sergeants mutinied against Sobel, writing a letter to Col. Sink indicating their unwillingness serve under the captain. Risking their own futures, the men unleashed a verbal volley undermining Sobel's authority and abilities. Several of the sergeants were accordingly punished for insubordination. Realizing how sour the situation was, Sink at last transferred the captain from Easy Company that February. He was replaced by Lt. Thomas Meehan from B Company. Meehan, a Philadelphian, possessed a kinder disposition. Winters was folded back into his former role. In the opinion of paratrooper Don Malarkey, "Winters quietly orchestrated the deal to force

Sobel out. Not for his selfish gain, mind you; that wasn't Winters's style. He was among the most selfless men I've ever had the privilege of serving with. No, he did it for the good of the men. He did it to save their lives." In any case, the company was glad to be rid of the irascible captain.[20]

That same month, on February 24, DeEtta Almon enlisted in the US Naval Reserves. Her three brothers likewise served in the navy. She remained in the service until December 7, 1945—the fourth anniversary of Pearl Harbor—and rose to the rank of specialist second class. Upon receiving news of DeEtta's enlistment, Dick penned a congratulatory letter:

"You are a Wave!"

Somewhere in England
20 March, 1944

Dear DeEtta-

There should be a lot of smart, modern things to say upon finding out that you've joined the Waves. But all I can say is what I feel. You've got what it takes. Congratulations, rookie.

This A.M. I jumped into my uniform and ran down to the company to take the reveille report (0530), and by gosh, there was a letter from you, nice and fat too. I jammed it in my pocket and went about business. At breakfast I started to read it and had the jolt of my life when you mentioned you were a Wave. Before, I'd honestly never thought a great deal about it. Oh, I'd noticed some Wacs back in the States and thought to myself, what a bunch of crazy kids. They're in this for one of two reasons, the glamour of the uniform or to get away from home. There are some, I know, who are as sincere as the blue of our colors, but they are about as few as the boys we have who like the army. Which reminds me, do the girls grouse?

That's a point that gets me. Some of these fellows could be in the army ten years and still consider themselves civilians. Hell, when you're in uniform you should be proud of it and quit the bitching about the army and being a soldier. Then when it is over, take it [the uniform] off and forget the army. But I guess it's only human to want what you don't have.

No doubt, that's why you joined the Waves—the uniform—yes, it's far more attractive than any of the others. If most of the men in the paratroops are honest with themselves, they'll admit it was the boots, patch, and wings that helped decide their minds to some extent. In fact, there have been times when I often wished I wasn't an officer. [At times] I'd like to beat the ____ out of somebody who was wearing [a] pair of boots and wasn't a qualified paratrooper.

Having your heart set on being an officer and then being disappointed must have [been] quite a shock. But, let me say, and with no meaning of consolation, it's not as great a thing as it may seem to you when you're on the outside. You certainly didn't join for the money that was in the job, nor do you intend to make a career out of it. Also, you'll find, when you're settled, that the big thing in being in the service is to be a cog in an organization, a cog in a smooth running machine. Yes, sure you wanted to be a big cog, an officer, but let me tell you something, the biggest cog isn't the most important in the service. It's the one that handles the men all the time, it's the non-commissioned officer, and you're destined to handle troops in that capacity soon.

On the same subject, you may envy the social life of an officer. Personally, that's my only holdback to future advancement. I have no desire [to], and refuse to, join in the parties and social gatherings [...] I am a half-breed, an officer, yes, but at heart an enlisted man. So I work and do my duty as I should, but when it comes to play I am in a bad position and only in athletics with the men do I enjoy myself. The happiest days of my army career were at Croft, making $21 a month, yet always a little money at the end of the month. I traveled more, did more, and had more fun than at any time since.

Most likely you'll think as I did, ye gods, what a waste of time this is, why don't they give us something to do to help win the war instead of fooling around. You'll feel guilty taking all the things they give you. The best remedy for the first, is keep your eyes open for the job you want then go get it. For the second, just get a little salt on your shoulders.

[...] Do the Waves ever go to the E.T.O.? Well, if you do drop me a line, I might still be here although I am anxious to get going. This is a battle of nerves over here. Gosh, I came over to fight. That's why I joined the paratroops, thinking, boy, here I go. But look at me, still prancing around the towns in the U.K. Oh, nuts!

Had a leave over here and got to see Edinburgh, Glasgow, Plymouth, Oxford, and London. London and Scotland, my gosh, what places they are. Not much fun traveling or going out over here, you can't get a decent meal, wartime leaves little amusement. And at night the blackout leaves you stumbling about, getting lost in strange cities, and wishing to God you could get out and do some real fighting. What I wouldn't give for a shake, some eggs, a couple quarts of milk and ice cream. If you ever come over let me know and I'll tell you what to bring and not to bring in addition to the poop they give you.

Well, rookie, if you ever find yourself with any problems, don't be afraid to ask questions. I'll be only too glad to help for it's better and easier to learn by another's experience than by knocking yourself out.

Love,
Dick

P.S. Never regret what you've done, for, by gosh, you've all my respect and admiration. With kids like you making sacrifices like that and taking it all so serious at home it helps a lot when we stop to think of all this trouble, suffering, and torture with it. Hell, yes, with kids like you in back of us we can't lose.[21]

In learning the operation of naval radar, DeEtta was not alone in her ambitions to serve. By 1944, over two million American women entered the industrial workforce for wartime manufacturing and preparedness. Some 86,000 ladies enlisted in DeEtta's branch of choice—the Women Accepted for Volunteer Emergency Service, popularly known as the WAVES. According to one historian, the public image of WAVES "was carefully presented—attractive and feminine, but not fussy, with hair pulled back but not constrained and with a strong, confident expression." Connotations of personal strength and power inspired women to serve in varied capacities.[22]

Writer Brenda Ralph Lewis, who herself lived in World War II London, attested to the uphill struggles women such as DeEtta confronted. "Once women, young and old, had secured war jobs, there was another hurdle: winning acceptance from the men whose enclaves they were invading—in unprecedented numbers." Almon paid little note to the glamor of her new position. Above all else, she desired to contribute—and Dick adored her for it. As was the case with minorities in the military, there was no better way to disprove inaccurate societal presumptions than to serve with valor and selflessness.[23]

Dick's desire to "beat the ____ out of somebody" who dared wearing jump boots without having earned them was a very real animosity expressed by paratroopers. According to Maj. Ben Vandervoort of the 82nd Airborne, "In those days parachute boots were as sacred to the paratroopers as their wings." Beloved infantryman cartoonist Bill Mauldin captured the essence of this mindset in a sketch depicting rotund, undeserving officers sporting jump boots as a disgruntled paratrooper observes nearby. "It's best not to speak to paratroopers about saluting," the caption claims. "They always ask where you got your jump boots." Paratroopers so loved the cartoon that one presented Mauldin a special gift: his own pair of jump boots.[24]

DeEtta is shown with her seafaring brothers in a December 1945 photo. Left to right are Robert, DeEtta, Harold, and Edwin Almon. DeEtta was the oldest of the siblings. A civilian sister, Maxine, is not shown.

"Any Yank gum, Yank?"

14 April, 1944

Dear DeEtta–

What a beautiful girl! What a uniform! What a present! You certainly look good in that G.I. outfit. It's hard to believe that the government issues such lovely outfits.

Your letter also was more than welcome. That's more reading material than I've received in months and receiving it after a long siege of rough going without a letup was almost as good as an ice cream sundae would be. Remember I haven't seen anything resembling the latter in the last eight months.

Of course as far as that goes it's been about that long since I've seen a pretty girl. I've decided to drop all judgment as to the beauty of the fairer sex until I come home for I am not sure what a good looking girl looks like anymore.

Hearing your observations and experiences as a "boot" brings back memories that run parallel in every respect: preparation for inspections and polishing and getting out of camp. Lots of fun but I feel like an old man looking back on those days. Actually you don't accomplish a darn thing, but by the time an inspection is over you're ready to take a break. One thing I can't appreciate though is walking around New York in a pretty Wave uniform. Must be rough!

[...] Gee, here it is 23:30 already and I started this about 19:30. It was such a nice evening out I had to go take a run and do a little wrestling. Just one of those days when you feel that you've got to do something about it being so nice. Especially after a long English winter filled with long, dark, foggy nights, blackouts at that, never seeing the sun all day, rain and mud all the time. But that's past now, spring's here and let's go.

You know that picture of Churchill reviewing paratroopers in England that you sent me? Well, "navy," that's my outfit. We gave the brass hats over here something to talk about. It was in all the newspapers and newsreels so I understand, although I haven't seen them. Yes sir, this is the outfit. You picked a good outfit for a girl, nice, neat, clean, no hard work, no walking, no sleeping on the ground, no eating iron rations. But for a man who wants action, well what's the use in bragging, most of the people know it now and before long the world will know it, so we'll let it go at that.

Did I tell you about the folks I am staying with? Boy, they're real. I am just like a son in this home. Better, for nobody ever bosses me around. They lost a son in this war, who was just about my age, and by some coincidence I've a lot of his characteristics, so I am receiving the best treatment.

Since I first came here there was a little girl of 13 [Elaine Stevens], just the age of my sister Ann, living here. Evacuated from London, of a poor family. Well, we get along pretty well and she's just like a sister to me. First thing I did was dress her up a bit. You can't buy a great deal over here but I had my shirts cut down, bought a sweater, scarf, gloves, shoes with my ration coupons. Now we step out once in a while to town, see a show, shop and eat, but outside of tea and toast there's nothing. Also take her to the officer's mess after church on Sundays. It's been a lot of fun for me, she's had a pretty good time, everybody's happy. Matter of fact I've often thought of bringing her back to the States. She's one of those kids you can't help but like.

Speaking of children, you should see the children over here. They love the Yanks. It seems as if the Yanks like the children too, for they give them anything they have. I'll bet I know fifty kids in this town and that makes it pretty nice. When you walk down the street there are always a couple walking along with you. The cry of every boy in England is "any Yank gum, Yank?" If you're driving along in convoy it's always "thumbs up" from every kid you pass, and to them it means something, they're sincere, and not trying to be cute as you'd find at home.

[...] You know with that picture of yours standing there it makes letter writing increasingly easy but [its] 0015 now, a big day starting in a few more hours, so I'd better hit the "old sack." However, you'll be my "pinup girl" now and so I should be able to get a few lines in once in awhile.

Just keep that clean, fresh, good-looking American atmosphere about you until I come home. What's more, just stay right in the States. I'll take care of this end of the job. Well I close now with a cheerio and

Love,
Dick[25]

On March 23, 1944, Winters participated in a massive airborne demonstration for Allied leaders. Winston Churchill and Dwight Eisenhower watched the spectacle from this platform.

Other than the thrill of seeing DeEtta in her first naval uniform, Dick was equally elated to conduct a demonstration for Winston Churchill. Throughout late March, the prime minister ventured to one US base after another to imbue solidarity with the former colonists. One of his first jaunts to an American unit included a visit to the 101st Airborne in Welford. Touring the interior of a glider, Churchill told the crew, commanded by Capt. Ira Hamblin, that "you look very sociable in here." The "Screaming Eagles" extended cowboy hollers and shouts of "Geronimo" to the prime minister while conducting field exercises and parachuting from C-47s. Inspecting thousands of paratroopers standing at attention with their polished jump boots and spotless M-1s, Churchill declared into a microphone, they "would soon have the opportunity of landing on the soil of Nazi-occupied Europe" in order to forge "a better and a broader world for all."[26]

The stogie-chomping leader of Britain foresaw the major test on the horizon. After three days of exploring American camps, he was rather impressed. "It has been a source of great interest to me to see how splendidly the American forces are equipped, the magnificent character of the officers and men, their martial bearing and the handiness with which they use all their powerful weapons," he attested to the press corps.[27]

Perhaps Churchill's glowing praise concealed a degree of apprehension, if not guilt. As correspondent DeWitt Mackenzie observed, Churchill "is uncomfortably aware that the vast numbers of the troops which will fight their way up the beaches from the sea on D-Day will be our [American] boys."[28]

Allied generals were fiercely determined to avoid calamity. Omar Bradley, the humble yet brilliant "Soldier's General," assured subordinates of success. He complained to officers that April, "[T]his stuff about tremendous losses is tommyrot." The destiny of "the whole war depends on this operation and I have no fear of its outcome," the commander of American ground forces confided. He calmly urged young leaders to be lenient on troops who initially exhibited fear. Allow them to overcome their trepidation, he instructed. Exert leadership. Lead by example. These were the simple albeit paramount ingredients of victory—factors Dick took to heart.[29]

Germans "will play dirty," Bradley warned. "I know of cases where he has booby-trapped the dead. Don't trust him very far. Sometimes they will come out waving white flags and then open fire on you." Better to kill than be killed, he advised.[30]

On a friendlier note, GIs developed a strong affinity for British youth, many of whom had never savored the joys of childhood due to the war. One American wrote his wife, "Children, it seems never had chewing gum before Yanks got here and since someone introduced it to them they have taken to it with great avidity." A GI seemingly risked being mauled if he did not carry sticks of Spearmint on his person at all times.[31]

Rules about going to all meals?
Rules about going back for seconds!

April 23, 1944
Somewhere in England

Dear DeEtta–

"Mathematically yours," what warmth, how tender. If fooling around with formulas and equations does that to you, it's about time to drop that line of work. I can see it's doing you no good, already you've lost all sense of beauty.

Your latest school sounds like a good deal. One of those setups where you really can learn something in the service and naturally I can see some hard work connected to it. Seems to me as though a rating of some sort should be connected to specialization of that kind.

That mess hall, barracks, washing machine, good bunks, movies, Washington 50 miles away, and a wash room right in the barracks, yes. I've heard of such things, never seen any though. The best setup I've had yet was at Croft, good barracks, pretty warm, and the wash room in the same building; that was the last I've seen a luxury like that. But do you know something? Right now I wouldn't trade anybody back in the States, or anybody over here tickets for the big show. No sir, I've worked hard and a long time for these tickets and now, by gosh, I am not going to part with them. But that mess hall sounds mighty good and I'll bet you have those old fashioned eggs that come in a shell and that milk that comes in bottles. We have the latest things over here: eggs, milk and everything else right out of the can. Then, too, you should try some K or C ration, or, best of all, a D. Of course you can't appreciate how good they are just by sampling them, but you should live off concentrated chocolate for a few days. Then let them make a rule "everybody must go to all meals, unless excused by the medics." Why, we must make rules about going back for seconds.

This Sunday afternoon in England is the kind I'd like to see more of, lots of good warm sunshine and me just sitting here eating it up, finding it hard to imagine that there's a war going on so close at hand.

You know that I am really not in the mood for writing a letter right now and I realize I am writing a letter that shows it only too well.

Censorship and other conditions of war and being away from home and a normal life for three years, put you at times in a condition where you can't write. To counterattack this I do one of several things, or a combination thereof. I sleep, take a walk, run, exercise, or work. Right now the fitting thing is to sleep and I've talked myself into it so I'll finish this later.

"Later" seems to have turned out to be at the end of another day. "The end of another day." Do you stand retreat in the navy? I imagine so. Back in the States we never bothered, over here we slick up every night and pay our respects to the flag. There's something I like about the ceremony, the sound of the bugle, men snapping to attention, presenting arms, and finishing off a day's work with the respect due our flag. That's something I guess you miss in the navy, I mean the soldiering part. Too bad, for that's one of the biggest thrills and satisfactions you get out of the service, to know you're really soldiering. Ah well, somebody must make up the navy.

Did I ever tell you about the English barber? Well, there's one to a village. He doesn't have a shop but comes around to your house by appointment. His price is only one shilling (20¢). Of course everybody tips him, but at even a shilling you're being cheated. He has a hard time getting used to the Yanks who are very particular and who insist on the short sideburns. The English all wack [*sic*] off their hair even with the top of the ear and to me it looks like the devil.

Well, sailor, it's time for this trooper to hit the sack, which is something I do too little of. By gosh, I never seem to be able to accumulate more than six or seven hours a day, but to be truthful, that's enough. I'd just like to see how much sleep I could store up on someday. For the present–

Cheerio,
Dick

P.S. This is a lousy letter. If you haven't read it as yet, don't bother.[32]

By May, the troops awaited the inevitable. Tenseness pervaded. Based in England, Sgt. Albert Robison conveyed home, "Street telephone kiosks were sealed a few days ago. All troops had their letters censored. Hospitals were at the ready, doctors and staff were warned to maintain continuous stand-to." Weekend passes became fewer. Men on holiday in Scotland were recalled. Service members were not as oblivious as their generals supposed. In an article entitled "Shadow of D-Day," the *New York Times* noted that correspondents in Britain were asked to end speculation of the invasion date. "The request was reasonable," the paper reflected, "for though the reporters do not know what date is D-Day, they do know a good many facts not familiar to the public or to the enemy." For correspondents, self-censorship prevailed in the name of a free press.[33]

That spring, DeEtta transferred to the Naval Proving Ground at Dahlgren, Virginia. Classified ordnance and weapons testing, fuse development, and computational analysis occurred at the site along the Potomac River. She tested cutting edge radar and computers. Regardless of her expertise, Dick was displeased by the very mention of naval gunners. "Don't tell me about the Navy marksmanship and figuring it all out. It's no secret anymore about how at Sicily the navy knocked down 400 paratroopers going in. I knew a lot of those boys. I've also had some experiences myself, that wouldn't pass censorship, as to the navy."[34]

In that May 6 letter, Dick vaguely referred to Operation Husky, the invasion of Sicily the previous July. Coinciding with the amphibious operations (the largest in history up to that point) were paratrooper landings undertaken by the 82nd Airborne Division's 504th PIR. The navy, largely unaware of the operation's airborne component, assumed it was under attack and obliterated several transport planes, ultimately killing 318 American brethren. Winters hoped history would not repeat itself in France.[35]

Lightening the mood, Dick jokingly reprimanded his favorite WAVE. "Remember when you talk to me, you're talking to the army, a commissioned officer, and I want no back talk, excuses, stand at attention," he kidded. "Ye gods, the navy doesn't know what attention means. Pull in your stomach, throw out your chest, pull those shoulders back, tuck in your chin, take that smile off your face, and stop making eyes at me. It won't do any good, you're on K.P. duty for life."[36]

Duties were constantly on his mind as invasion preparation mounted. "Now all I do is work," he explained. "Work to improve myself as an officer, work to improve them as fighters, as men. Make them work to improve themselves. Result—I am old before my time, not old physically, but hardened to the point where I can make the rest of them look like undeveloped high school boys."[37]

Ten days later, on Mother's Day, Dick's burgeoning invasion curiosity was on full display. "You know I often wonder myself when the big show goes on," he admitted. "Never really worry about it, but just wonder. Whenever it does, you can start powdering your nose and getting ready to step out, for it won't be long when they let a certain bunch in there. As a matter of fact, the rest of the services could just go home awhile and read about it in the newspaper. Seriously though, I don't know if we'll be staying to police up the area after the show's over or not." D-Day was three weeks away.[38]

Whitsun–Children's Day
S/Sgt. Leo Boyle marries Wyn Hawkins

21 May, 1944
Somewhere in England

Dear DeEtta-

In your letter it sounds like you're trying to guess D-Day when you say, "by the time you receive this letter you'll most likely be on your way." Unless you're on the inside, or know a good looking G-3, you might as well give up. I've seen many reputations and pounds (English money) fall by men trying to do the same. What difference does it make if it's today, tomorrow, or next year? When they decide to go, O.K. Until then, just relax.

Today is Sunday and I've tomorrow off until 1800. Now, boy, isn't that the nuts? Two days off in a row doesn't happen often. Think I'll take my friend Elaine to town and see a show. The other night they brought one out to camp, *The Palm Beach Story*. That's about the best show I've seen since I left the States. Usually the shows are years old or English, either way it's just a way to pass the time and not really entertaining.

In church they had what they call Whitsun, Children's Day. I've gone twice already and there's still another service this evening but think I'll miss that one. It sure is enjoyable to watch those kids get up there and recite, then recall how I used to be in the same shoes not so many years ago. One little girl, about four, with a pretty little pink dress and white bonnet-shaped hat stole the show. She was up and down, yawning, stretching, singing with her music upside down, waving to friends in the audience, and then fussing with her new dress, hat and shoes. Quite a show.

Yesterday we had two weddings here in camp. One officer married a girl from Scotland and a fine bonnie lass she is, too. And a S/Sgt. from my company married a local girl. I went to the Sgt.'s wedding. That was the first church wedding I ever attended and what an ordeal that is. That's worse than jumping from a plane in flight. Not for me. Why my legs were quivering and I was just an onlooker. Men being men, and men being what men are, there naturally were a few tricks, besides a lot of the usual ribbing. They stole the ring just before he left for the church, unbeknownst to him, and returned it during the ceremony just before the time for the ring so all were sweating that one out. Next they had some signs, "Target for tonight. This is the result of careless talk," placed at strategic places. Then, as they were leaving the church a beautiful smoke screen was placed upwind and in the confusion the bride was whisked away in a taxi. They brought her back in half an hour but if time hadn't been so valuable, I'll bet that she'd still be missing.

A few minor jokes, not exactly of the parlor variety, were also pulled. But one of the best fell through when one of the boys pulled a detail at the last minute. They had an old lady's rig and a shotgun for him and he was to walk in the church beside the groom. It's best it did fall through for I am afraid the town folks wouldn't have been able to see any humor in that episode.

[...] Well, it's time for chow and I can't miss anything like chow and keep up my strength, so I'll have to whip along. However, don't "Wave" at any trooper until you're sure it's the right guy. Then you can start "Waving" and throwing all your affections all over the place and it'll be O.K. by me.

Oodles of love,
Dick

P.S. No cheerio this time.[39]

On May 20, Easy Company's S. Sgt. Leo D. Boyle married Winifred Louise Hawkins at the local church. That same day, Lt. Ronald Speirs of Dog Company wedded a member of the Auxiliary Territorial Service. Such marriages between GIs and British women were not uncommon prior to the Normandy invasion. The American Red Cross estimated somewhere between 40,000 and 60,000 Anglo-American couples tied the knot by that point of the war. Furthermore, some 20,000 babies were born out of wedlock despite the widespread availability of prophylactics to Allied service members.[40]

On a broader scale, GIs exerted energies elsewhere. The British Isles bristled with the sights and sounds of military maneuvering. In every direction, the nation's lush countryside served as an obstacle course during this "friendly invasion" of coalition forces. A photograph in the May 10 edition of the *Gettysburg Times* revealed an English sky dotted with countless parachutes unfurling in the wind. The caption discreetly read, "The sky over this unidentified base in England is filled with paratroopers and parachutes carrying their supplies during pre-invasion maneuvers."[41]

As Dick witnessed firsthand, top brass reviewed paratroopers that spring in an endless tide of inspections. In mid-May, the British royal family observed one of the largest airborne exercises ever staged. According to one reporter, "They witnessed a sky-darkening fleet of gliders that landed and filled a field like a jammed parking lot. They saw hundreds of parachutists drop in faultless precision." The demonstrations bolstered optimism among the civilian populace.[42]

Some American officers were secretly less optimistic. Capt. Harry C. Butcher of Eisenhower's staff wrote in his journal on April 4, "I am concerned over the absence of toughness and alertness of young American officers whom I saw on this trip. They are as green as growing corn. How will they act in battle and how will they look in three months' time?"[43]

Notwithstanding the perpetual procession of generals, most infantry training was undertaken in the anonymity of British woods and meadows.

The highly-skilled men of the 101st Airborne participated in a wide range of physical activities to hone tactical skills. Expected to embark upon a forbidding night jump in the early hours of D-Day, the paratroopers were the tip of the invasion spear. Other than conducting practice jumps, the men (who received an extra fifty dollars per month as "hazardous duty pay") perfected squad movements, prepared foxholes, established communication with division artillery, and embarked on twenty-five mile marches. After one demanding trek, a paratrooper wrote, "Glancing down the line you were of the opinion that everyone had that combat expression, an unshaven face showing extreme weariness and disgust, caked mud from head to foot, and every jump suit looking as though it had come out second best in the ordeal of the fences. You finally dragged your weary body those last few tortuous kilometers, and throwing yourself across the bunk, you said…combat can't be that rough!"[44]

The rigors of maneuvering paid off. Correspondent DeWitt Mackenzie was mesmerized by the robust agility of "those daring adventurers" who plummeted into hostile territory. "When the Allied forces finally have stormed their way onto the European continent in the approaching invasion we shall find, I believe, that we owe great things to airborne troops," he suspected. The Nazis took "full note" of the feared invaders from above and prepared to stymie advances by flooding and mining Normandy's pastures.

In Mackenzie's estimation, a squad of airborne men within Hitler's fortress was "worth a legion outside for it bids fair to be a terrific job to get amphibious troops ashore." The paratroopers' physical prowess and surreptitious style made them indispensable in the art of covert warfare, paving the way for ground forces. "The paratroopers are temporarily self-contained when they hit the air, so far as equipment and goods are concerned," Mackenzie added. "Their tasks are myriad—all tough ones—such as destroying enemy communications and capturing or even building air fields. Once the paratroopers have established a base, the regular air transports and gliders get into action with more men and equipment."[45]

The price of victory was expected to be extreme. Dwight Eisenhower was told by one subordinate that perhaps 80 percent of his American paratroopers could perish in the invasion. As the supreme commander later confessed, the "unbearable burden" of potentially sacrificing "the flower of our youth" was the most "soul-racking problem" he ever confronted.[46]

CHAPTER FOUR

HOT AS A BAKED POTATO

June to August 1944

"Every night at taps I'll meet you at the north star."

2 June 1944

Dearest DeEtta-

Received your letter of May 24 yesterday and enjoyed sharing your first visit home since you've started the latest chapter of your career. This type of life that we're experiencing is really worth all the trying experiences, aches and pains we must bear. We realize this all the more when we are lucky enough to go home and have a taste of what a soft and wonderful life we had at one time.

I know what you felt when you started nearing home, the trees and the country started to look better, more fresh and clean. Then when you hit Montana Ave. you thought it looked like a street that St. Peter designed, and home, well it's like a doll house, so small, petite, clean, things are so convenient and handy, and, oh boy, the soft bed and two clean sheets. Perhaps that's something you don't fully appreciate but if you go without them for a couple of years and sleep on the ground with nothing to keep you warm but your shivers, then a bed looks mighty cozy.

It's time for chow so I'd better run or I'll be left filling up on water. Just stand by.

English weather is really something to write home about, just like summer one day and the next you'd think it was a fall day. The funny part about it, these people think nothing of it, while we expect it to go warm and stay warm at this time of the year.

Had quite a thrill the other day when I read in the *Stars and Stripes* (that's the soldier's overseas newspaper), that on D-Day all theatres, ballgames, and non-essential business establishments will close and people will be asked to go to church and pray. The size and magnitude of a united feeling like that just sends the chills right up and down a fellow's spine. When we're at home a fellow doesn't usually think beyond his local acquaintances. Go to another part of the country and it's your home state, and anybody from your hometown is a buddy. So when you feel that and think that all those people are sending their best wishes and prayers to you, a fellow can't help but feel good.

Boy, I am telling you, writing a letter under and obeying these censorship rules is a job that is a job. You're really limited.

Brother, another interruption. They just made me go see a show, *Air Force*, but I left after the first reel for I'd seen it a long, long time ago.

Sorry I can't make that date to go for a boat ride, but I'll tell you what, every night at taps I'll meet you at the north star [*sic*]. The old north star is a soldier's guiding light when he's lost, alone, and feeling mighty funny in the pit of his stomach. That's when he feels good, when he can look up and know that there's somebody else looking up there also.

Well, it's time to hit the sack so I'll say good night, mate.

Love from your trooper,
Dick

June 5, 1996–
Summary of Last Four Letters Before D-Day

My last four letters to DeEtta bring back memories of doubt that I would be alive to see the flowers bloom in another spring.

6 May 1944–

I hope the payoff for all this training is that "Shep" (Howell) will live to go back home to his girl. He did!

16 May 1944–

It was very important to me to remember my mother and Mrs. Barnes on Mother's Day–I might not be here next year.

21 May 1944–

Church services–will I be here next year to share another "Whitsun Children's Day?"

2 June 1944–

Everybody in America is asked to go to church and pray when the invasion is announced!

5 June 1944–

We take off for Normandy.[1]

The symbolism of the North Star resonated with Winters. Amid all his troubled days ahead, he took solace in Polaris, knowing that others, perhaps DeEtta, might also have been gazing at its magnificence. Winters was certainly not the only one looking upward on June 2. The invasion window, only days away, was largely dependent on suitable weather. As Dick suggested, the unpredictability of English weather made for a nerve-wracking process of meteorological speculation.

Awaiting improved conditions, the men of Easy Company on June 4 made final preparations for their aerial journey across the English Channel. Liftoff for D-Day was scheduled that night. Francs, ammunition, and toy "cricket" sound makers for identifying comrades in the dark were distributed. Pvts. Forrest Guth and Joe Liebgott cut comrades' hair for fifteen cents each. Amused by the spectacle, Col. Sink announced, "The Germans are telling French civilians that the Allied invasion forces would be led by American paratroopers, all of them convicted felons and psychopaths, easily recognized by the fact that they shave their heads." The bit of news offered levity in those hours of restlessness. Seeking further distraction, Lt. Raymond Schmitz challenged Dick to a boxing match behind the tents. Winters, the former wrestler, instantly won the duel—inadvertently cracking two of Schmitz's vertebrae. Schmitz was absent for the Normandy landings as a consequence. (Sadly, Schmitz died in action three months later in Holland.) Contrary to their hopes, no paratroopers set across the Channel that night. Foul weather and high winds prevented the monumental enterprise from taking flight. Eisenhower postponed the operation for twenty-four critical hours.[2]

In the meantime, soldiers double-checked their overwhelming supplies of personal equipment and weapons. The menu options of gear included T-5 parachutes, reserve chest-pack chutes, rifles and machine guns of various denominations, grenades, medical supplies, British-issued leg bags, gas masks in black rubber pouches, web belts with ammo pouches and canteens, sidearms, knives, compasses, cans of colored smoke, map pouches, musette bags, rations, field glasses, bandoliers, entrenching tools, extra clothing, Hawkins mines, and yellow "Mae West" life preservers—just to name a few. On average, each paratrooper carried one hundred pounds or more of equipment when he lunged into France.[3]

Paratroopers prepare their mounds of equipment before loading into a C-47.

The long-awaited moment arrived the following night. The weather cleared. A near-full moon was expected. The tides, though strong, were still favorable. Eisenhower issued the order. Operation Overlord commenced. The supreme commander referred to the biblical struggle as a "great crusade," one which would liberate those shackled by Nazi tyranny. Col. Sink likewise released a motivational statement to his regiment. "Tonight is the night of nights," he declared. "May God be with each of you fine soldiers." Mounted with gear and faces blackened, the men of the 506th PIR waddled to their C-47 transports around 8:30 that evening. British anti-aircraft gunners nearby openly wept at the scene. As the planes ascended from the runways, Winters reflected, "Every man, I think, had in his mind, 'How will I react under fire?'" They were soon to confront that challenge.[4]

Whizzing over the Channel in vast formations of hundreds of planes, some paratroopers observed the mammoth naval armada below. Vessels of every conceivable size chugged closer to France's shore. Success was dependent upon the airborne and amphibious troops linking near the beachhead. Fighting as shock troops, paratroopers were presented an unrealistic expectation from the outset. Gen. Maxwell Taylor, 101st Airborne commander, promised his regiments, "Give me three days of hard fighting, then you will be relieved." The pledge proved overly optimistic.[5]

Shortly after 1:00 a.m. on June 6, the planes thundered over the Normandy coastline and rolled into a thick bank of clouds. When the invaders emerged from the dense overcast, all hell broke loose. The night sky was set ablaze by the fluorescent vibrancy of tracer rounds and flak. Lt. Buck Compton, a compatriot of Winters, heard a crackling sound beyond his plane and spotted bursts of explosions illuminating the heavy clouds. As Compton attested, other flights suffered even closer brushes with death. "Bullets from the antiaircraft fire streamed inside the planes, caging the soldiers in.... Some pilots strayed off course. Some panicked and dropped their men in the sea, drowning them all. Some flew too low—with soldiers plummeting to the ground without enough time for their chutes to deploy."[6]

Temporarily confined to their planes, the parachutists anxiously awaited the green-light signal to jump. For some, the experience felt as if they were standing inside a ticking bomb. Sgt. Ralph Bennett of H Company recalled, "When the red flickered to green nobody moved. I could hear people shouting, 'For Christ's sake let's go, let's get out, what's happening up there?'" Upon reaching the doorway, Bennett found his lieutenant hunkered in fear. Some men could not cope with their first taste of battle.[7]

"How do you prepare yourself mentally?" Winters later pondered of the D-Day experience. "Each man must do that himself. Each man must prepare himself mentally to make that jump." When his moment arrived, Dick did not hesitate. He jumped "immediately."[8]

Lt. Thomas Meehan, Winters's company commander, prepared himself with a grim prognostication. In a final letter to his wife, Anne, Meehan confessed, "I'm afraid I am a pessimist with little faith in the goodwill of mankind. Looking it over, thinking about it brings the realization that any peace will be compromise, not everlasting." Meehan's plane exploded near Sainte-Mère-Église in the earliest moments of D-Day. All passengers and crew were lost. Upon the death of his superior, Winters became interim company commander.[9]

Parachute infantrymen resembling small armories leapt from planes at incredibly high speeds and low altitudes. Red hot tracers zipped past their heads and through their chutes. The clusters of parachutists scattered to the wind. Troopers landed miles from their designated drop zones. Overburdened by the gear on their backs, many drowned in the flooded pastures. Bewilderment and adrenaline dazed many as they fell from the night skies. Unscathed by his descent, Dick pressed through thick hedgerows as the countdown to the beach landings commenced. His M-1 broke loose during the jump, leaving him armed only with a knife. He first encountered Pfc. John D. Halls, a radioman from Able Company. Their small squad grew as Winters randomly assembled men. They pushed onward.[10]

For others, confusion reigned supreme. One soldier declared, "There was gunfire coming at us all the time. . . . [F]rom the first second we landed we were uncertain what our next step should be." In a nearby culvert his companions discovered a German lurking in the shadows. Taking him prisoner, they inquired where all the Americans were.

The German anxiously waved his hands and answered, "All over!"

And the whereabouts of the Germans?

"All over!"

The battlefront was in every direction. Worse yet were apparent cold-blooded murders. "[W]e saw some paratroopers hanging from trees," reporter Robert Cromie observed. "They hadn't had a chance; their harness and chutes had caught in the trees as they floated down and they were just shot up and bayoneted where they were." Tales of German atrocities provoked vengeful desires among Americans. Anecdotes fueled bloody score-settling openly practiced by both sides. Few were sinless in the turbulent free-for-all.[11]

This German Fallschirmjäger paratrooper died in the Normandy hedgerows. An American knife sheath, one the German presumably captured, hangs from his waist. The knife itself is lodged in his neck. A photo rests atop the corpse's face. This grim tableau speaks to the violent nature of battlefield retribution.

Winters was in the thick of the maelstrom. On June 9, he began cataloging "memory joggers," concise pointers that loosely chronicled his D-Day trials. He recorded a list "of what had happened, what I had observed, and the sequence they happened in." Two weeks later, he began composing his thoughts in diary form. "I wasn't writing to anybody," he recalled. "Just my memories for myself. Nothing in mind at all. I just wanted to make a record of it." With a sense of history in mind, Dick jotted a rich account of perhaps the most consequential day of his life.[12]

D-Day Diary

22 June 1944

Dear Diary:

Today is D+16 and I've decided to tell my story as I sit here at the First Aid Station along the M.L.R. [Main Line of Resistance] with artillery shells shattering the silence of the afternoon.

Leaving Aldbourne was a tough job, a fellow couldn't say a thing to anybody due to security. But they knew we were pushing off, then when I went to say good-by, as if I was off for another maneuver, it got me to see them cry and take it as they did. As we roared down the highway for Hungerford, I waved farewell to my adopted sister, Elaine, who had started down the highway ahead of me.

We pulled into the same marshalling area we had on the dry run a month previous, that was May 27, from then until June 5, we did very little except get ready, which is no little job in itself to see that every man has his every item called for. Then of course there was the briefing, a shower every few days, and a show. The S.O.S. [Services of Supply] did a nice job on feeding us, P.X. supplies came in every day so all we did was sleep, eat, brief, get ready.

Personally I did very little briefing, I just couldn't seem to get interested. But I did have the situation well in hand.

Church services were attended a lot better than usual, but not what you'd expect from a group about to start an invasion, which is something I really can't figure out.

Sweating out the $10,000 jump was something that never occurred to most. They simply relaxed and enjoyed the rest. A few did sweat and they were easy to spot for they kept asking questions about the enemy, situation, equipment, etc.

General Taylor gave the boys a little pep talk and asked for three days hard fighting and then we'd be withdrawn. Now at D+16 that's a standing joke, and has been for the past 14 days. My estimate of the situation is that we're here for ten more days.

The afternoon of the 5th, we were told tonight is the night. So I spent the afternoon getting ready and taking a two hour nap. After supper things were in a great up-roar getting ready. A final check was made of all equipment, the rest was packed away. A last minute look. Faces blackened, weapons checked. Then news came that Rome was captured, which wasn't any great thrill, at this time, for we were too intent on our own job at hand.

At 20:30 we lined up by plane loads and marched off for the hangers. As we passed buddies, friends and fellow officers, there was usually a stiff smile, nod of the head or pat on the back, but very few showed any emotions at all. It seemed like just another jump, nothing to get excited about. On the way to hangers we passed some British anti-aircraft units stationed at the field, and that was the first time I've ever seen any real emotion from a Limey, they actually had tears in their eyes, and you could see they felt like hell standing there watching us go out to battle.

At the hangers each jump master was given two packs of papers, one a message from Gen. Eisenhower, the other from Col. Sink. Each man synchronized his watch, was assigned a truck and whisked off to his plane.

At the plane the first thing I did was unload all the parachutes and equipment and see that each man had his. Then in a huddle I passed out the poop sheets, gave them the schedule we would have to follow. 22:15 in the plane ready to go. 23:10 take off, 01:20 jump, good luck, God Bless you and see you in the assembly area. With that done we went to work harnessing up and it's here that a good jump master or officer can do the most for his men. For in getting all that equipment on, tied down, try to make it comfortable and safe and then a parachute over top calls for a lot of ingenuity, and sales talk to satisfy the men that all's well. By 22:00 all were ready but myself for it's no good getting ready yourself and then helping the men. So I whipped into my equipment fast and furious, mounted up and was ready to go. One incident at this time is worthy of note: One of the boys, Pvt. [Robert T.] Leonard had a terrible load, in fact like others in the stick, I had to push him up the steps into the plane, he had such a big load. Well "Jeeter" [Leonard's nickname] was in the plane ready to go, so was everybody else so I made a final check of all kit bags that held our equipment and his, I found one basic load of M-1 ammunition. Poor "Jeeter" had everything but ammunition. The sad part about it is that he just didn't have any place to carry it. So I told him, see me at the assembly area and I'll give it to you, which was O.K. for there was to be no shooting on the jump field.

At this time I handed out the second motion sickness pill, the first being given at 22:00. The idea being to do away with air sickness and the butterflies in your stomach when you're scared.

All was pretty quiet, a little bitching about all the equipment we had to carry, but outside of that it was pretty quiet, most of us were just thinking good and hard.

Take off, on schedule, nice and smooth. Usually on these rides everyone goes to sleep and tonite I had to fight going to sleep. I just had to stay awake so I'd be able to think and reset quickly. But those pills seemed to slow down feelings of emotion. Pvt. [Joseph E.] Hogan tried to get a song going after awhile [and] a few of us joined in, but it was soon lost in the roar of the motors. I fell to making a last prayer. It was a long, hard, sincere prayer that never really did end for I just continued to think and pray the rest of the ride.

When we hit the channel it was really a beautiful sight, but I just couldn't appreciate its full bounty at this time.

Twenty minutes out, came back from the pilot and the crew chief took off the door. I stood up, went to the door and had a look. All water, nice formation. No fire yet. We passed those two islands off shore, then we were over land. "O.K. boys! Stand up and hook up, best to be ready to jump at any time now, and if we do get hit we won't be taking it sitting down."

It's 01:10 red light, ten minutes out, all's quiet. Ah, there's some anti-aircraft fire, blue, green, red tracers coming up to meet us. Gee, it seems to come slow, they're pretty wild with it. There, looks like they might hit one of our planes. Look out, they're after us now. No good, shooting straight at us, so they start out right for you, but seems to make a curve and fall to the rear. Now they're heading for us, coming close you can hear them crack as they go by. There they hit our tail. Straight ahead I can see the lights set up on a jump field. J-C there's the green light, we're doing 150 MPH and still eight minutes out. O.K. let's go—Bill Lee G-D there goes my knee pack and every bit of equipment I have, watch it boy! Watch it! J-C they're trying to pick me up with those machine guns. Slip, slip try and keep close to that knee pack. There it lands beside that hedge. G-D that machine gun. There's a road, trees, hope I don't hit them. Thump, well that wasn't too bad, now let's get out of this chute.

So as I lay there working free from my chute, machine gun bullets whistling overhead every few minutes, more M.G. tracers going after planes and chutes still coming in, a big fire on the outskirts of town—turned out to be a plane on fire—and the church bell tolling out a warning to the countryside of the invasion by parachutes. That sent a back tingling sensation down a man's back.

The only weapon I had was a trench knife I'd stuck in my boot, which was stuck to the ground before I went to work on my chute. Despite this deplorable situation of landing in enemy territory with only a knife I still wasn't scared. Don't ask me why.

Before jumping I'd thought of cutting the top of my chute off and using the silk as a raincoat, protection against the cold and camouflage. But now the only thing on my mind was to get the hell away from those machine guns' bullets and that town.

Just as I started off, trench knife in hand, another chutist [*sic*] landed close by. I helped him free of his chute, got a grenade from him and said let's go get my equipment. He was hesitant of taking lead even with his Tommy gun. So I said "follow me." It wasn't long until we were away from that machine gun. But to find my equipment would take us near the road that had another M.G. shooting down it, so I said "the hell with it, let's go," and we started to move North away from the strong point of St. Mere Egleise [*sic*], which we were to find out a few minutes later when I cricketed and received an answer from one of my platoon Sgt's. [Carwood C.] Lipton, who had run across a sign post and a few other men. We hooked up with them, about 12 men, and started down the road. In a short while we ran into a group of about 50 from 502 [PIR] and a [Lt.] Col. [Robert G. Cole] in charge, so I attached my group to him. With this force we turned East toward the [Utah] beach.

The rest of the night was spent in walking down the road, while the Col. and Maj. [James W. Vaughn] tried to find their way to their objective. My intentions were to stay with them until we reach the beach, then cut loose and go South to my own objective. To do that with 12-15 men tho [*sic*], would be foolish if I could stay with 50 more. The only real excitement we had all night is when we ran into four wagon loads of Germans with horses and saddles. Most likely saddles for the reported Prussian Cavalry in the area. We knocked off two wagon loads and the others escaped.

About daybreak we were close to the beach and going through some M.G. fire and else an occasional shell from our own Navy off shore.

About 06:00 we bumped into Capt. [Jerre S.] Gross of D Co.—killed two days later—with about forty men so we joined forces and headed South for our own objective. In a few minutes we bumped into the Bn. Staff and about forty more men, so the Bn. once more was a fighting unit.

We hadn't gone far when we came across some dead Jerries and I was still looking for a weapon when I found an M-1 under a wagon seat of a German wagon. So I was happy once again, a little further along I had a revolver, belt, canteen, gas mask and lots of ammunition so I was feeling ready to fight. Especially after I bummed some food from one of the boys.

E Company now consisted of 2 L.M.G., 1 bazooka (no ammunition), one 60 MM mortar, 9 riflemen and 2 officers. We were running across a lot of dead Boch [*sic*] as we moved down the road for our objective, but very little fire. Suddenly some heavy stuff opened up on the head of the Bn. as they moved into a small town called LeGodChemin [Le Grand Chemin, 2nd Battalion Headquarters]. The column stopped, we sat down content to rest. In about ten minutes Lt. Geo. Lavenson came walking down the line and said "Winters they want you and your Company up front." So off we went. Up front I found Capt. [Clarence] Hester, [Lewis] Nixon and Kelley in a group talking it over. Seemed like Kelley had taken his Company up to a position where he could see the 88's but couldn't do anything about stopping their fire. Capt. Hester showed me where a machine gun was and about where an 88 was situated. That was all I knew.

First thing I did was have everybody drop all equipment except ammunition and grenades for that's all we'd need, if things went good or bad. Then I placed one of my two M.G. in a position where he could give us a little covering fire as we went more or less into position. Next I divided the group into two units. One went with Lt. Compton, the other with myself. He took one hedge, I another. When we reached the hedge that led up to our position we stopped. Here I placed another M.G. fixing on the 88 pointing blank at us with instructions not to fire unless he sees a definite target so he wouldn't give his position away, for he was without cover from the gun. Then we worked up to Lt. Compton's hedge row. Here I spotted a Jerry helmet and squeezed off two shots—later found a pool of blood at this position, but no Jerry. Then I sent Lt. Compton with two men up a long hedge to grenade the position while the rest of us gave him covering fire. I fired occasionally to fill in spots when there was a lull in the covering fire due to putting in new clips. They took too long getting up and we spent more ammunition than we should have but in return we received no enemy fire.

Just as Compton was ready to throw his grenade I started up with the rest of the assault team so that we were all jumping into the position together as the grenades went off. At the same time we were throwing more grenades to the next position and in return receiving small arms fire and grenades. One man, [Robert "Popeye"] Wynn, of W. Va. was hit in the butt and fell down in the trench hollering "I'm sorry Lt. I goofed off, I goofed off. I'm sorry." Over and over again. At the same time a Jerry potato masher sailed into the middle of us, we all spread out as much as we could. But Cpl. Joe Toye of Reading, Pa. just flopped down and was unlucky enough to have the grenade fall between his legs as he lay face down. It went off as I was yelling at him to move for Christ sake move. He just bounced up and down from the concussion and then bounced up unhurt and ready to go. A couple of us had tossed some grenades at Jerry at the same time, so we followed up our volley with a rush, not even stopping to look at Wynn. A Pvt. Lowraine [Gerald Lorraine] and Sgt. Suernen were with me as we pounded in on them. They both had Tommy guns and I had an M-1. As we came into position three Jerries left the 88 that we had found working our way up and started running. It took only a yell to the other two and we all opened up on our corresponding men for we were strung out, one, two, three, and so was Jerry. Lowraine hit his men with the first burst. I squeezed a shot off that took my man through the head. Suernen missed his man who turned and started back for the gun, but he'd only taken about two steps when I put one in his back that knocked him down, then Suernen settled down and pumped him full of lead with his Tommy gun. This fellow kept yelling help, help for about five minutes. I know he was out, but finally I had one of the boys put a couple through his head just in case he was only wounded, but kept yelling just the same. We had just finished off these three when out stepped a fourth about 100 yds. away. I spotted him first and had the presence of mind to lay down and make it a good shot. All this must have taken about 15 or 20 seconds since we rushed the position. My next thought was Jesus Christ somebody will cut loose in a minute from further up the trench. So I flopped down and by laying prone I could look through the connecting trench to the next position and sure enough there was two of them setting up a machine gun, getting set to fire. I got the first shot in however and hit the gunner in the hip, the second caught the other boy in the shoulder. By that time the rest of the group were in the position so I put Toye and Compton covering up toward the next position and three to go over and look over the 88 and three to cover our front. Then I retraced my steps, looked Wynn over, who was still sorry he goofed off, saw that he wasn't too bad and told him to work his way out and back himself for I couldn't spare anybody to help him. He took off.

Just as I came back Compton, who had been fooling around with a grenade let out a yell, "Look out!" We all hit for cover but there was no cover for you couldn't get out of the trench and right in the middle of it was a grenade set to go off, which it did, but for some damn reason nobody was hurt. Then a Jerry scared to death came running down the trench with his hands over his head, so he was our first prisoner. We had a lot of trouble getting him out tho [*sic*], and finally one of the boys hit him with some brass knuckles and he lay there moaning for about a half an hour until I went over, kicked him in the pants and let him know that it was high time he got out, and he did as we wanted. No sooner had this happened than I spotted three Jerries for some damn reason walking toward our position along the hedge in a very informal manner. I got our range for about 200 yds. and left them come at about 225. Somebody must have yelled at them for they stopped and seemed to listen. That's when I gave ready aim and just then this guy Lowrainne cuts loose with a Tommy gun which isn't worth a damn over 50-75 yds. One of us wounded one of them, tho but after that it was pure hell for they had machine guns on us all the time just cutting the top of the trench.

It was time we took the second gun I thought, so I left three behind and we charged the next position with grenades and lots of yelling and firing. Don't think anybody hurt anybody that time, but we did pick up those two I'd injured when they tried to put a M.G. up.

At this time ammunition was low as hell. I needed more men for we were stretched out too much for our own good and those Damn M. Gunners never came on up after us as I'd instructed. So I sent back for some, after about half an hour the M.G's. finally got there so I put them in place and decided to take the next gun. Two men from another Company had come up also.

On the attack one of these boys, John D. Hall[s] was killed. We took the position and four prisoners and then again had to hold up.

I sent all four prisoners I then had back and at the same time asked for more ammunition and men. Finally I spotted Capt. Hester coming up, went out to meet him and he gave me three blocks of T.N.T. and an incendiary grenade of ______. I had these placed in the three guns we had already taken. Also he told me Spears [Ronald Speirs] was bringing five men up.

So while waiting I went about gathering documents and stuffing them in a bag. I found one good map showing all the 88 positions and M.G. positions in the peninsula. I sent these back and directed the destruction of the radio equipment, range finders, etc.

Finally Spears arrived and led an attack on the final gun which we took, destroyed and then withdrew for the machine gun fire we were receiving from the house and other positions was pretty rough. First the machine guns pulled out then the riflemen. I was last and as I was leaving I took a final look down the trench and here was this one wounded Jerry we were leaving behind trying to pull this M.G. on us again so I drilled him clean through the head—as I found out later—and then pulled out.

On the way I found [Warrant Officer Andrew Hill] dead. He had been killed trying to work his way up to us.

In all we had four dead, six wounded and accounted for 15 dead and 12 captured. Enemy forces about fifty.

When we came out I put the M.G's firing on the position as well as a 60mm mortar as a sort of harassing fire. Also it was here I took my first shot of cider. I was thirsty as hell, I needed a lift and when one of the boys made me the offer I shocked them all by accepting. I thought at the time of it slowing down my train of thoughts and reactions, but it didn't.

The Bn. sent for some tanks to help clean this job up and then left for the objective. At that time Lt. [Harry F.] Welsh and [Warren R.] Roush came down the road with about thirty more men. I then organized them into two groups. Had them stand by when the tanks came up.[13]

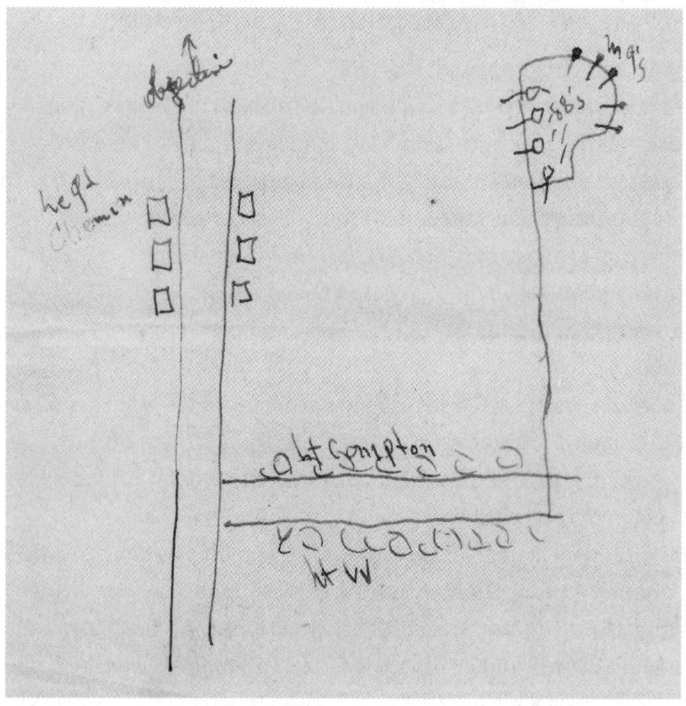

This map of Brécourt Manor was later drawn by Winters to accompany his D-Day journal entry. The perspective faces south. The cluster of buildings at Le Grand Chemin is shown at left. Winters indicated the routes he and Lt. Compton took to attack the German artillery. Enemy machine gun positions can be seen in the far right corner, behind the cannon.

Winters and his men covered substantial, dangerous ground on June 6, 1944. Early on D-Day, several troops within Dick's impromptu squad were unarmed, their weapons lost in the jump. The roving paratroopers were glad to encounter Lt. Col. Robert G. Cole, Maj. James W. Vaughn, and approximately fifty men from the 502nd Parachute Infantry

Regiment. Only moments after this fortuitous rendezvous, the paratroopers set an ambush on a small German wagon train. Weaponless and outranked, Winters could only watch as the trap was sprung.[14]

The clash was over as quickly as it began. Most of the Germans lay dead afterward. Maj. Vaughn was also cut down in the brief but fierce melee. Dick retrieved a German pistol from a corpse. The Americans thereafter advanced toward Utah Beach. As the sun rose, Winters arrived at the battalion rally point, Le Grand Chemin. Cole's troops were soon after among the first paratroopers to link up with the 4th Infantry Division pouring in from the Channel. Five days later, Cole led a bayonet charge near Carentan that earned him the Medal of Honor. Sadly, Cole perished in Holland that September.[15]

Having recaptured an M-1 rifle from a dead German, Winters and company set out to join the fight in earnest. The presence of four 105mm artillery pieces at Brécourt Manor afforded them the opportunity. "We cut them down," Winters said of the German defenders. In hindsight, he was in awe of his men's valor. Particularly evocative were the deeds and words of "Popeye" Wynn following his wounding by an enemy grenade. "That thing fell right down in that trench with me," said Wynn of the *Stielhandgranate* hurled at him. "And I was trying to scuttle my way out of the way of it and it went off.…I felt like it blowed my butt over my head." Winters was dumbfounded when Wynn apologized for being wounded. "My God!" Winters reflected. "It's beautiful when you think of a guy who is so dedicated to his company, to his buddies, that he apologizes for getting hit. But that's the kind of guy he was. That's the kind each one of them was."[16]

Wynn was not the only man worthy of praise. Pfc. Gerald Lorraine of the regiment's Service Company successfully petitioned Winters to join the attack. Lorraine received the Silver Star for his D-Day actions and earned the award a second time that fall. Others paid the ultimate price during the battery assault, including John D. Halls, the first paratrooper Dick encountered in the predawn darkness.[17]

Winters's clash at Brécourt Manor yielded substantial ramifications. The dismantling of the artillery lessened the havoc raining down upon Utah Beach, undoubtedly sparing lives. The action was likewise of great personal significance to Dick. Not only did he capture an enemy map indicating artillery emplacements, but the encounter marked the first time he fired his weapon in combat. It was the first time he killed men. Decades later, a West Point cadet asked Winters if he enjoyed the sting of battle. Did he find the experience empowering? "No, it did not," was the reply. "It was not so much a feeling of happiness as it was satisfaction, satisfaction that I got the job done and that I had proved myself to my men.…Brécourt gave me confidence in my ability to lead. That's why it remains so special to me."[18]

"Take it on from the flank," he instinctively thought of the enemy position. "This is part of your training. It's not something that you're dreaming up and creating on the spur of the moment. This is all part of the training that's kicking in." Success does not mean "you made a brilliant decision."[19]

Brilliant or not, men perished in the heat of combat. "On D-Day morning," Winters recalled in 1996, "Warrant Officer Andrew Hill (Regt. Hq.), was trying to join me in the German connecting trenches where we were trying to knock out their four 105m cannons." The fire was coming in thick and heavy. "As W.O. Hill was crawling across the field, at one point he raised his head to see where we were. He was hit between the eyes and died immediately. When he died his right arm was extended straight upward, exposing his wrist watch." After seeking additional ammunition, Winters retraced his steps, rediscovering Hill's remains and timepiece. Dick thought, "I could use that watch." Turning to fetch it he muttered to himself, "This is crazy. That watch isn't worth the risk." He grabbed it nonetheless. When he returned to England that July, he presented the timepiece as a souvenir gift to thirteen-year-old friend Elaine Stevens.[20]

This iconic photo taken by Easy Company paratrooper Walter "Smokey" Gordon was snapped in the town square of Sainte-Marie-du-Mont on June 7, 1944. The front row includes (left to right) Forrest Guth, Francis Mellet, David Morris, Daniel West, Floyd Talbert, and Campbell Smith. Members of the 4th Infantry Division from nearby Utah Beach are in the background. Forrest Guth photo.

While Winters's diary painted a personal portrait of battle, Associated Press reporter Wes Gallagher rendered a broader panoramic. "Airborne troops have seized bridges and roads, and joined sea-landed troops at some points," he scribbled on June 7. The Cherbourg Peninsula was aflame with firepower, strewn with tattered silk parachutes, littered with discarded crates. German broadcasts proclaimed Allied beachheads were smashed and countless airborne formations were "wiped out." Berlin radio nonetheless conceded "the airborne assaults were spreading great confusion behind German lines." Some occupiers "had been duped by parachuting sacks of straw loaded with explosives that blew up when they touched" the ground. Despite the apparent effectiveness of hit-and-run tactics, Gallagher concluded, "There still was no sign [Hermann] Goering had begun to risk his weaker sky arm with big scale attacks." The defiant airborne men were grateful for Goering's apparent indecision.[21]

On D+11, Dick wrote a concise announcement of survival to DeEtta.

"If you're ever in a tight spot."

V-MAIL

17 June, 1944

Dear DeEtta–

Just a note to let you know I am O.K., doing fine, and making a tour of France. That's about all rules and regulations will permit me to say, but I've found out that it's the essentials that count.

If you read the newspapers, (I haven't seen one for a long, long time), you'll get the big picture which is more than I know. In fact, I am just dying to see a newspaper to find out what is going on in this war. However, as far as the details of the big—well I'll tell you that stuff later.

Once you wrote and said "if you're ever in a tight spot, remember you must come back." You'll never know how much that helped. So thanks a million!

If you receive this so-called letter with that address, it'll be due to some smart mailman.

Love from your trooper,
Dick[22]

In the days following the invasion's opening salvo, the 101st Airborne maintained the advance. A seesaw of battles engulfed the community of Carentan, located approximately ten miles inland from Utah Beach. In preparing a counteroffensive, German officers hoped to divide the Americans and push them back to the sea. Conversely, US forces aspired to capture and hold Carentan to consolidate their beachheads and form one continuous front. Winters did not escape the clash unscathed. A machine gun ricochet pierced the tongue of his boot and lodged beneath his skin during the assault into the town. He was hobbled for several days but there was no time for rest or recuperation. Through June 14, the division faced one of its most imposing challenges in combat. Intense hedgerow and street fighting was followed by a fierce German counterattack later known as the Battle of Bloody Gulch. Here, Easy Company played a crucial role holding the line. Winters personally spurred his men into the fight when they were gripped by fear or confusion.[23]

Like Confederates defending the Sunken Lane at Antietam, the paratroopers were in a concealed, fixed position at the base of a long, open slope. Naturally, the GIs had the advantage of automatic weapons, but the situation was no less precarious. Unlike their Civil War ancestors, the troopers of the 506th PIR trained for the unpredictability of combat as such. According to author Brad Graham, the constant shifting of paratroopers prevented the enemy from "locking in." Pockets of men in reserve filled defensive gaps with flexibility. "As a combat leader, Dick Winters knew to move from one end of his line to the other, encouraging the men and telling them to keep firing," Graham continues. "The basic problem, from the German point of view, was their inability to find a weak spot to exploit." The subsequent American success at Carentan created a firm lodgment solidifying the beachheads.[24]

Dick's concise post-D-Day note to DeEtta offered little information other than that he was alive. His frustration over a lack of newspapers underscored the value of periodicals—an amenity often absent in foxholes. Interestingly, *Stars and Stripes* staff writer Jack Foster published an in-depth summary of the fight for Carentan the very same day Winters composed his V-Mail. The article accurately summarized the fierce nature of the brawl:

June 14–The next bridge was mined, according to the paratrooper corporal, so we stopped where he and his four men had an advance post west of Carentan. Bombs and artillery had blasted a path through the town for the troopers. Now they were dug in for the night 600 yards from Nazi pillboxes.

"It's been bloodthirsty!" said the corporal. "They have been giving us trouble with heavy guns, but we keep chasing them along this road. Is our artillery coming up?"

It was, and we told him about the lines of tanks and guns we passed a few miles back. Captured German trucks were in the procession, loaded down with shells for our cannon. Munching on a big onion, the corporal calmly pointed out a German artillery position on our left. As he waved a shell burst nearby in answer.

"We don't worry too much about it, though," he went on. "Their shooting isn't so hot."

These troopers had been fighting since D-Day. All of this little group were forced to bail out when their plane was damaged a few miles from their objective.

"It was really tough then," broke in a private. "We were damn busy. The corporal there wiped out a machine gun nest all by himself and the rest of us have been killing them all along. But the glider guys are the ones who have really done the job."

Wherever you go it's the same story. Paratroopers praise glider men, glider men extol troopers. I decided to leave when the corporal noticed my Navy uniform. "The Jerries wear blue clothes sometimes, bud. I wouldn't go around here dressed like that. We shoot first," he warned. I took the hint and crowded deep in the jeep between Lt. Col. Ernie Parks of Savannah, Georgia and Capt. John R. Parkhill of Tampa, Florida. Parks gave some German pineapple grenades to the soldiers. "These will come in handy, colonel," said the corporal. "We'll get some of the bastards for you."

Rolling back to Carentan we saw ample evidence of Allied accuracy with bombs. At a railroad crossing a whole train had been blown from the tracks. It was a German troop train and we heard later that our planes had strafed its passengers as they scurried from the wreckage. Tracks and ties pointed skyward as high as 25 feet.

The town is draped with Tricolors. Men who arrived here only a few minutes ago are already billeted in empty houses. The civilians help them find quarters. They were confused this morning when the town changed hands several times, but now they are at home with the Yanks, who are passing out chewing gum and candy to grateful kids.

The Germans fought hard to keep Carentan. Dead of both sides line the shoulders of the road in. Dead cattle in the fields show how heavily the Nazis mined the area. At several spots piles of machine gun shells mark bitter skirmishes. Three bridges at the outskirts were demolished by the retreating Huns.

Our men are confident that they will hold the town this time. Every arriving tank and gun reassures them. A paratrooper riding a beautiful horse showed us the Yankee spirit as we watched him direct traffic in the center of the town. "Come on back tomorrow," he shouted to us. "I'll buy you the best drink in town as soon as we slack off!"[25]

Having completed his lengthy D-Day account, Dick spared another moment to write DeEtta on June 23. "Received your V-mail and airmail letters that were sent on D-Day," he wrote. "Under the conditions I received your mail, its presence is most welcome and valued beyond estimate." Despite his detailed diary entry, Dick was not at liberty to convey his invasion observations. "If I could describe to you the story of the start of the invasion to the present situation, it would make an interesting story. However, that's more than we're allowed to say, since we're limited to saying we're in France and the telling of personal encounters without disclosing any names of towns, places, etc."

He vowed he was doing the utmost to help win the war. His paratroopers had "done more than they'll ever receive credit for." History shows he was incorrect on that point. "God, but I am sick of iron rations," he complained. Dick ate nothing but K and D rations for eighteen days. The pitiful diet hurt his teeth and soured his appetite. Yet, "I'd rather be a trooper than a swab," the lieutenant ribbed.[26]

On June 27, an article about Dick entitled "Wounded at Carentan, Commended for Bravery" appeared in the *Lancaster New Era*. The newspaper picked up a correspondent's syndicated report chronicling Dick's recent heroics. "According to the dispatch," wrote the *New Era*, "Lt. Winters showed valiant action under enemy fire near St. Come Du Mont and Carentan where he also received a leg wound and is now recuperating in England."

The article stated, "He was given orders to take his company and silence a battery of four German 88s which were shelling the beach and after capturing two prisoners, they were finally able to silence the battery. He then went into the front lines when the SS troops counter-attacked Carentan the night of June 12 and the morning of June 13. He was commended by his CO, the dispatch stated, who said that it was Lt. Winters' personal bravery and battle knowledge that held a crucial position when the going was really tough."[27]

On the same newspaper page, several Lancastrians were classified as killed or missing in action. Dick's parents breathed an uneasy sigh of relief.

The important message: "I am now a captain."

July 2, 1944
Somewhere in France

Dear De Etta-

Not much to report from the beachhead today, there is not much that can be told.

The French people are becoming more and more friendly as the Boch [*sic*] are pushed further back and they become used to the idea of Americans being around.

To those who have lost everything it must be hard to feel anything but hatred. They've all lost at least a little by our coming, yet they seem to take great pride in flying their flag once more. They wave to us as we go by and call "Viva La France," or hold thumbs up or V for victory. It seems like the feeling is the same the world over.

The life of a conqueror isn't bad for a while. You're a paratrooper who lives off the land for we can't carry anything extra. So to be victorious is a necessity to life. We win or die. When we win we're on top of the world. We win!

The natives aren't too bad off in general. In the country the people have plenty to eat. Some hurt in the cities. But they have all the meat and butter they can use. Bread is rationed, and of course now they have their garden vegetables.

Just about everybody wears wooden shoes for work, leather for dress. But I understand this was a custom in times of prosperity as well. Also, I noticed when the women go to church that they all have silk stockings, or something that looks like silk.

Life, here of late, has been very nice. Why right now I sit here with a sound power telephone to my ear listening to some of the first American music I've heard for two months. Before that I never heard a radio back at camp in England or America. Boy, when it comes to popular music I am not hep. Now I've music from the radio I picked up from an old friend of "Herr Krauthead," who won't be needing it anymore. And I am munching on my first candy bar in over a month. What's more it's a Hershey chocolate bar. I am not tired, of course I am hungry, but that's always a good sign that I am normally healthy. Say, here comes the "Hit Parade," what a treat. Now they're playing "Broadway." I know that one but this song, "Russia," never heard of it.

Your prayers for my safety certainly helped a lot, more than you know. I don't know what else could pull a fellow through. I found out just what is essential and what isn't in life. In my prayers before I always thanked God for what He'd done for the world in general and asked that they be given a break in the future. For myself, I always thanked Him for a lot of things that I found out were insignificant. That I was still alive each night was the big thing, the only thing. And the only thing you ask for the future is that you'll be alive tomorrow morning and be able to live through the next day. That's all that matters, that's the only thing as far as wanting anything for yourself that's important. All other things are extra, unessential, and you can't be bothered or burdened with unessentials [*sic*], not when battle is the payoff.

Say, I haven't received any mail from you for a long time—about two weeks. Hope it's just accumulating someplace. In fact the last one I received was at the time you were pulling K.P. in a bellhop's uniform. Isn't that a silly outfit for a man or woman to be wearing?

Did you notice my change of address? Take another look. Yep, it's true. I am now known as Captain Winters, Company Commander of Easy Company. So please take note and never make the mistake of addressing me as Pvt., Cpl, Lt, or ---. However, it'll be O.K. to say

Your trooper Captain,
Dick[28]

On July 2, 1944, Winters was among a number of soldiers presented the Distinguished Service Cross by Gen. Omar Bradley. Winters was promoted to captain the previous day. Winters is fifth from the right. Gen. Maxwell Taylor stands at the far left. Bradley can be seen with his three-star helmet on the stage.

Interactions with the liberated French were telling. Sgt. Dewitt Gilpin of *Yank* magazine recognized the "split-second relationship" formed between the civilian population and the Allies. "Raymonde Jeanne, who works in the general store at Ste. Mere Eglise, looked out of her bedroom window the night of June 5 and saw an 82nd paratrooper in the street," said Gilpin. "She threw him a rose and, unless Raymonde is romanticizing the incident, he kissed it and walked out of her life with the rose in one hand and his grease gun in the other."[29]

"The French remember," Gilpin insisted. Townspeople marched with bowed heads to makeshift cemeteries each Sunday to place flowers atop the graves of "adopted" American sons. "Gone, of course, is the pre-invasion conception of some Normans that our coming would be a costless thing that would not disturb the economics of life," Gilpin added. "The peasants and townspeople paid for their liberation in lives, in wrecked homes, and depleted dairy herds. Some grumble about these things, but the majority think the bigger sacrifice was made down on the beaches. And the same majority seem to understand why most of the GIs, unlike Raymonde's gallant trooper, were very rough with them on D-Day."[30]

Throughout the night of June 5, recalled Alexandre Renaud, mayor of Sainte-Mère-Église, "we watch in the trees, on the houses, on the church. And all night the four machine guns that the Germans had in the church steeple keep shooting. But we are happy, because the Americans have come and we want to help them so much," he exclaimed. "But in the morning when I go out and find the captain of the paratroopers and speak our welcome to him in English, he refuses to shake my hand. I felt very bad. Now we understand that the Americans at first could not trust anyone." Alexandre's wife, Simone, placed flowers on the graves of American dead, wrote to parents of the deceased, mailed headstone photos to families, and later hosted returning veterans for reunions. She is still lovingly remembered as the "Mother of Normandy."[31]

Mademoiselle Andrée Manoury of Carentan took seventy-two English lessons in anticipation of invasion. She wished to serve as a translator to assist American and British liberators. Sadly, an Allied bomb annihilated the German gas depot near her home, forcing her family to flee. Such was the dreadful cost of liberation. Despite the ruin of their towns, the French were free once more—and their calvados was heartily shared.[32]

Once beyond the beaches, Americans quickly learned the perils of German trickery. "Those first outfits, the men who went in June 6, found German soldiers posing as French civilians, they met their first fanatic Nazis kids—the sixteen- and seventeen-year-olds who fight to the last bitter end, and then blubber like babies when they are finally captured," wrote Ralph Harwood of *Stars and Stripes*. The enemy came in many sizes and ages.[33]

"P.S. Did I tell you I received the D.S.C.?"

15 July 1944
England

My favorite sailor–

Those church bells that just tolled 2100 made me stop a moment for they brought back memories of the last time I heard church bells ringing. That was in France, D-Day, H-hour-5 (1:00 A.M.), and they weren't tolling a request for us to come to church but an alarm to all the countryside that we'd arrived. What followed of course is history but it sure gave me a funny feeling. Machine gun fire and rifle fire didn't scare me. But those bells, being all alone with only a knife, gave me the feeling of being hunted down by a pack of wolves.

Say, I am sorry that my mail hasn't been coming through, but I feel sure the situation has improved by now.

Received your record, along with a lot of your back mail yesterday, and I'd like to say you've certainly been right on the ball. The first opportunity I have I'll see what that record has to say.

Returning to England, my adopted parents, and a seven day leave, all at one time, has really been wonderful. However, I am spending most of my time right here at camp, resting in the laziest manner I know. I expect I'll go to London though and see some shows and do a little shopping for clothes that I had pilfered from me while we were gone.

Some of the local boys seem to have formed a band and they're out in the square playing a few selections. It sounds darn good, in fact any kind of music would sound good to me right now.

Everybody in England gave us a wonderful homecoming. They forgot all about being reserved and dignified and broke down. It sure was nice and appreciated by all.

You mentioned about your officers going on picnics with the enlisted personnel and your thinking more of them for it. That may work in the navy, but I don't think it does, for I've noticed it throughout. You lack military discipline and respect for rank. I've been a buck private, and when I was I didn't want to fool around with the officers. All I wanted from them was good leadership. Now I am a captain and I find that buddy stuff is out. I am all in favor of knowing each and every man, getting in bull sessions with them, etc., knowing their background, likes, dislikes, capabilities, and weak points. I want to be their friend and the guy they go to when they want a favor or they're in trouble. But I am not their buddy, I am their captain, and when I say something, that's it, you jump. If you're going to have things like that then you can't go around on picnics with them and so forth. Oh, I know those officers are well liked that do things like that, but in the end their ideas and principles break down. I've only been around three years in the army, but I can see that the old army is the right army, and the longer I am around, and the more I see of it, the more I am convinced. You can't make a decision as quickly and thoroughly if your buddies are concerned in a life and death situation. I've seen it, kid.

Say, I've got a little something I'll wrap up and send up some day when I get the mood and urge to move. It's a scarf I had made out of a piece of parachute silk that was used on the beachhead in France. Attached I'll stick a captain's bar. Of course you won't be able to wear the insignia on your shoulder or hat, but they may let you stick it around your throat, or some place.

Well, be good, but don't look for me in your chow line for I am afraid the boys and girls in the navy would find me a bit tough to get along with.

Say, incidentally, just what the hell are you Waves supposed to be doing to help win the war? I mean, now you're learning radar and a lot of stuff. How are you going to use it? Where and when it'll do you or anybody else any good ----. Don't feel insulted now. Just go down to the PX and have a pint of ice cream on me. Oh -----------.

Dick

P.S. Did I tell you I received the D.S.C. for a little job on D-Day? Knocked out some artillery that was taking shots at your navy and troops landing on the beach.[34]

The paratroopers sustained a costly month in Normandy and savored a needed respite in England. The literary Pvt. David Webster commented, "The losses on the jump had been heavy—dead paratroopers scattered like blown leaves over all the roads, fields, hedges, and villages." The "Screaming Eagles" returned to Aldbourne as other divisions pummeled their way across France. The troopers were issued fresh jumpsuits. Battle-tested veterans coldly greeted replacements. Men were granted leave, reoccupied old pubs, and rekindled romantic flames. "We knew, though," continued Webster, "that our luck couldn't last indefinitely…we looked at England with loving eyes, knowing full well that our time was running out." At a memorial service for his fallen comrades, Webster perused a list of 231 men who would fight no more. How much would the list grow after battles to come?[35]

Winters sought solace in camp—welcoming the quiet pleasures of books and sleep. Although interrupted by the occasional rattle of a German "buzz bomb," he enjoyed a number of London shows during leave. That July, DeEtta mailed a letter expressing her longing that Dick was a stateside private instead of an officer in harm's way. Winters was riled by the thought. "If I'd still be a private after almost three years of army life, I'd go nuts," he howled. "I'd be worse than 'sad sack.' No responsibilities, no thinking to do for myself, no problems or excitement, no nothing.… Then to have somebody doing the fighting for me! No thanks! I'll just stay right where I am and dodge bullets for a living." Apparent in his post-Normandy correspondence, Winters occasionally expressed cynicism and impatience. The war was already changing him.

His frustrations often melted in light of DeEtta's upbeat disposition. Enclosed in his July 27 letter was a sliver of silk parachute salvaged from Normandy. He also mailed DeEtta captain bars as a keepsake pin. "I hesitate sending it for if you wear it you might be picked up for impersonating an officer," he quipped.[36]

"If those mosquitoes don't ease up, I'll be glad to 'hurry home.'"

6 August, 1944
England

My favorite Wave–

You know I am really being put to shame each and every day. For not a day passes that I find a letter or two in my mail box. [Y]et here I go on writing my same ration of letters: two per week, one home, and one for the "Navy." How do you suggest I remedy the situation?

Say those mosquitoes must have really been tough, and then imagine having to get up and hunt through your belongings for Noxzema [*sic*] in the middle of the night. Oh, my, but the navy's rough. Sometime remind me to tell you of those mosquitoes outside of Carentan when we were fighting on the edge of some swampland. They flew in formations and one night actually lifted a parachute I was using for camouflage right off me.

Don't say things like "hurry home." Ye gods, a war's toughest thing to fight is just the simple thing of waiting patiently. You wait for transportation, chow, pay, meetings, problems, take-off time, the attack, the enemy. So actually there is little fighting, just a lot of waiting and training while you wait. Of course it's easier to wait if you just keep your shirt on, don't get excited and wear yourself out with anxiety. As a result you're a better fighter, do a better job, time goes by much quicker, and all is well if you have patience. So just stand at ease.

Yes, "Chicken," I am still receiving the *Reader's Digest* and blessing you every time I do. Good reading matter is hard to get hold of over here. Just last night I was up until 0200 reading the *Digest*.

[...] My father writes and tells me he received a letter from you. Very nice. Thanks a lot. My folks worry too much about their son. In fact, I worry more about them worrying about me than I do about myself. Boy, was my dad proud when he heard I'd made captain and won the D.S.C. Then, I've been getting a few write-ups in the *Washington Post* and in the hometown papers, so he thinks I am a regular hero. Well, anything to keep him happy.

Had a pass this week and took my best girl to town to see "Snow White and the 7 Giants." Funny part about it is I enjoyed the darn show myself. You remember Elaine, don't you, my blond from London? She's evacuated for the summer to get away from the buzz bombs. You should see her hair. It's absolutely the most beautiful blond hair I've ever seen, long, silken, and just as smooth as honey. She's only 13 but I'll bet in about ten years she'll be a knockout. When you see kids like that suffer from war, it hurts. Just about five years now she's been away from home, parents poor as hell, education will most likely stop in another year and then what can a kid that age do? I get a kick out of taking her to officer's mess once in awhile and keeping her in spending money. Reminds me of my own sister.

Oh, yes, some day I'll get up enough energy to write a letter sitting up, then maybe you'll be able to read it.

Love,
Dick

P.S. My gosh, I forgot this was supposed to go to my cousin, Jack. How do you like this scotch envelope from Scotland?[37]

During World War II, over three million Britons—including children like Elaine—were evacuated from metropolitan areas due to German bombing. The feared "buzz bombs" (an early cruise missile) seen by Winters were particularly debilitating on a psychological level. "The consensus is solid that the buzz bomb is a more frightful weapon than the kind dropped by planes piloted by humans," noted writer Robert Bunnelle. "People generally view it like the frenzied thrashing of a mortally wounded animal. They hope it will stop but are pretty well resigned that it or something worse will likely continue to the war's end."

Civilians did their best to carry on—just as they had done during the Blitz in 1940–1941. They camped out in "improvised nooks of comparative safety" and maintained a strong sense of community. Dick greatly admired the citizenry's determination to survive and rebuild. The pulsating hum of incoming bombs nonetheless shook residents to the core. "The buzz bomb," concluded Bunnelle, "has a greater ability to create an impression that it has got not only your name on it but also your street address."[38]

No use telling you all the good news in one letter.

7 August, 1944
England

Seaman Almon–

After reading your letter of the first I've decided to take your suggestion and submit a recommendation for a court martial to prove the point, you can't get too friendly with the E.M. (enlisted men) and hold their respect. As in this case, things are out of hand when you start telling me what the score is in handling problems of a delicate nature, etc.

Then, too, it was most interesting to read about how you "take orders whether we like them or not, and obey and make the most out of whatever happens." Why you poor, poor dears. You mean to say they give you things you don't like to do? But I am mighty proud of you for making the best of all those difficult situations and problems you face. I'd like to shake the hand of each and every Wave—between here and the States. The way you must suffer, though, just makes me so mad, I could go out and kill a whole mess of Germans, or even down a quart of ice cream.

Another point is the way you speak of your officers. God almighty, I'd hate to be an officer in that outfit. Why there'd be just no telling when a person might get hit on the back of the head with a powder puff. Then you think we don't worry about the social life of our men. Hell, what do you think we take them out running every day for? So they can stay away from these women and thus the venereal rate stays down. That's our biggest problem. Then we also have beer parties, movies, little things like getting laundry, dry cleaning, haircuts, ball games, things that are done after working hours. But it's no problem, no worry, no special way of doing it, but it's done.

Now don't think that when I knocked out that battery of 88s on D-Day that it was to save the navy. Hell, no, it was for those poor "dog faces" trying to get ashore. The fact that it helped the navy is a side issue.

Next the scarf. By now you've most likely received it and are disappointed in finding that it's green instead of white. You see our chutes are camouflaged for combat. You've been looking at the "U.S. glory jump picture."

> Then you bitch about my not telling about being wounded. My gosh, is that supposed to be something interesting? Now, if I'd been killed or something, that'd be something to write home about. But being "pinked" in the leg is about as interesting as cutting yourself while shaving. The only difference is you get a little Purple Heart. People write a few very sad letters when they read about it in the paper. Wish you all kinds of good luck, hope you pull through and that _____, nuts! Someday the damn thing will work out and I'll show you what it was. As yet I don't know myself how big it is.
>
> Now I am sick and tired of all this unnecessary bitching! Get on the beam, soldier, and let's see a little more cooperation and work and less mooning and brooding.
>
> Capt. R.D. Winters
> C.O., Co. E, 506th Para. Inf.[39]

Winter's witty sarcasm did not dampen DeEtta's spirits. She could hold her own. As Winters later attested, her jocular rebuttals demonstrated her strength of mind and lifted his spirits. Near war's end, he described her as the "only person who ever gives me the devil." Through their written words, the two kept each other in line.[40]

The chatter often took a serious turn. Winters realized that to be a commander is to be lonely. In his August 7 letter, Dick conveyed the importance of objectivity regarding subordinates. As he later confessed to Cole Kingseed, "A commander cannot show partiality or favoritism to any soldier, officer or enlisted, in his command. There is simply no time to develop personal relationships or worry if you are liked. You do your best, and at the end of the day, you look in the mirror and hope you were a good leader." This philosophy marked a change in attitude from Dick's days as a platoon leader, when he thought it important to gain familiarity with his men. Although in the service herself, DeEtta functioned as Dick's confidante rather than a comrade. Transparency notwithstanding, DeEtta expressed shock upon learning of Dick's Normandy wound in a secondhanded manner. His omission of key events in his correspondence underscored his strict adherence to self-censorship. Perhaps he also wished to spare her from the disconcerting news of the battlefront.[41]

"Yep, I like to go to church."
Totally frustrated–can't tell you about cancelled missions to jump outside Paris, etc.

19 August, 1944
England

Dear DeEtta-

Your letters have been arriving quite regularly although not as frequently as they did for a period just following D-Day. Today I received your song hits and as I expected, there are only a few that mean anything to me, and their tunes are at least a year old.

You mentioned in your letter of the 8th that you had a couple of clippings from the *Washington Sun Star* on Carentan. That would be mighty interesting reading to me. I heard they gave us a pretty good writeup, but as yet haven't seen it. Usually though, they manage to get things mixed up royally. In fact, being a member of the distinguished and upstanding organization of the Waves, you may not understand the meaning of the word, "Snafu," but that usually covers the situation quite well.

That family of yours sure goes all out in the war effort. Four kids in the service! Too bad though they just picked the wrong branch.

Now, then, you want to transfer, figures petrify you, you're frantic and I can see you're all flustered and in a state where you declare you simply "can't do the work, suh." Don't get frantic, take it easy. Do you think you can stand it for, say another year? Well, by that time I imagine they'll be telling most of the skirts to go home and put on the lipstick to welcome the boys. Another year, at the outside. Now, if you transfer, you simply have to be trained all over for some other job, unless you have some unskilled job, which will take time, space, and money. So, instead of being an asset, you'll just be a debit. That's about as sensible as me deciding to join the Air Corps or the navy at this stage of the game, after having been trained in my own line of work. Oh, you women! Sometimes I wonder if the dear Lord did you justice.

Say look, Squirt, I don't want to disappoint you but I doubt very much if this captain will make it back to the States this fall. You see, it's going to be a little late in the year when this job's done. Then, being the type that likes to stick to a job till it's done before I quit, I think I'll try and go down to the South Pacific, either with the paratroops or without them, all depending on what they decide to do with them, and help finish that job. Those of course are my present plans, however, they're subject to change. I just wanted to let you know how I feel.

One thing about this being overseas and away from home isn't so good. Ye gods, I find myself not giving a damn one way or another. Maybe I'm spoiled or something but I don't give a damn if I write or don't, and if I get mail, good, but it doesn't bother me one way or another. Then, what's to do when I do get home? Nothing so wonderful, no job, no idea what I'd like to do. Sometimes it worries me, at other times I just have a negative feeling. But I guess what I need right now is to get out and run, or walk, or sing, or do something to change my frame of mind. It'll be a run.

Well tomorrow is Sunday and I am all set for church, buttons shined, boots polished, ribbons all over my tunic. Yep, I like to go to church. The way I feel about it, it is a very special privilege to be able to go at all and I don't want to miss a chance.

Well, I'll see you in church and later at the gangplank.

Your trooper,
Dick[42]

P.S. Wrote this damn letter a week ago and never could get any stamps.

DeEtta's letters accurately reflect the prominence of Carentan in press reports. Because of frequent strategic shifting, Dick had little opportunity to read of the battle in which he played a considerable role. He already pondered what history would say of the moment. DeEtta collected several newspaper articles chronicling paratrooper actions, particularly those featured in the *Washington Sun Star*. Col. Sink informed *Star* correspondent Walter McCallum that, "It was Lt. Winters's personal leadership which held the crucial position in the line and tossed back the enemy with mortar and machine gun fire. He was a fine soldier out there." DeEtta beamed with pride.[43]

Fellow war correspondents covering the clash included Don Whitehead of the Associated Press. Known as "Beachhead Don" due to his battlefield durability, Whitehead offered stirring frontline perspectives to readers. "SS troops and parachute troops fought frantically in a mad effort to break through between the two beachheads," he explained.[44]

"The Krauts fell from trees and out of the hedges like flies," exclaimed Capt. Harry Vold of the German counteroffensive. Whitehead described some enemy troops being brutally crushed under the treads of their own tanks as the clash spiraled out of control. Yanks staving off the assaults were "hard pressed" until American armor came to the rescue. The paratroopers arose from foxholes and wildly yelped in celebration. "You'd have thought you were at the Giants-Dodgers game," remarked Pvt. John Boretsky. The battle reduced the town to a blackened shell. Another reporter grimly concluded, "Carentan may go down as one of the bloodiest of the war." Considering his recent exploits, Winters fancied his return to England.[45]

Company Commander's meeting–Sunday afternoon.
Another mission–later cancelled.

26 August, 1944
England

My favorite Wave–

Glad to know you've received and are pleased with the scarf. If you can't wear it, perhaps it'll do a good job camouflaging the dust in preparation for inspection.

Squirt, I know just what you mean when you tell me about being bored. I enjoyed the rest at first myself, if you can call it a rest. Actually I guess it's just a mental relaxation. I know darn well the army is no place to relax physically. As for the "devil finding evil things for idle hands to do," well, that seems to be the normal trend.

[...] Well this afternoon I was all set to hit the sack for an hour or two and catch up on some rest this damn training schedule has been denying me. You see in the army we work nights as well as days and such things as an 8 hour shift is strictly for the S.O.S. and navy boys. Just as I settled down with a sigh of contentment and happiness at thoughts of what a way to fight a war, the thing happened that keeps me on a constant edge—a C.O. meeting. That's S.O.P. (standard operating procedure) when you're getting set for some relaxing.

[...] Well yesterday I celebrated my third anniversary in the army. As I look back it seems like a lifetime in some respects and as if I've aged three times three. Then again, it isn't so long and I've been pretty lucky right along. There are not many in this outfit that have done as much in the same period of time. In fact, I know of none. Ahem. Then, too, if I stick in this parachute outfit for two or three more years, salt my money away at about the same rate I have been, I'll have a pretty darn good foothold on this financial situation.

Ah, yes, but what I really want is to get this war over. Amen! And the sooner they put me back in the fight the better I'll like it, for it's no good letting the other guy do it for you. Just doesn't feel right.

You ask for some requests again—thanks.

1 doz. pens
½ doz. Waves
1 qt. ice cream—any flavor
2 doz. Kisses
&
Love,
Dick

Picture taken by P.R. the day we returned from Normandy.
Backdrop a stone wall.[46]

Dick once more took refuge with the Barnes family that summer. Upon his return from Normandy, "Mother Barnes" declared, "I'm so proud of you. I just knew you would do good." In the challenges to come, Dick had no intention of letting her down. He regularly attended church in his unblemished dress uniform and spotless boots. He prayed for guidance and safety. The frequency of his writing waned as his physical regimen intensified. Dick was no longer concerned with the trivial demands and expectations of life. He simply did not want to fail his men.[47]

The portrait Winters sent of himself to DeEtta from Aldbourne that summer offered little indication of fear. "I was told not to smile in order to project the proper warrior image," he later confessed. Showcasing his new service ribbons and his chiseled jaw, the photo captured a changed man—a twenty-six-year-old combat veteran whose days on the battlefield were far from complete.[48]

"I've seen death," he said. "I've seen my friends, my men, being killed." The experience forever changed him.[49]

CHAPTER FIVE

NO TIME TO MOURN

September to November 1944

"I can make it until Christmas," Winters thought. Such was the optimistic longing of Allied service members swept by liberation fervor in the late summer of 1944. Veterans of Easy Company embraced the thrilling potential of jumping into Berlin for a grand finale. The lively deliverance of Paris, the seeming disintegration of the once-mighty *Luftwaffe,* and rumors of a dwindling German army bolstered the confidence of Allied generals and enlisted men alike. Emotions swelled further on September 4 as British troops handily conquered Antwerp, Belgium—one of the largest deep-water ports in all of Europe. Presumably, the seizure of the centuries-old city on the River Scheldt would unleash an unflagging tide of supplies from the sea. Leaders were too buoyant in their aims to end the war before 1945. A mixture of hastiness and brashness on the part of strategic planners unveiled dire repercussions for untold thousands of combatants.[1]

Deferring to the wishes of British general Bernard Montgomery, Dwight Eisenhower relinquished plans to attack Germany via a broad front. The result was a narrow and rapid strike into Holland, codenamed Operation Market-Garden. The bold endeavor was incredibly complex and daringly multifaceted. Several airborne divisions would overwhelm

Dog tags listed the details of life. They were also grim tokens of wartime danger. Winters's stainless steel tags bear his name, serial number, the year of his last tetanus shot, his blood type, and religious faith ("P" for Protestant). He wore these tags in battle.

According to Winters, he always tried to save "a little money at the end of the month" for leisure activities and creature comforts. Early in his military career, he often wished more dollar bills filled this wallet—inscribed with his Lancaster address.

Winters's officer identification card was issued to him on July 31, 1942. He officially qualified as a parachutist two months later. When he was subsequently promoted, Winters crossed out his previous rank and inserted his new rank.

"Three miles up, three miles down," was the phrase often used to lament the forced marches to the summit of Currahee Mountain overlooking Camp Toccoa. Plenty of dirt was kicked up on this trail as the troops built endurance and bonds of camaraderie.

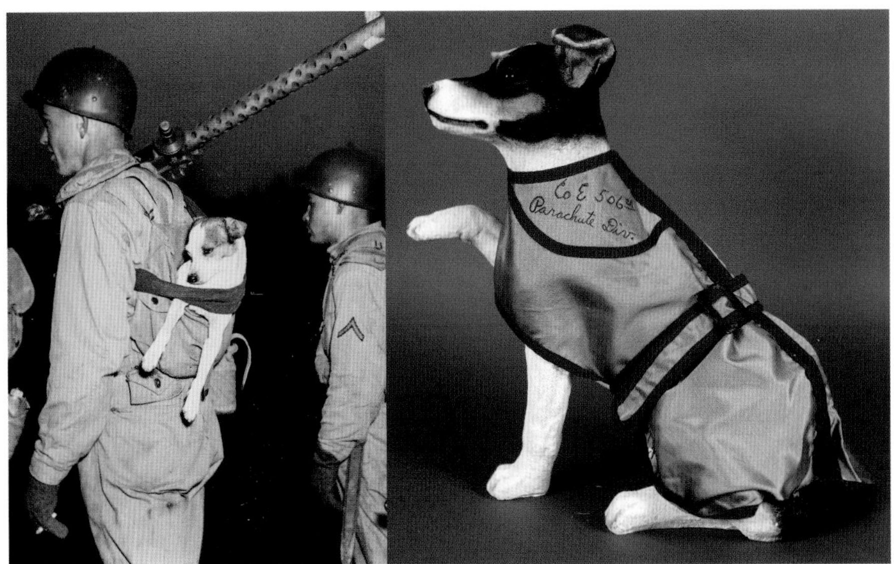

During the Atlanta march, Dewitt Lowrey of Easy Company retrieved a dog following the column and tucked it in his pack. The dog, fittingly named Draftee, was presented the ceremonial coat at right, and became the company's mascot until it was gifted to the nurses of Fort Benning.

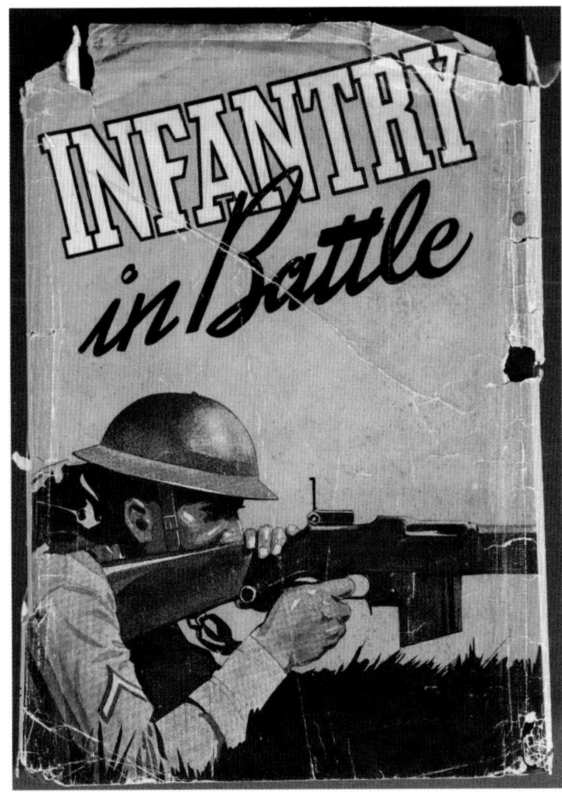

On February 19, 1943, Winters purchased this copy of *Infantry in Battle* at the Fort Benning post exchange. His many notations throughout the book underscore his eagerness to become an effective field officer.

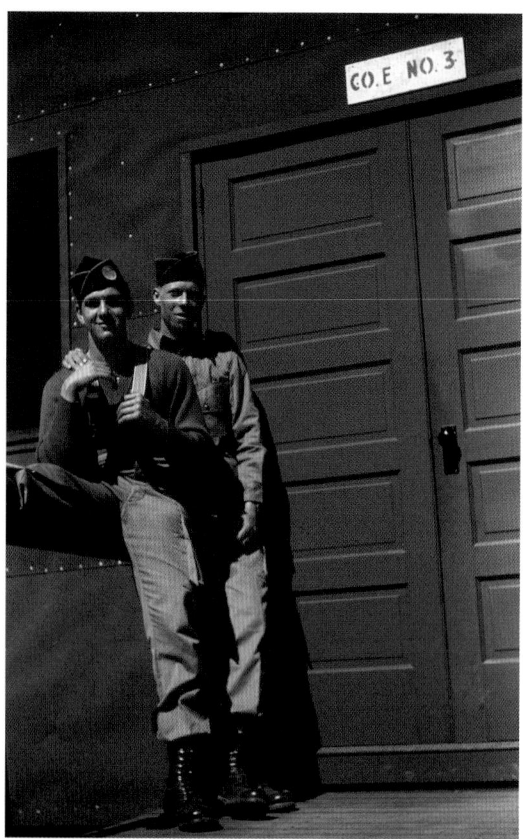

Soldiers Bill Guarnere and James L. Diel enjoyed a moment of levity at Camp Mackall, North Carolina, in 1943. Guarnere, despite later losing a leg in Belgium, lived to old age and considerable fame. Tragically, Diel died in the Netherlands on September 19, 1944.

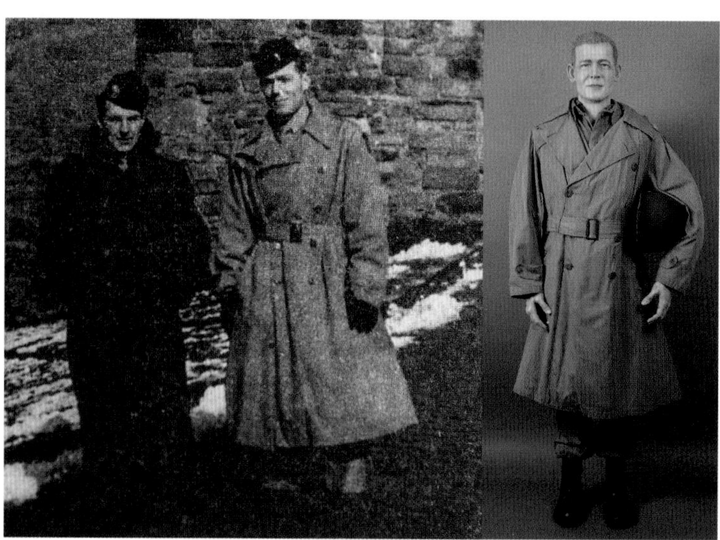

Winters can be seen wearing this officer's overcoat alongside paratrooper Buck Taylor while on leave in Scotland, February 1944. "London and Scotland, my gosh, what places they are," Dick marveled in a letter to DeEtta Almon.

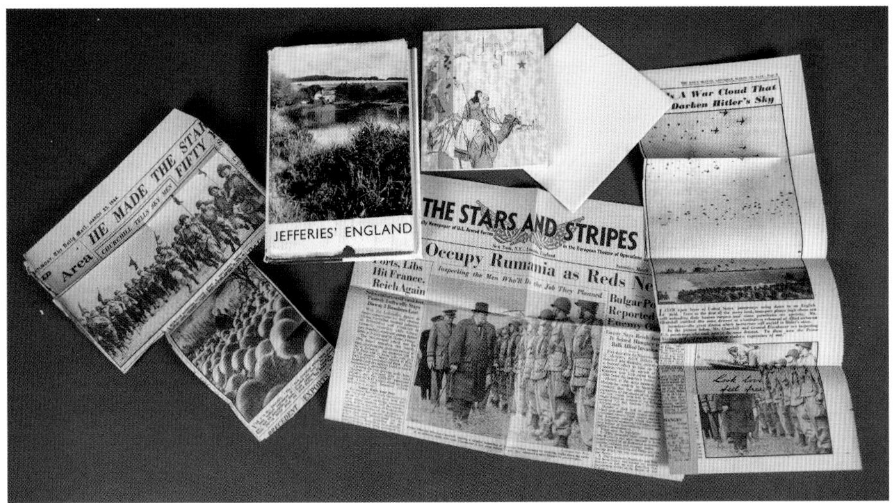

Dick Winters collected these newspaper clippings that chronicled Winston Churchill's March 1944 visit to the 101st Airborne in England. The copy of *Jefferies' England* and the Christmas card were presented to Winters as gifts from the beloved Barnes family—his host in Aldbourne.

At left, Winters is seen in this M42 jump uniform during the airborne demonstration conducted for Dwight Eisenhower and Winston Churchill in March 1944. Winters's name can be seen written on the breast pocket at right. The lieutenant added sleeve pockets for extra gear.

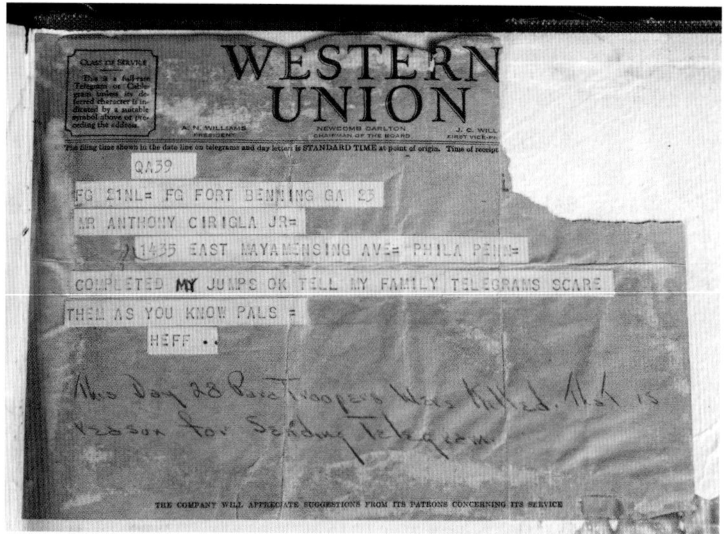

WESTERN UNION

CLASS OF SERVICE
This is a full-rate Telegram or Cablegram unless its deferred character is indicated by a suitable symbol above or preceding the address.

A. N. WILLIAMS PRESIDENT | NEWCOMB CARLTON CHAIRMAN OF THE BOARD | J. C. WILL… FIRST VICE-PR…

The filing time shown in the date line on telegrams and day letters is STANDARD TIME at point of origin. Time of receipt

QA39

FG 21NL= FG FORT BENNING GA 23

MR ANTHONY CIRIGLA JR=

1435 EAST MAYAMENSING AVE= PHILA PENN=

COMPLETED MY JUMPS OK TELL MY FAMILY TELEGRAMS SCARE

THEM AS YOU KNOW PALS =

HEFF ..

This Day 28 Paratroopers Was Killed. That is reason for Sending Telegram.

THE COMPANY WILL APPRECIATE SUGGESTIONS FROM ITS PATRONS CONCERNING ITS SERVICE

As the 101st Airborne finalized D-Day preparations in England, aspiring paratrooper Edward "Babe" Heffron was completing jump school at Fort Benning. On the night of his final jump, one of the planes crashed and killed a score of passengers. Heffron sent this telegram to a friend in Philadelphia announcing his safety.

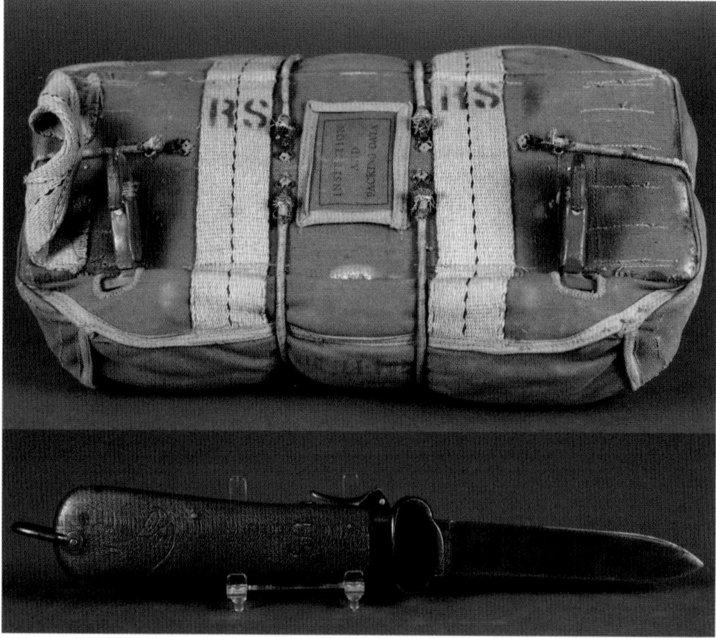

The T-5 reserve parachute at top was a secondary chute strapped to the chests of paratroopers. The "RS" stenciled on the back designates the paratrooper who wore this chute as being under the command of Col. Robert Sink. Below, paratrooper Dick Hoover carved the 101st Airborne's "Screaming Eagle" into a captured *Fallschirmjäger* Gravity Knife.

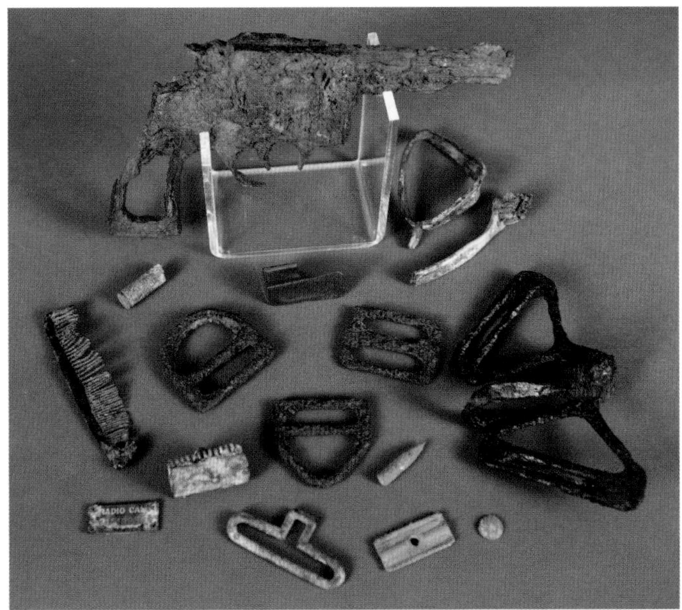

These charred items were recovered from the crash site of C-47 Stick #66 near Beuzeville-au-Plain in Normandy. Mangled buckles, razors, toothbrushes, a pistol, and an airborne "cricket" symbolize the twenty-two men aboard who perished. Among the dead was Dick Winters's company commander, Lt. Thomas Meehan.

The many battlefields Dick Winters crossed were seen through these Nash-Kelvinator M3 6x30 binoculars, manufactured in 1944. Winters painted a white spade and hash mark, representing the 2nd Battalion of the 506th Parachute Infantry Regiment, on the leather case.

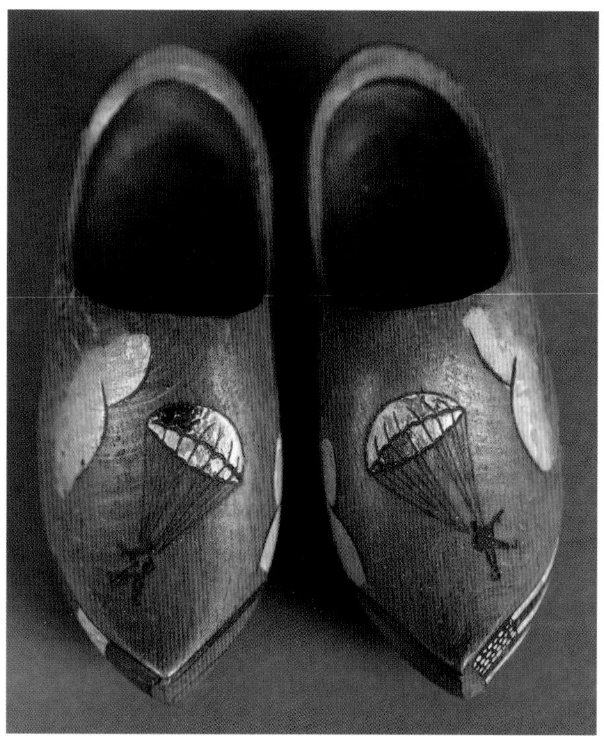

These wooden clogs were crafted by a resident of Sainte-Mère-Église to commemorate the Normandy invasion. These handmade shoes are indicative of the ways in which the French expressed the joys of liberation. "Just about everybody wears wooden shoes for work," Winters observed of the French.

Winters carried this weathered M1911 pistol throughout much of the war in Europe. The .45 caliber sidearm can be seen in several photos of Winters in the field. In nearly all cases, however, Winters preferred the reliable M1 Garand over his pistol.

During the Battle of Carentan, Winters confiscated these German *Fallschirmjäger* gloves as a prize of war. Winters can be seen wearing one of these gloves fifty years later in the photo at right.

CAPT. WINTERS AWARDED DSC

Capt. Richard D. Winters, 418 S. West End Ave., and 24 other members of the 101st Airborne Division were decorated Wednesday at an U. S. Air Base in France with the Distinguished Service Cross, by Lt. Gen. Omar Bradley, commander of the First Army.

The country's second highest military award was given to the Lancaster officer, son of Mr. and Mrs. Richard N. Winters, of the S. West End Ave. address, for silencing a battery of four German 88's which were holding up the advance of beach units in the opening of the French invasion.

Capt. Winters

Capt. Winters, who successfully completed the mission with the aid of seven enlisted men, later was wounded in the leg. He is now recuperating at an Army hospital in England.

The officer's valiant act was previously recorded by war correspondents, who quoted his commanding officer as saying it was Capt. Winter's personal bravery and battle knowledge that held a crucial position when the going was really tough.

A graduate of Franklin and Marshall College, class of 1941, he entered the Army in August of that year. He was commissioned at Fort Benning, Ga., in July, 1942, and has been overseas since Sept. 1, 1943.

Capt. Winters is the second Lancaster service man to be decorated with the Distinguished Service Cross since the invasion of France began.

Technician Fourth Grade Elmer G. Shindle, 424 Dauphin St., was given the same decoration on July 6 by Gen. Bradley.

On July 2, 1944, Gen. Omar Bradley pinned this Distinguished Service Cross on the chest of Dick Winters. The lieutenant received the medal for his actions at Brécourt Manor on D-Day. Dick's parents clipped the corresponding article from the July 13, 1944 edition of Lancaster, Pennsylvania's *Intelligencer Journal*.

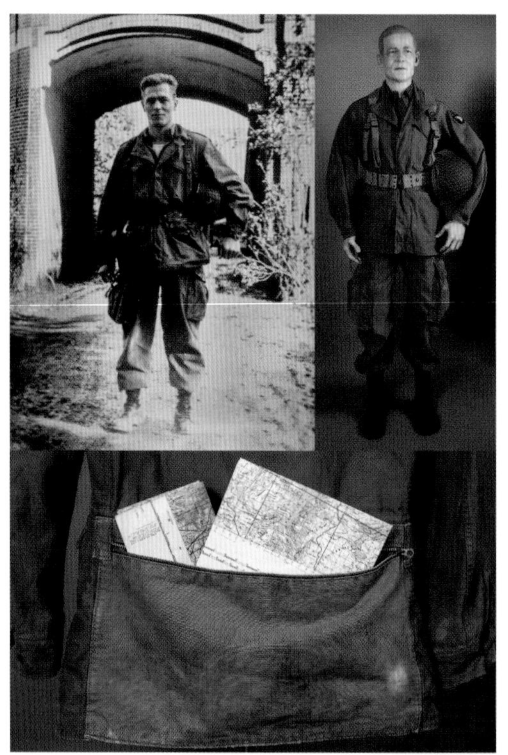

To avoid the eyes of enemy snipers, Winters often concealed his rank by turning up the collars of this M43 Field Jacket. A zippered pocket on the back was likewise less conspicuous than carrying a map case. The iconic photo at top left shows Winters sporting this jacket at the Landgoed Schoonderlogt Estate in Holland in October 1944.

B10 Flight Jackets were intended for Air Forces personnel to combat extreme cold. The coveted jackets were acquired by officers in the 101st Airborne as well. Winters was prompt to cover the area meant for an Air Forces patch with a "Screaming Eagle." A close-up of his name tag can be seen at bottom.

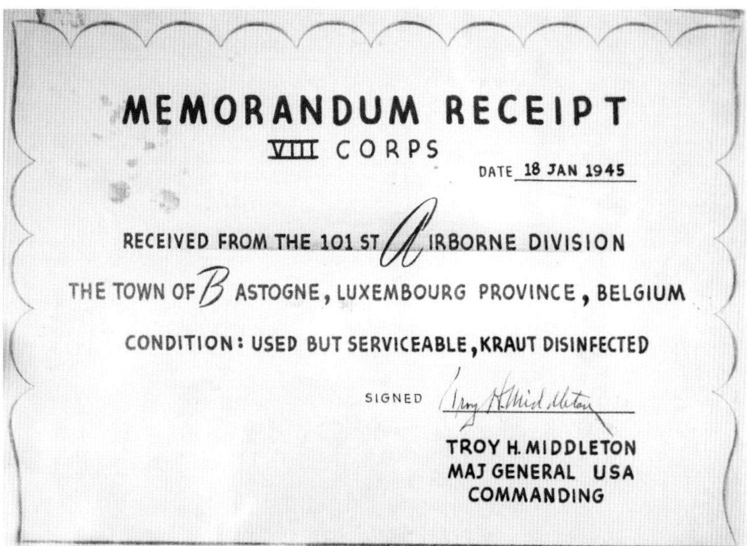

MEMORANDUM RECEIPT
VIII CORPS

DATE 18 JAN 1945

RECEIVED FROM THE 101 ST AIRBORNE DIVISION
THE TOWN OF BASTOGNE, LUXEMBOURG PROVINCE, BELGIUM
CONDITION: USED BUT SERVICEABLE, KRAUT DISINFECTED

SIGNED Troy H Middleton

TROY H. MIDDLETON
MAJ GENERAL USA
COMMANDING

101st Airborne commander Gen. Maxwell Taylor wryly insisted on a memorandum receipt for the transferal of Bastogne to the VIII Corps following his division's iconic defense of the town during the Battle of the Bulge. Maj. Gen. Troy Middleton, commanding, gladly complied.

This prisoner uniform from Dachau concentration camp remains a grim reminder of the horrors of the Holocaust. The red triangle on the chest denoted the prisoner as a political enemy of the Reich. Winters and his paratroopers helped liberate the oppressed at Landsberg am Lech, a subcamp of Dachau, in April 1945.

Once into Germany, American servicemen seized war trophies with great fervor. GIs often wrote their signatures on the white field of captured Nazi banners. The soldiers of the 101st Airborne's 907th Glider Field Artillery Battalion did so with this flag in the spring of 1945.

As prolific souvenir hunters, soldiers of the 101st Airborne absconded with Adolf Hitler's silverware and linens from Berchtesgaden. Note Hitler's initials on many of the items.

Sgt. Herbert Clark of the 506th Parachute Infantry Regiment removed this emblem from Reichsmarschall Hermann Göring's luxury Mercedes in Obersalzberg. Paratroopers also used the automobile for target practice to test the rumor of the car being bulletproof.

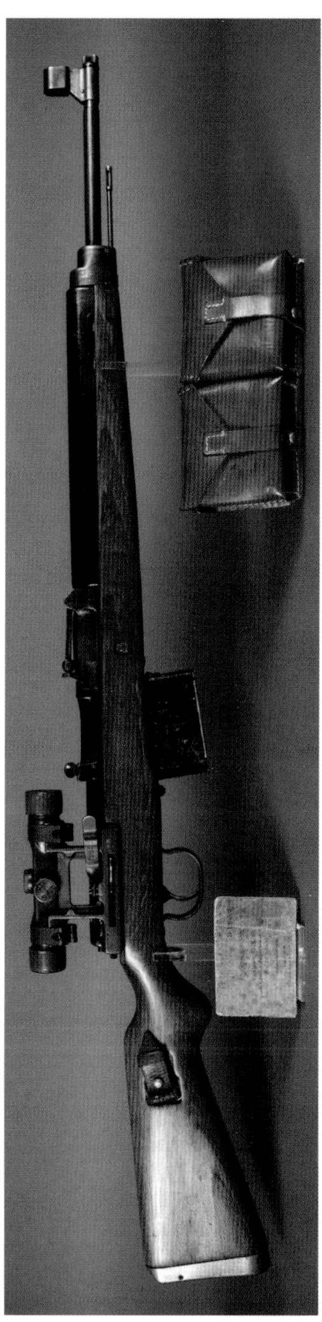

Winters acquired this German G43 sniper rifle as a war trophy in Kaprun, Austria in spring 1945. Unlike the German soldier's typical bolt-action Mauser, this weapon was a semi-automatic rifle.

This 506th Parachute Infantry Regiment sign stood on the outskirts of Zell am See, Austria, during the 101st Airborne's occupational duties in the summer of 1945. Paratrooper Darrell "Shifty" Powers called the area, "Fine country to be soldiering in."

When Winters returned to Lancaster in December 1945, his parents insisted that he have a portrait taken in which he was smiling while in uniform. His officer's Class A dress jacket features several of the decoration ribbons DeEtta mailed him.

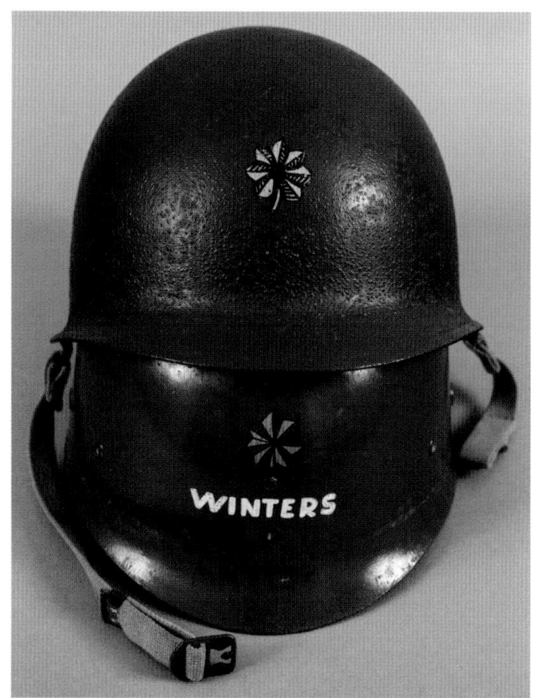

Major Winters sported this Korean War era helmet and liner while serving in the New Jersey National Guard in the early 1950s. Thankfully, he never had to wear them in combat.

This banner was one of several guidons used at Easy Company reunions in the decades following World War II. Veteran Bill Guarnere helped spearhead the gatherings and later wrote in his autobiography, “It was important to me to keep in touch with the men.”

Dick and Ethel Winters traveled to Wilmington, North Carolina for DeEtta Almon's eighty-fourth Birthday on May 14, 1996. Dick presented her transcribed and annotated copies of his wartime letters from half a century prior. Dick and DeEtta are seen here on her birthday.

Following the 2001 release of HBO's *Band of Brothers*, Winters became a historical celebrity. He signed the helmet at left with his famous "Hang Tough" mantra. Shown at right is one of the helmets actor Damian Lewis wore on the set of the miniseries. The helmet was given to Winters by Lewis and features both their autographs.

German defenses guarding vital bridges stemming northward across the Netherlands. Armored units were to leapfrog alongside their paratrooper brethren to the Rhine River and then batter their way into the heart of Germany. Ultimate success depended on logistics and timing—both of which would break down with ruinous outcomes.[2]

As the generals designed their hopeful campaign, Winters supervised a period of readjustment and reconditioning for his company. Anxious to fill the void of officers and non-coms lost in the Normandy campaign, Winters set forth branding the next generation of unit leadership. Among those promoted was Carwood Lipton, bound to leave his own indelible imprint on Easy Company's storied history. Winters selected Lipton after he recommended then-acting 1st Sgt. James Diel for a battlefield commission. Once approved, Diel transferred to F Company. One comrade referred to Lipton as "the best non-commissioned officer in the whole army." Winters's marrow-deep trust in the West Virginia sergeant never wavered.[3]

At the same time, the company's battle-tested warriors greeted many replacements with lukewarm indifference. For now, few Normandy veterans wished to befriend boyish, unproven substitutes who seemed prime candidates for early graves. As Winters awaited the next jump and reflected on his third anniversary in the service, he privately recommitted himself to his guiding principles: he would see the war through to its conclusion; he would not lead his men astray. Further embodying his status as a father figure, Winters prepared Toccoa veterans and fresh rookies for the rigors of combat. By September 10, Easy Company was once again in the marshalling yards of England, gearing up for a desperate gamble only days away. Amid the hustle of briefings and equipment checks, Dick welcomed a brief interlude to pen professional advice to DeEtta. She would not hear from him again for over two months.[4]

10 September, 1944

My favorite ripple–

Guess I've really been one hell of a correspondent for the past few weeks. But we've really been setting a pace and when I do find time to write, there's just nothing left to give me the push and always there's that lack of something to say. But that never gives you a reason or excuse for not having a letter waiting for me when the mail orderly hands me the mail.

[...] Oh boy, that brings to mind a couple of pictures a friend of mine sent me. They were taken right after we came from France and are to be used on the publicity angle of being decorated, etc. Honest, I didn't know I looked that mean and tough. I am actually afraid to send them home to my mother for I know she'll worry and wonder what this army's doing to her son. Her son, the boy who could never even get mad enough to raise his voice. However, I don't feel quite so hard inside as I did there for a while, but I guess I still look the part. As for a twinkle in the eye, sometimes I think it must have been frozen to death, but there may be a day when it'll warm up, but never as long as there's a war on and I've got to push a company.

You're right about wondering about the casualties between now and the end of the war. Ever since the second week of the invasion that's been my greatest concern. Victory is ours but the casualties that must be paid is the price that hurts.

Your new barracks sounds ducky. Am I right when I get this double bunk system? Do you mean something like a double bed? Never heard of anything like that in the army unless you're out in the field and you sleep together for warmth.

Sounds to me like the varnish is wearing off this thrilling chapter in your life of being a Wave.

Now you're taking calisthenics and you put on two pounds as a result. What are you doing? Putting on weight for the football season? Now if you want to take off weight, you must do it every day and in addition, take it easy on the chow and liquid intake. After about two or three weeks, if you've been real conscientious, you'll see some results. This may sound like a lot of bunk to you but there are few days when I don't run between 2-2 ½ miles, do 80 pushups, 60 situps on a foot locker, a couple of splits, and some leg and trunk exercises after the day's work is over. As a result I keep in pretty good shape. Not what I'd call wrestling shape, but good enough for army work. It keeps you alert, builds up your endurance, and keeps you supple.

As ever,
Dick[5]

At home and overseas, apprehension regarding mounting casualty rates was inherent and potentially debilitating. A frequent churchgoer, Winters contemplated the spiritual elements of survival. Even more pronounced in this religious temperament was Darrell "Shifty" Powers, a Virginia outdoorsman and perhaps the most talented marksman in Easy Company. Of his own endurance, Powers later wondered, "Maybe it was a special angel looking over my shoulder, don't rightly know, but I had dodged bullets aimed at my direction. Unlike most men in Easy Company, I had no Purple Hearts. In a company that suffered 150 percent casualties, I was an acute rarity."[6]

For the time being, Winters remained confident in his own willpower. The profile photo Dick mailed to DeEtta proudly radiated the stalwart demeanor he relished as an officer. Innocently describing himself as a once-gentle boy "who could never even get mad enough to raise his voice," the captain revealed how dramatically the war altered him emotionally and physically. Winters recognized he would never again be an innocuous college lad.

More importantly, Dick constantly aspired to be the best possible leader. When his company returned to England from Normandy, he assembled a training schedule for replacements and veterans. He also smuggled live ammunition to England "to give the replacements the feel of advancing in an attack under covering fire." Such a plan was not without potential hazards. The risk nonetheless proved worthwhile. He wanted his men to be proficient in laying down a base of fire and having the ability to advance under that fire. "If it is done correctly," he argued, "the job gets done and you save a lot of casualties. You can talk about it;

you can go through dry run exercises; but the men only get the feel of it with actual experience." Winters was not above bending the rules if such actions molded better soldiers.[7]

Dick's strategies were thoroughly put to use in the outfit's next campaign. Some forty-five years after the fact, Winters composed recollections of that operation in sharp detail:

At our briefing [for Operation Market-Garden] we were told that the 101st and 82nd A.B. were to be attached to the British 2nd Army. We would be going to Holland where our job would be to secure bridges over canals and rivers and then to hold the road open so that the British 2nd Army could make an end run to Arnhem and thus have a clear path to Berlin, ending the war by Christmas. The 101st had four bridges to secure in Eindhoven and one over a canal at Zon. The 82nd, who would jump north of the 101st, had bridges to secure over the Maas River at Grave, and over the Waal River at Nijmegen. The British paratroopers were to secure the bridge over the Rhine River at Arnhem. [...] We had the easy part of this mission.

[...]The jump [on September 17] was easy, compared to Normandy. The only danger I personally felt was the need to get off that drop zone as soon as possible in order to prevent getting hit with falling equipment. It was just raining equipment: helmets, guns, and equipment bundles.

In view of the fact that this was a daylight jump, the assembly of the troops seemed to take much longer than it should have. We were taking far too long to get to the objective. I thought, "Next time, please drop us on the objective."

The 2nd Bn. was sent down the main road towards Zon. [...] We had a column of men on each side of the road, and we heard a German machine gun open up. There were no casualties. D Company covered the right side of the road, E Company the left side. We pushed forward. When we were about 25 to 30 yards from our first objective, a bridge, it blew. For the second time that afternoon, we were caught in a hail of debris, this time of wood and stone. I remember hitting the ground with Nixon, to my left, and as the stone and timber came down, thinking to myself, "What a hell of a way to die in combat!"

The German rear guard, having accomplished their mission of blowing the bridge, quickly withdrew, after we fired a few bursts of machine gunfire into their position.

After halting further covering fire, I can remember lying on the bank of the canal, watching Major [James L.] LaPrade, 1st Bn. C.O., tiptoeing from rock to timber to rock, trying to make his way across the canal without getting wet. He had his .45 pistol in one hand as he tried to keep his balance. It struck me as funny, carrying a .45 like that was ridiculous. I thought to myself, "For God's sake, man, carry an M-1 rifle if you're expecting trouble. Give yourself a little fire power. Furthermore, carrying an M-1 makes you look like another soldier, not an officer. Snipers like to look for officers.

We got across by dark, and I remember sleeping in a wood shed that night to keep out of the rain.

[...] When we reached Eindhoven, in order to reach our objective, which was to secure the bridges, the biggest problem was pushing the troops through the crowds of people. This was unbelievable. The streets were full of civilians, smiling, waving, offering drinks or food, even bringing out chairs and encouraging men to sit down. This was so different from France, where we had been suspicious of civilians being snipers.

I still was afraid of snipers, German snipers, after just seeing [Robert B.] Brewer get hit [in the throat]. I put my map case under my pants belt, and then pulled my fatigue jacket over the map case and the binoculars, to hide them both. I turned the collar of my jacket up to hide my rank. I always carried an M-1 rifle; it just felt good to know that I could take care of myself at all times. I tried to look like just another GI.[8]

As Winters and company vainly attempted to press through the throngs of jubilant townspeople, nurse Koos van Schaik of the Dutch Red Cross was ecstatic amid the celebratory mayhem. "The American paratroopers have taken the road from Eindhoven on north," she recorded in her diary. "Motorcycles and dispatchers are shooting in and out of the convoy." Soldiers and civilians ecstatically waved back and forth at each other. Orange streamers denoting liberation fluttered from every home. "It is so overwhelming that we cannot comprehend that this is real," van Schaik continued. "A few days ago we were standing on this very spot watching the Germans retreat. The people laugh and cry at the same time." An elder approached and buoyantly inquired, "Nurse, is it peace now?" One could only hope.[9]

The joyous reception in Eindhoven was largely unexpected. "They just came out into the streets," Winters said of the euphoric crowds. "It was a party like you've never seen before in your life. You'd never seen people more happy in your life." Decades later, Dick teared up as he reflected on the symbolism of the moment. In the United States, he said, "we have great pride in the fact we have freedom of speech, freedom of religion, freedom from fear, and freedom from want—the Four Freedoms. And these people had that denied to them." In fact, the Dutch had been unsure if they would ever have liberty again. "Freedom is so important that we take it for granted," Dick concluded, "and it shouldn't be taken for granted."[10]

Celebration notwithstanding, the advance haltingly forged ahead. With a column of tanks in support, Easy Company set forth toward the town of Helmond which, according to the Dutch Resistance, was a pillar of German defenses in the region. Before Helmond could be reached, however, the 506th PIR became ensnared in a contentious struggle at Nuenen (where van Gogh once painted picturesque scenes). A slew of enemy tanks suddenly emerged, grinding the American advance to a chaotic halt. "Company E was pinned down so quickly," wrote Winters, "that we found it almost impossible to move. Most of the men were pinned down in ditches by the side of the road. We had only a few buildings that we could use as cover to move around and set up some return fire." The paratroopers thwarted a relentless tide of German attacks in a series of

Paratroopers of the 506th PIR socialize with residents of Eindhoven following the city's liberation, as seen in an image taken by Dutch photographer H. Teune. The soldier at left is Harold Boye, an immigrant from Denmark who was killed less than three weeks after this photo was taken.

firefights that raged until nightfall. The GIs heaved their wounded into trucks brought up by Lt. Nixon and thereafter disengaged from the fight.[11]

Returning to Eindhoven, Winters encountered a scene starkly contrasting the one he witnessed earlier in the day. The *Luftwaffe* wreaked widespread damage on the city as Allied convoys inched through the crammed streets. The community's blocks were aglow with flames. Over 1,000 casualties were inflicted. Winters felt abject pity for the downtrodden civilians. "The Dutch, who, just that morning, had been so happy to be liberated, and who had cheered us on as we marched out toward Helmond, were now outside, closing their shutters, taking down their flags, looking very sad and disappointed," he observed. "They obviously felt that we were deserting them and they felt they were right back where they had been, in an occupied country."[12]

The dejected members of Easy Company felt little better. Winters's mood soured further when he reported to battalion headquarters that evening. There, he discovered officers enjoying dinner in a holiday mood. Lt. Col. Strayer spotted his subordinate entering and inquired, "How did it go today, Winters?"

"I had fifteen casualties today and took a hell of a licking!" the displeased captain retorted. The room immediately quieted. Winters abhorred the bitter sting of defeat.[13]

Following a day of rest and reorganization, the 101st Airborne was given word from the Dutch Underground of enemy movements in the vicinity of Veghel and Uden, some fifteen miles to the north. Troops from 2nd and 3rd Battalions were dispatched in trucks from Eindhoven to investigate the matter. Winters, Nixon, and Welsh were among the passengers in the first serial of trucks. Shortly after the modest convoy rumbled through Veghel, Germans tied the loop and ostensibly cut off Easy Company's route of escape. With this sudden development, Winters assured his outfit, "Men, there's nothing to get excited about. The situation is normal; we are surrounded!" The ominous stretch of road became part of the infamously-named "Hell's Highway." In Uden, Winters and company linked with three British tank crews who initially seemed indifferent to the unfolding predicament. In moments like these, paratrooper Clancy Lyall was no admirer of the British tankers' prim customs. "Every day at ten, two, and four they'd stop those sons of bitches, get out of the tanks and make tea....The war's over at those times." For three days, the troopers resided in Uden alongside their aloof allies.[14]

Lt. Col. Charles Chase, executive officer of the 506th PIR, appeared only slightly more concerned by the developments. Winters reported to Chase and was promptly ordered to establish a defense of the town. "That, to the best of my memory," recalled Winters, "was the only time

I talked to Lt. Col. Chase for those three days. Sink was a hands on kind of man, always moving around, checking up on Bn. and Co. CPs. Chase, evidently, felt that since he had told me to take care of the defense, he had done his job."[15]

After overseeing the placement of roadblocks on the town's perimeter, Winters and Nixon hurriedly dashed up one of the twin bell towers of the impressive Church of St. Peter. The brick house of worship dominates the town's skyline to this day. With their field glasses, the two officers witnessed heavy fighting to the south. "The land," Winters later observed, "is flat; there were a few scattered trees, but the view was basically clear from the church tower at Uden to Vechel [*sic*]." Winters and Nixon ascended the tower sporadically between firefights until a German round literally clanged the bell above them. "We came down the stairs of that tower so fast," remembered Winters, "I don't think our feet touched the steps more than two or three times." The officers landed in a heap below, laughing at their skittish withdrawal from the observation point. The ornate bell tower was too close to heaven for comfort.[16]

At the southern edge of town, Winters designated a store owned by the Van Oer family as the company command post. Situated nearly in the shadow of the church at a road junction, the small mercantile seemed an ideal strongpoint. The Van Oer's "were 100 percent cooperative and receptive to having the troops move in with absolutely no time to prepare for us," Winters explained. "They just moved to the cellar. For some years after the war, their daughter, Nel, was a pen pal of my sister, Ann. We moved furniture and rugs to one side and brought in the machine guns, ammunition, Molotov cocktails, and explosives, and set up a defensive position." If tanks rolled into the street, the cocktails could be dropped onto the armor from the store's second floor.[17]

The Van Oer Home in Uden. US Army photo.

Frustration with the British tankers persisted. "Damn mad," Winters discovered an absent English lieutenant curled in front of a fireplace with a Dutch girl.

"Are my tanks still outside?" the officer inquired to Winters.

Dick unleashed a livid reprimand. His outburst "did not improve British-American relations" that night, he conceded.

Challenges of accountability aside, Winters was content with his positions and confident the town could be held. "There was no talk of retreat or withdrawal and certainly nobody thought of surrender." The following day, the remainder of the 506th PIR arrived in Uden, having doggedly pushed through from Veghel. Shortly thereafter, the Germans once more cut the road in two.[18]

At 3:00 a.m. on September 25, the regiment was ordered to counterattack and reopen the link to the south. The Americans departed in a heavy predawn rain, which increased the sullen mood. Supported by a half squadron of British tanks, the advance was tediously slow as the regiment attempted a flanking action. Dispersed to avoid concentrated fire, the men yet endured withering volleys from machine guns and tanks. Nixon barely evaded death when an enemy round punched through the front of his helmet, merely bruising his forehead. According to Winters, Nixon seemed to be one of the lucky few in 2nd Battalion who lacked a Purple Heart.[19]

Little headway was made. Combat persisted until nightfall. In the near distance, Winters's armor support stood mangled in flames. The burning tanks illuminated the woodlots with a ghostly aura. Machine gun rounds inside crackled like popcorn in a kettle. Nixon implausibly scavenged a bottle of schnapps and consumed its contents as he watched the tanks sizzle in the eerie darkness. His blank stare bespoke the numbing psychological toll of combat.

Hours later, Dick heard the engines of the opposing German vehicles rev up and slowly fade away. The enemy was withdrawing. Sunrise on the 26th revealed abandoned enemy emplacements. Americans moved across the formerly contested terrain unhindered. All the while, steady downpours persisted. His boots soaked and in tatters, Winters sought a new pair from the heaps of German dead. No boots in his size were found.

On September 28, the 101st Airborne relocated to a sliver of terrain between the Lower Rhine and Waal Rivers north of Nijmegen, known as the "Island." The lush pastures were sprinkled with dikes, orchards, and charming villages once rendered on canvas by Impressionists. Awaiting the paratroopers were the battle-tested Germans of the 363rd *Volksgrenadier* division. Customary outpost-patrol activity ensued in the following days as Easy Company gained a sense of enemy size and positions. Maneuvers through the intersecting roadways and dikes set the stage for a hallmark moment of Winters's military career. Nearly two weeks after that collision, Winters penned a detailed after-action report describing his bold risk on the fifth of October.[20]

Hqs. Kidnap White
U.S. Army
17 October 1944
Subject: Action of 1st Pltn. E Co., on 5 October 1944
To: C.O. 506th Prcht. Inf. APO 472
P. The following is a history of the 1st Pltn. of E. Co. on 5 Oct. 1944.

At 0330, 5 Oct. 1944, 4 men left E Co. CP at Randwijk to observe enemy action and adjust artillery at 0420 to report they had met a party of the enemy. [The enemy was] at the road crossing three fourths of a mile west of the CP and just about half way between our right flank and the left flank of the unit on our right. This was covered by patrols. Taking one squad of the platoon in reserve in the company, we went up to make an estimate of the situation. When we realized the last bit of cover [was] about 800 yds. from the reported enemy on the crossroads, firing was observed flying in all directions and apparently shooting at nothing.

An attempt to put artillery fire on this point failed when we couldn't reach the artillery F.O. with our 536 radios. A short reconnaissance showed that we had two covered routes of approach, one was on either side of the dike but the one which was on the river side was a ditch deep enough to provide cover. Leaving two men as security on the right, the rest of the squad advanced to within 250 yds. of the crossroad. Upon making reconnaissance, seven Jerries were observed setting up an anti-tank weapon. The squad was advanced, men were assigned definite targets, and given a complete fire order—the group completely accounted for. The squad then moved forward to the ditch 50 yds. to a point where the ditch ran parallel to the road leading to the river and also to the enemy.

The rest of the reserve platoon and the two MG's from the section of MG's attached to the company were ordered to come forward. They were ordered to come forward and arrived in 30 minutes and reinforced the firing line. While we were awaiting this group's arrival, the enemy attempted to work a rifle grenadier through a drainage pipe to place fire on us, but accurate rifle fire stopped this and also seemed to keep them from employing their automatic weapons.

The situation at this time found us in a position where we weren't receiving a great deal of fire but with our small force we could not hope to build up a static line of defense, which wasn't in the tactical position to start with; if we were hit we had no line of withdrawal which would be of any value to us. Also it appeared that the enemy was over the dike and would be cutting us if nothing was done. The decision was made to make a bayonet charge. Lt. [Thomas] Peacock, with a squad, worked down to a covered route to their left flank. S/Sgt. [Floyd] Talbert had a squad on the right and another squad was in the middle. The 2 HQ MG's were the base of fire and the 60mm mortars was firing from a range of about 250 yds. where it had been firing harassing fire on the junction of the road where we figured the enemy would be passing.

On a smoke signal the base of fire started and the mortars ceased firing, and the three rifle columns made a 175 yd. dash across a level pasture, through and over fences. Upon reaching the road, which was raised 2 ½ ft., we could see approximately a company of what we found out later to be SS Troops laying in one big group where they had evidently stopped to take cover from mortar and MG fire. They soon took off on the double, then the MG of the center squad opened up on them at point blank range, along with rifle fire and grenades. This, however, drove them into the MG and rifle fire of the squad on the right which had arrived just a few seconds later than the middle section but in time to rake the whole group from the flank and from the rear as they ran. These two squads had efficient fire on them on the level ground for 250 yds. Then long range MG fire was harassing them for another two hundred yds.

What evidently was the second company of the second assaulting group came pouring back over the dike towards the river when all this firing started and received fire from about 250 yds. The attack was held here, for it was evident that despite our success we couldn't maintain our attack with the small force we had across open terrain in pursuit of the enemy.

The squad on the left was occupied with a small group of enemy and accounted for nine prisoners and six dead.

Communication by 300 radio was perfect and artillery fire was placed on the withdrawing enemy, difficultly. [H]owever, it accounted for a reasonable percentage of the casualties.

A platoon of Fox Co., reserve company for the Bn., was asked for and, while waiting, the artillery continued and reorganization and distribution of ammunition continued. Our own casualties at this time was one killed and four wounded.

> When the platoon from Fox [Company] arrived, we decided to try and force our way to the river, turn right, and work our way along the cover by the bank to where we believed the enemy was withdrawing across the river.
>
> The buildings along the river were reached without casualties, although we had to pass through a light concentration of artillery which wasn't too effective because it was wide. Once we were at the buildings they had to lift the fire for fearing of hitting their own troops. Just as we finished cleaning out a squad of enemy, we were hit on the right flank from the rear by a reported force of seventy-five enemy. Being in the minority, we set up a base of fire to the front and to the right and withdrew to the road, that being our only route of withdrawal. At all times two squads were acting as rear guard.
>
> Just as the last elements of our group reached the crossroads, a terrific and accurate mortar and artillery concentration hit us and continued to account for casualties. We moved both platoons 300 yds. to the right and left, respectively, of the crossroads and out of the danger area, but the first concentration or two caught us and accounted for eighteen men—all wounded—none killed. They were not bunched up as the concentration covered an area of two hundred yds. in which they were hit.
>
> Artillery and mortar fire was returned and platoons stood by to guard this avenue of approach.[21]

A division press release heralded Winters's attack as a model of small-squad tactics. The public relations statement declared, "As they spotted the advancing, knife-wielding men in 'para-boots' the Jerries got up as one man and took off in the general direction of Berlin. The manner in which they ran might have been called 'double-time' in their army, but to the Americans, it looked like an effort to break all existing dash records en masse."[22]

Winters considered the action his men's acme of heroism. His rough-hewn report was composed with the hope of attaining decorations for worthy subordinates. Not desirous of personal accolades, the captain typed his entire assessment without incorporating the word "I." All credit was due to the boys in the ranks. "This absence of the first person pronoun,"

Winters later admitted, "and being forced to write it on the front line whenever I could find a few minutes, accounts for the awkwardness of the description of that day's action." In contrast to his personal letters, the summation of combat was technical and detached.[23]

The attack itself was anything but impersonal. Winters experienced an otherworldly, hyper-focused state of awareness during the engagement. Everything around him seemed to unfold in slow motion. This suspension of time was inexplicable to Winters, even decades after the fact.

"We were making a frontal attack," he said of the moment. There was no other choice. There was little room to maneuver or hide. With bayonet fixed, he charged the enemy at full speed. His men could not keep his pace.

"I was running faster than I ever ran before in my life. Everybody else was moving so slow. I couldn't understand it."

With his men yards behind, Winters jumped atop the dike, alone, and stood before two companies of unsuspecting Germans. "I'm in a different state of mind that I've never been in before," he confessed. "Hope I never get there again." He described this surreal sensation as being "pumped up." His next actions remained long-ingrained in his memories. "In jumping up on the dike," he continued, "there's this young soldier right across the road from me.... He was directly on the other side of that road from me, about two steps away, because it was just a narrow dirt road coming up from the river."

The young German combatant was a lookout, an obviously ineffective one. "That was his job, to keep them informed. He didn't do it.... And I came up directly across from him—eyeball to eyeball. And he was just as shocked as could be. I leveled off at him," said Winters. "The thing I can never forget was that he smiled.

"And as he smiled, I shot him."

The youthful adversary crumpled to the ground.

The remainder of the paratroopers scaled the rim of the dike and annihilated the enemy. With automatic instinct, Dick emptied clips of ammunition into the fleeing Germans. "We had them boxed," he concluded. His comrades mowed down their antagonists with alarming accuracy. The incident on the Island was Winters's most dramatic demonstration as a tactician. His assault was a resounding success. It also carried profound emotional weight.[24]

Col. Sink offered a fitting tactical assessment of the charge. "By this daring act and skillful maneuver against a numerically superior force," reported the colonel, "the use of an important road junction was denied the enemy in their withdrawal across the Neder Rhine River. Also, heavy casualties were inflicted upon them by this small force." Sink concluded the men were to be "commended for their daring and aggressive spirit and sound tactical ability." The deed was arguably more daring than the actions at Brécourt Manor. Interestingly, Winters received no decoration for the assault.[25]

Personal heroics and warrior instinct aside, luck was with Winters that day. Flowery rhetoric or not, his emotions were genuine. As Winters attested in his memoirs, the events of October 5 "sealed feelings of camaraderie and friendship that were beyond words. You can't describe it. You have to live through it, but you never question it." The day also marked the last time he fired his weapon in battle—an amazing feat when considering what lay ahead.[26]

This scene of GIs entrenched in one of Holland's many dikes is telling visual testimony of how the countryside's undulating terrain played a considerable role in combat conditions. National Archives.

Despite heartfelt bonds of affection, Winters's remaining time as commander of Easy Company was short-lived. Four days after his iconic attack on the crossroads, Dick was transferred to 2nd Battalion headquarters as an acting major and executive officer. Lt. Fred "Moose" Heyliger emerged as one of the battalion's most capable officers during this time of transition. On October 22–23, during Operation Pegasus, paratroopers under Heyliger helped over one hundred British airborne troops flee to the Allied sector under cover of darkness. The entrapped Brits had been hidden by the Dutch Resistance following the calamitous defeat at Arnhem the month prior. Heyliger was commended for his role in the escape feat. Among those in the successful raiding party was Pfc. Bradford Freeman, who took pride in the daring operation.

By the final week of October, enemy patrols continued pressing through American company outposts. On Halloween night, Winters accompanied Heyliger to Welsh's position. The two proceeded down a narrow path until a voice cried out from the darkness. "Halt!"

"Moose" froze, having forgotten the password. Before he could explain himself, three shots thundered forth, breaking the calm of night. Heyliger shriveled to the dirt, shot in the right shoulder and left leg by one of his own men. Welsh quickly arrived on scene, helped Winters apply tourniquets, and administered morphine. As the bloodied lieutenant was evacuated by ambulance, Dick remorsefully uttered, "I hope he makes it."[27]

Overcoming a tremendous loss of blood, Heyliger survived his wounds thanks to the handiwork of talented surgeons. His road to recovery was long and uncomfortable, but he was grateful to be alive. Days later, "Moose" appraised his healing process to Winters:

Nov. 7, 1944

Dear Dick,

Here I am laying flat on my back taking it easy. I want to thank you for taking care of me that night. It sure was a stupid way to get knocked off.

I lost a hell of a lot of blood and so far I have had six transfusions in all. I am getting my color back slow but sure now.

I arrived here naked as a jay bird. Didn't have a thing. I know you have my wings and pistol, but I am sweating out the clothes in my bed roll and the rolls of film in my musette bag.

[...] Jesus, Dick, they put casts right over my wounds and it smells as if a cat shit in my bed. I can't get away from that stink.

Well, this is short, but my right arm is very weak. Remember me to all.

As ever,
Moose[28]

While autumn temperatures and hopes for the war's prompt conclusion declined, the division withstood daily mortar fire in Holland. The Germans lacked neither ammunition nor high ground from which to expend it. Dour weather added to the tedium. "[M]ud everywhere, water in the foxholes, everything soaking wet," Winters complained. "Not being able to get away from the mud and rain became very depressing as the days went on and on."[29]

In their spare time, the sodden members of Easy Company sought alternatives to the equally watery British rations known as the 14-in-1. "Parts of this ration were good," Winters surmised, "but let's face it, we were spoiled by our K-rations and C-rations and even the crummy D-ration tasted good at times." Troopers such as Ed Stein rectified the issue by brewing homemade stew in a large barn. "They threw everything they could find in that pot: the oxtail soup from the British 14-in-1 ration, carrots, cabbage, some pork, anything they could scrounge," Winters recalled. "Then, just as the cook hollered, 'Come and get it," a mortar round came through the roof of the barn and landed in the pot of stew. Nobody was hurt, but the cook was slightly burned by the stew."[30]

Between dodging mortar shells and scavenging for grub, some paratroopers engaged in more nefarious mischief. Countless Dutch homes, damaged and abandoned, became susceptible to pillaging by both sides. Winters devoted a fair portion of October and November to distributing justice to known offenders. Though monotonous, the duty proved less demanding than the torments of combat. Over the previous two months, the division suffered some 3,300 casualties. The strategic shortcomings of Operation Market-Garden left many a soldier bereft. Gratefully, the division was relieved from the line two days after Thanksgiving and relocated to a rest area near Reims, France.

Regardless of the lost hopes of the campaign, Hollanders were grateful for the effort. Later in life, Winters took special note of the wartime recollections of Piet Huisman, who witnessed the failed endeavor to liberate his country. In hindsight, Huisman concluded, "We were very lucky to come through the war alive and healthy.... We learned a lot in this war. People must cling together in the face of adversity, be polite to others, and appreciate what there is to share. We made a lot of good friendships during the war." Winters had similar thoughts in mind when he composed a November 14 letter. He finally had a moment to break two months of silence with DeEtta.[31]

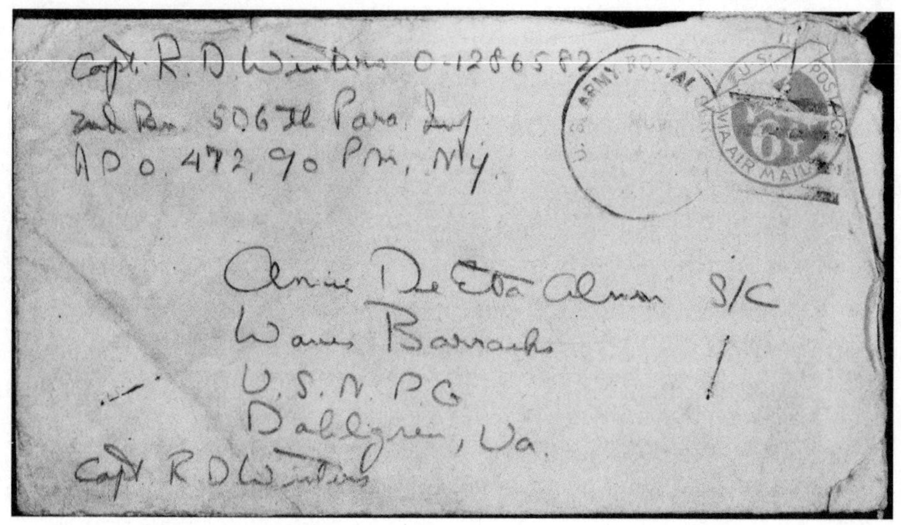
Capt. R. D. Winters 0-1286582
2nd Bn. 506th Para. Inf
APO 472, c/o PM, NY
DeEtta Almon S/C
Waves Barracks
U.S.N.P.G.
Dahlgren, Va.
Capt. R D Winters

This envelope, dated November 1944, was one of dozens DeEtta received from Dick throughout the war. The envelopes carried messages of humor and hardship alike.

Wearing dog tags: "DeEtta Almon??"

Dear DeEtta–
14 Nov. 1944
Holland

My favorite Wave–

My luck is still holding up and now I am just a little superstitious that it's your dog tag that holds the charm. I lost my own dog tags the first day and since receiving yours, I've been wearing it. Hope your folks aren't informed someday that you're missing in action. That sure would be something—a Wave M.I.A. with the 101st in Holland.

The pictures you sent of your camp look to me like a storybook setting for an army camp. If I could only put my boys in a place like that for about two months! I am not saying they'd do nothing but rest, for in the army that's one thing that never happens. You never take time off to rest or do nothing, no matter how tired or what you've gone through. But what it would do is give them a chance to clean up and warm up and maybe get a few hot meals. Also they could get over that jumpy feeling.

Sent my kid sister a flock of German & British insignias to stick on her "junk coat" as she calls it. Boy I'll bet that thing is really something, all kinds of American shoulder patches and insignias, British & German.

[...] Had the chance to go to church the other week for the first time in two months. Of course it wasn't exactly fancy but it was church. We had it in a barn with some cows and horses crunching on some hay and adding a delightful aroma to the setting.

Another ray of sunshine is the radio which plays on occasion. About all we can get is some German station and they have a gal announcer we call "Annie," who tells us what to bring if we we're captured, what a dog Eisenhower is, and how the Roosevelt family is now running the country. Then they announce the names of those captured, telling us how nice it is, since for them the "war's over." However, between times we hear some pretty good American recordings of dance bands.

Say, on looking over a few of your back letters, I see you're telling me what to do, as letting you know, if I am wounded. Sister, we just don't talk about stuff like that, unless we're kidding. Everybody has the idea that "they may get the other guy, but never me." Actually it's all luck.

Wish you wouldn't have bothered with those Xmas presents. I am in no position to send anything in return and consequently feel sort of guilty about receiving.

Well, I've run out of questions and things to say, so I'll just close as usual with

Love,
Dick[32]

The superstitious nature in which Winters cherished DeEtta's naval dog-tag was not a unique tendency. The safeguarding of good luck charms and sentimental tokens among GIs emerged as a common pastime. As veteran Paul Fussell acknowledged, "the most popular military rumors are the ones fostering irrational hopes and proposing magical outcomes.

Closely related by the motive to influence the future mystically are wartime military superstitions." Eisenhower pocketed a collection of seven coins he rubbed prior to impending operations. Airmen sported St. Christopher medals around their necks. All too often, treasured talismans reflected romantic interests or sexual conquests: brassieres, nylons, panties—all "especially lucky items, not to be parted from." Ever the upright sentimentalist, Winters's token reminder of DeEtta was decidedly chaste.[33]

A GI tradition as prevalent as expressing superstition was souvenir hunting. The amassing of battlefield relics occurred in manners both benign and malicious. Winters attested to the problems looting posed in maintaining military discipline, but the acquiring of squarely-earned battlefield trophies was another matter. The collecting of patches for Ann's "junk coat" served as a temporary means of escape from the more onerous obligations of a frontline captain. For many, attaining souvenirs became a fixation. Men avidly sought confiscated Luger pistols, Crosses of Iron, and Nazi flags as mementos of battlefield triumphs. Even as he endured shellfire following his wounding on the Island, Pfc. David Webster yearned for combat trophies. "A German poncho caught my fancy as I approached a grassy embankment two feet high," he recalled. "Make a good souvenir for my sister's boy, I thought. I scooped it up and ran on." He hobbled toward the regimental aid station, poncho in hand.[34]

Officers generally dissuaded enlisted men from scavenging during battle. "Don't become a souvenir sap when you get on the Continent," *Stars and Stripes* warned three months prior. "Some Yanks are like pack rats—they load themselves down with everything in sight when they pass an enemy position. Souvenir collectors are a nuisance to the Intelligence boys, too. Lots of valuable information on the enemy has been destroyed by GI souvenir saps." Scores rejected the sound advice. To the victor belong the spoils. "If they picked up a few trinkets," Winters said of his men late in the war, "I had no problem."[35]

Dick's vague mention of the German radio personality named "Annie" refers to the propagandist better known as "Arnhem Annie." The malevolent, English-speaking broadcaster introduced popular big band music interjected with ominous threats and overtures enticing surrender. Among Annie's more repeated offers was to "just bring a toothbrush, overcoat, and blanket and come across the river where you will be treated like kings." Not to be outdone by rhetorical one-upmanship, paratroopers of Company A crossed the frigid Rhine and left the aforementioned items with a saucy note intended for Annie. Most GIs ignored the radio propaganda and simply enjoyed the music.[36]

Regardless of Nazi hogwash, fate was on the minds of all. According to Fussell, every combatant contended with flagging confidence in his hopes of survival as campaigns persisted. A soldier who withstood consistent fighting often experienced two stages of rationalization and one stage of realization regarding mortality: It *can't* happen to me; It *can* happen to me; and It *is going to* happen to me. Any infantryman was susceptible to this psychological fatigue. "Inevitably, all will break down if in combat long enough," Fussell concluded. As Christmas approached, Winters himself drifted toward this straining mindset—and ever closer to the breaking point.[37]

"I hope when it's my turn it isn't too bad," he thought. "Hope to live through it."[38]

CHAPTER SIX

IT'S ALL LUCK

December 1944 to April 1945

"The last time I saw Paris"

13 Dec. 1944–France

My favorite Wave–

Remember me? I'm that two-headed paratrooper who used to write on occasion.

This writing, or should I say, lack of writing is something I can't honestly explain. In the past two months I don't believe I've written more than three or four letters. Can't say I haven't had the time, although I've been darn busy, but the thing is I can't get in the mood. As near as I can explain it, it goes like this: I've not answered, get a big bang out of reading it, looking at the pictures, sniffing the perfume. Next, I promise myself "yes, I'll write her the first chance I have, but right now I must study this manual," or do this or that. Or if I can't find something to do or an excuse, I've just got to relax.

Don't ask me why I've suddenly reached a point where I can't write. It's not you, my parents, or anybody. It's just me. Can't seem to find anything to say, that is something worth saying. And if you've nothing worthwhile to say, why write?

You talk about those marines jumping when guns go off—it just ain't funny.

Do you ever re-live an important or thrilling experience in your life? Well, "Twerp," I've been knocking myself out.

Not to change the subject, but ----, the last time I saw Paris! Her heart was young and gay. What a town that is. Boy, it really is all they say about it. Even after taking into consideration the fact that I hadn't been around civilization for some time, it's still some town. Went on a tour and found out how many people were beheaded here and how many nuts and bolts in the Eiffel tower and all the rest of the worthless information. Took in a couple of good shows, bought some clothes, and best of all, got to sleep between two sheets on a bed with springs. Yep, and I even had a good hot bath. Boy, what a time!

Did I ever tell you what I think of the navy? Remind me some time. But first I've got to finish this war.

By the way, who won the Army-Navy football game? Somebody told me navy refused to play.

You know I've got a piece of white silk I've been going to send you for Xmas for three months now and I don't believe I've ever sent it. But right now, while I'm in the spirit, I'll look it up, enclose it, and forward same. It will be late, but it's what we'll call your Xmas present for '44. Next year it'll be a grass skirt so don't complain.

Pardon me, but if I recall correctly, you mentioned in one letter that you're equivalent to a sgt. now. That's just fine, but remember this, Sgt., what you need is leadership to get the job done, not the power of rank.

Well, sailor, it's 2300 and for want of something better to do, I think I'll read a little from my Bible, nothing like a war to make a believer out of me, and then hit the sack. So, till reveille, I dream of -----,

Dick

To make a ring for the scarf, take a piece of suspension line, hold ends together, place flame of match under and, result—it will weld together. I'd do it, but nobody is around.[1]

Preparations were underway for a major German counteroffensive as Dick savored a much-needed holiday in the City of Light. Adolf Hitler, with his troops slowly being pushed back within their own border, sought to reverse the Allied advance. Setting his sights on the port city of Antwerp, Belgium, the Führer hoped to split British and American forces while also driving them back to the sea. The daring gamble would be spearheaded

Winters and fellow GIs enjoy leave in Paris in early December 1944. This photo was taken in front of the Arc de Triomphe. Winters is fourth from left. The City of Light was a bit gloomy that day. Even so, Dick later wrote, "That place tops anything yet."

by refitted divisions just days before Christmas. Their intention was to roll through the steep and thickly forested region known as the Ardennes. Standing in the way was a mixture of fresh and recuperating American divisions dispatched to this sector considered beyond the enemy's reach. December 16 opened with a massive Germany artillery barrage followed by a flood of troop columns pouring into the American zones. Unsuspecting GIs were left vulnerable due to a lack of air support caused by blinding fog. The sudden onslaught created a large salient stretching some forty-five miles wide and seventy miles deep. The Battle of the Bulge had begun.[2]

To blunt the oncoming tide, Eisenhower mobilized the 82nd and 101st Airborne, both of which were recovering from the failed Operation Market-Garden. The latter was stationed at Camp Mourmelon near the historic city of Reims, France. The division suffered nearly 4,000 casualties during its previous campaign, and its members embraced a Christmastime recess. Rear echelon amenities and a highly anticipated football game between the division's 502nd and 506th Regiments set the tone for an optimistic new year. Those hopes were dashed in an instant on the evening of December 17 when the men's weekend passes were revoked and all were ordered to marshal for battle.

Brig. Gen. Anthony McAuliffe, serving as acting division head for Maxwell Taylor—summoned to Washington prior to the incursion—prepared his officers as best he could. "All I know of the situation is that there has been a breakthrough and we have to get up there," he informed subordinates. There was little time for assembly and, within hours, the paratroopers funneled eastward in a convoy of cargo trucks. Foregoing blackout regulations, the vehicles barreled through the winter haze with headlights turned on. "[W]e were in a hurry and living dangerously," recalled Winters. Snow was falling, an ominous indicator of the battle's dreadful conditions.[3]

Upon reaching the crossroads town of Bastogne, Belgium, McAuliffe was ordered to halt and dig in for a defense. The modest city was to become one of the significant pivot points on which the fate of the campaign hinged. A few miles away, the 101st Airborne convoy was halted by a stream of battered, retreating infantrymen of the 28th Division. Many were in a dazed stupor as they stumbled to the rear. Others yelled, "Run! Run! They'll murder you!" Winters was embarrassed by the spectacle. "They were just babbling," he remembered. "It was pathetic. We felt ashamed." Considering what the men of the "Bloody Bucket" division had endured over the past month, this may have been an overly harsh judgement on Winters's part. With the roads bottlenecked, the paratroopers continued their trek on foot.[4]

Matters were grim from the outset. On December 19, Germans feigning as civilians overran a division supply area west of town and later captured substantial medical stores. At one point, Dick was told that a supporting artillery piece had only three rounds. The Americans lacked adequate winter clothing, medicine, and rations—forcing them to scavenge.

Lt. George Rice of the 10th Armored Division attempted to partially remedy the dire situation by driving jeeploads of ammo and grenades to undersupplied paratroopers. "I will never forget him for being a conscientious officer and getting us a couple of loads of ammunition at the last second, and taking it right out from under the Germans," recalled Winters. "I was battalion executive officer, but when he started throwing that ammunition out of that jeep…I'm on my hands and knees fighting the rest of the guys for a few rounds of ammunition, because I didn't have any either!"[5]

Improvisation became an art form as supply routes closed. When Easy Company corporal Gordon Carson was transported to an aid station after suffering a thigh wound, he was aghast to see so many maimed men lying about. "Hey!" he bellowed to a medic. "How come you got so many wounded people around here? Aren't we evacuating anybody?"

"Haven't you heard?" the medic replied.

"I haven't heard a damn thing."

"They've got us surrounded—the poor bastards."[6]

The violent standoff persisted as the battalions daily thwarted enemy advances. On the morning of December 22, a delegation of Germans approached a farmstead defended by the 327th Glider Infantry Regiment. The figures emerging from the haze hoisted a white flag, offering terms of submission. The only way the besieged Americans could avert complete annihilation, they warned, "was [the] honorable surrender of the encircled town."

Receiving the offer, the typically soft-spoken McAuliffe indignantly crumpled the note and blurted, "Us surrender? Aw nuts!" This initial response evolved into his iconic, formal reply to the German commander: "N U T S !" The German envoys were puzzled by the one-word response.

"Is that reply negative or affirmative?" one German officer inquired.

"The reply is decidedly *not* affirmative," explained Col. Joseph Harper.

The colonel added an exclamation point to his clarification as the enemy departed: "If you don't know what 'Nuts!' means, in plain English it is the same as 'Go to Hell!' And I will tell you something else: if you continue to attack, we will kill every goddam German who tries to break into this city." The incensed emissaries stormed off.

The phrase "NUTS" became ubiquitous with the division's defense of Bastogne. Lifting the men's spirits, the word's defiant, dual interpretations led to chuckles in the snowy foxholes. Sgt. Bill True of Fox Company declared of McAuliffe, "That guy has balls!"[7]

The bitter weather dampened these rare moments of levity. "It stayed below zero most of the time," remembered paratrooper Vince Speranza. "We were told it had been the coldest winter in Europe in twenty years. Almost no one had a winter coat. Most of us had only a field jacket, a sweater, and cotton long johns. We had no gloves, no wool beanies, and no galoshes. Our feet were always wet, and we lost almost as many men to trench foot as to bullets." Speranza avoided some anguish by daily alternating two pairs of socks, tucking a set in his shirt to dry each night. Not all were graced by such luxuries.[8]

Rick MacKenzie, one of the few correspondents to venture to Bastogne, huddled for warmth in a command post cellar when a nearby explosion jarred the room. Col. Clifford Templeton entered the basement and informed MacKenzie at his typewriter, "An H.E. [high explosive] shell came through the roof and exploded in your room." The reporter then recognized the sinister truth of his slim survival. "Here in Bastogne was reality," he mused. MacKenzie walked to his former room and the grisly scene within. His bedroll was "chewed up" by the blast, and his four roommates were dead. The correspondent dropped to one knee in prayerful contemplation before returning to the command post. "That was a close one," Templeton cheerily announced. But the consolation "brought no comfort."[9]

A glimmer of hope appeared the next day when skies cleared and the paratroopers at last obtained fresh supplies dropped from cargo planes. One lieutenant noted, "We sent every available truck and jeep out to the drop zone to help collect and transport supplies for Regimental HQ. Consequently, the company gathered dozens of parachutes as well as canvas sheets....Layered onto logs, this waste material drastically improved our living conditions and provided us warm bedding." Meanwhile, the contrails of German-bound Allied bombers were spotted from the ground. American fighters simultaneously helped foil enemy headway in the immediate vicinity. In the coming days, some 2,000 parachutes dropped nearly 500 tons of equipment.[10]

The support, both logistical and psychological, boosted the division's energy. Illustrating the fortitude of his men in a Christmas Eve announcement, McAuliffe explained, "We are giving our country and our loved ones at home a worthy Christmas present and being privileged to take part in this gallant feat of arms are truly making for ourselves a Merry Christmas." Two days later, George Patton's Third Army battered through the German lines to support Bastogne. Weeks of desperate winter fighting remained until the enemy was fully thwarted.[11]

Angst over news of the Ardennes offensive, plus infrequent correspondence from Dick, stirred consternation in DeEtta. Reports of the Bulge suggested the multi-nation clash had grown into the largest battle in US Army history. Christmas 1944 was an unhappy one. She was certain something dreadful had happened to Dick.

German prisoners dig into the frozen, snow-covered soil of Bastogne to make temporary graves for American dead. Over time, Winters grew hardened to such scenes. US Army photo by Al Krochka.

First letter mailed from Bastogne.

V-MAIL

Jan. 6, 1945
Belgium

My favorite Wave–

Just a note to let you know that mysterious feelings you've been having about me being wounded, back in the States, and all that is just a point to prove how far wrong a woman's intuition can be.

Thanks a million for all the letters, especially when I realize how many I've sent.

Read the papers and keep an eye on the 101st and you'll know generally where your paratrooper is spending his time.

Haven't received your Xmas package as yet but that gives a fellow something to look forward to.

Love,
Dick[12]

Contrary to DeEtta's divinations, Dick was spared injury in the Battle of the Bulge—barely. His regiment hunkered in the woods north of Bastogne on the road to Foy. Known as the Bois Jacques (Jack's Woods), the setting could have resembled a vista from a Germanic fairy tale had it not been for the bullets and shrapnel. Foy itself was unoccupied by the GIs because the enemy had advantage of high terrain encompassing the town. Entrenched on good ground of its own within the woods, the 506th PIR maintained arm's length from the enemy—like a predator awaiting its prey.

The trees of the Bois Jacques were often planted in straight rows, therefore diminishing the levels of concealment soldiers sought. The pines were doubly problematic because, like in the Hurtgen Forest weeks prior, trees themselves became projectiles when struck and splintered by shells. After heavy bombardments, some trees resembled large, shaved pencils protruding from the earth. The frozen soil proved nearly impenetrable for picks and entrenching tools.

Many expressed doubt in their likelihood of surviving the horrid environment. In one letter, Easy Company's Don Malarkey described himself as "a fugitive from the law of averages, which isn't good." Reflecting upon the death of his friend, Warren "Skip" Muck, Malarkey described his dreary reality: "Each day more of my friends would leave for a better world.... I could never describe the terror that strikes you when you're under terrific artillery barrages when the exploding steel seemingly pounds you into the ground and makes your head reel, your ears pop, and your heart stop beating." When men were wounded, Winters said their comrades "felt glad for them," for they were able to escape. When a man perished, "we found that he was at peace." Existence itself seemed a nightmare.[13]

Winters, as the battalion's executive officer, helmed a variety of challenging tasks. Beyond contending with logistics and the common perils of combat, he served as the observant bridge between company-grade officers and superiors. Lewis Nixon simultaneously acted as intermediary in the communication chain linking the battalion command post with Col. Sink. Forays as such were demanding, dangerous, and—due to the dense fog and snow—often befuddling. This confusion proved especially so for an oblivious enemy soldier who wandered too far astray to relieve himself. Winters noticed the man walking in a carefree fashion through the fog and within American lines. After the squatting German was done with his business, Winters bellowed out, "Kommen sie hier!" Realizing his vulnerably awkward predicament, the intruder surrendered with little complaint. Armed with only a full bowel when he initially stumbled into the lines, the German was the singular enemy combatant to infiltrate Winters's defenses.[14]

Even mundane aspects of soldier life were no less arduous in the Ardennes. A shortage of food on the frontline was emotionally and physically draining. Similar to his Normandy experiences, Dick recognized an exclusive K-ration diet as nothing enviable. When the opportunity for a meal of hot beans presented itself, Winters naturally allowed his enlisted men to eat first. He later admitted, "I made a tactical error in that I allowed several soldiers to return to the chow line for seconds before going through the line myself." As a result, his scrumptious repast "consisted of five white beans and a cup of cold broth." So much for the privileges of rank. Nonetheless, those in the company recognized Winters shared their hardships.[15]

The desire for any degree of warmth pressed men beyond reasonable bounds of logic. Alongside Lt. Harry Welsh, Winters took solace at a modest campfire one particularly frigid evening. Unsurprisingly, the Germans responded in kind with a shower of mortar rounds—landing one directly amid the small gathering of officers. As Winters regained his composure, he noticed a bloodied Welsh tearing his trousers open to examine the severity of a wound. "He wasn't castrated," Dick recalled, "but it was too close for comfort."[16]

The debilitating circumstances bore down on men's souls. They endured "night after night, not knowing how long" the battle would persist, noted Winters. Defenders of Bastogne gazed onto no-man's-land with fatigued, thousand-yard stares. Approximately one-third of casualties were frostbite victims. Soldiers driven to exhaustion had the capacity to ignite breakdowns in discipline. Demoralization festered in the raw conditions, offsetting the accountability of even dependable personnel. For those on the edge of mental collapse, Winters offered them a change of pace. Removing them from the immediate dangers of foxholes, Dick temporarily converted battle fatigued GIs into runners, stretcher bearers, or simply granted them short leave in Bastogne. The momentary hiatus often refreshed the minds of those on the emotional brink. Winters remained focused and diligently surveyed the battalion's welfare. As to his own well-being, the cold did not curtail his daily shaves.[17]

By December 31, the 101st Airborne was no longer on the defensive. As Eisenhower said of the big picture, "The present situation is to be regarded as one of opportunity for us and not of disaster." Seizing the opportunity required American divisions to reclaim the territory lost over the prior two weeks. For Dick Winters and company, this drive compelled them to aim their guns at Foy, and Noville beyond. But first, the *Luftwaffe* presented a sinister New Year's gift to the "Battered Bastards of Bastogne." The bombs of fifty German *Lehrgeschwader* aircraft rained destruction on the Belgian crossroads on January 1.[18]

Amid the hardship, Winters's self-awareness peaked. Though he cared deeply for his men, he had to maintain emotional distance in order to function as an officer. To dwell on each casualty was to welcome shattered nerves. "You look around and see men hit every day, or getting frostbite or combat fatigue," he remembered. "Each day the line gets thinner and thinner. Every morning my present for duty roster kept going down. I couldn't focus on each man's loss. I had the rest to worry about." Nobody was fully immune to the hysteria of the battlefield—not even Dick's most trusted dependents.[19]

After discovering Sergeants Joe Toye and Bill Guarnere each with a leg severed, Lt. Buck Compton cracked. The sight of their smeared blood and severed limbs in the snow was more than he could bear. A shell-shocked Compton wandered toward the rear in a hypnotic state of horror. Dick confronted him, declaring, "Buck, you're an officer; you've got to get a hold of yourself. I can't excuse you for this."

"I can't take it anymore," Buck confessed. "I just can't take it anymore. I'm sorry." Aside from losing dependable platoon leaders and non-commissioned officers, the ranks of staple Toccoa men dwindled day by day. All throughout the regiment, the unfolding crisis exerted pressure on green replacements and the men charged with their care. Sgt. Lou Vecchi of I Company recalled, "One night I led a group of around fifteen soldiers out to a forward OP. They were all replacements of one sort or another and begged me not to leave them alone. They were so inexperienced and scared that I had to stay with them."[20]

Quiet reservations about the abilities of strained men permeated the ranks as the regiment prepared for a final attack on Foy, north of Bastogne, on January 13. Over the course of several previous days, multiple companies of the 506th PIR attempted to dislodge the enemy from the hamlet and blunt German counterattacks. Because the town was in a geographic bowl, the tactically precarious position was difficult for Americans to hold with permanence amid the seesaw battles. Seizing the town and evicting the Germans would permit the division to advance in domino fashion toward Noville, past Rachamps, and onto Houffalize.[21]

Broader accomplishments were contingent on the actions of individuals. The night prior to the attack, Sgt. Carwood Lipton expressed doubts in Easy Company's commander, Lt. Norman Dike. The lieutenant seemingly disappeared when needed most. With no other officers readily available, however, Winters was stuck with Dike—at least until the latter committed an unforgivable error. That moment arrived the following morning.

Two hundred yards of white pasture separated the regiment's wooded position from the enemy-defended structures of Foy. Agility and speed were perhaps the two dominant factors determining the assault's success. The column darted from the tree line with the support of heavy machine guns, trudging as quickly as possible through the mounds of snow. German firepower intensified with each step forward. Then—only a few dozen feet shy of the village's edge—the advance abruptly froze. Dike, paralyzed by indecision or possible injury, halted the company on the far end of the plain. Winters was enraged. Every unnecessary second in the open prolonged an already lethal situation. For all intents and purposes, Winters was now the battalion commander. He had to act. Stopping himself from venturing into the melee and leading the attack personally, Winters anxiously sought any nearby officer to do what Dike could not. Out of the corner of his eye, Dick spotted the gung-ho but effective Lt. Ronald Speirs of D Company.

"Speirs, get over here!" Winters screeched above the gunfire. "Go out there, relieve Dike, and get that attack moving!" Blind to the confusion and carnage, Speirs raced into the action and relaunched the charge that ultimately secured the town. Speirs remained Easy Company commander for the war's duration. Dike was relegated to a desk job at division headquarters.[22]

After a month on the line, the 101st Airborne was placed in reserve on January 17 and ultimately relocated to Drulingen, 162 miles away. The Ardennes was the division's most torturous campaign. One-third of Dick's regiment became casualties. Total German losses in the Battle of the Bulge hovered around 80,000 men—a proportion not easily replaced. Hitler's gamble temporarily stalled the Allied juggernaut but did not reverse the inevitable outcome.[23]

In more lighthearted terms, Gen. Maxwell Taylor (who rushed from Washington so as not to miss the entire campaign) wryly insisted on a memorandum receipt for the transferal of Bastogne to the VIII Corps. A soldier artist hastily rendered a certificate that Maj. Gen. Troy Middleton gladly signed. The receipt read: "Received from the 101st Airborne Division–The Town of Bastogne, Luxembourg Province, Belgium–Condition: Used but serviceable, Kraut disinfected."[24]

Surrender of the city was never considered, Winters insisted. "We never talked about it. We never thought about it. How can you? If you're going to be sitting around pitying yourself…the first thing you're going to do is you're going to convince yourself you *should* surrender. That never happened."[25]

"I, too, will never forget this past Xmas or New Year's Day"
Pride in being a leader.
"Wherever the book opens"

Somewhere–
Jan. 22, 1945

My favorite Wave–

Well, today I received three letters. Quite a day. Two from you, 26 Dec., 5 Jan., and one from my dad.

First I tried to answer my dad's letter, and it was a miserable attempt, to thank him for writing. Gee, it's been so long since I've done any writing, I've almost forgotten how. I can't spell, and despite the fact that the weather doesn't cause me much physical discomfort, I sure go frigid mentally. Can't think of anything to say except thanks for writing, don't worry, I am still O.K., still ducking at the right times. This censorship stops a fellow cold, and as for writing about love and all that, well I am about as brilliant as Li'l Abner along those lines. I just ain't got it!

Just reread your letter of Dec. 26th. It's darn good. You must have been full of the honest to goodness Xmas spirit when you wrote that one. By now you have most likely forgotten what you had to say. You described Xmas at home, the church service, and choir, Xmas dinner, etc. I, too, will never forget this last Xmas and New Year's Day.

But now this letter of the 5th of Jan.—what a change! You've just received my letter of the 16th of Dec., the day before I took off, and you're ready to fight, or at least tell me to go to hell and let it go at that. Well, well, just go right ahead. Don't let my feelings interfere with yours. If you want to fight, might as well do it now while I don't have much zip left, [be]cause I am a fighting man when I am going strong. Also, might as well fight the Germans, the army, and you at the same time instead of individually. I feel like I can take care of the whole bunch and still not knock myself out. At least I am not really worried about a fight from you for all you can throw are strong words and right now they don't even faze me, just sort of bounce off. It's something like a close shell—you just hit the dirt when you hear it coming, wait till the shrapnel stops singing overhead, then go on your way. Sometimes a piece of spent shrapnel hits you, might leave your leg or arm stiff and a little black and blue, but you're not hurt enough to stop. So it goes in any kind of a fight. You get hit, sure, you're bound to, but that doesn't mean you're out or that you're even hurt, unless you want to think so. So go ahead, start a fight. One more won't make any difference either way.

Now I do believe you think I, as well as all other soldiers, raise all kinds of hell when we do get a pass to a place like Paris. Well, you've been around; you know the navy. It's the same in the army, only more so overseas. But that doesn't mean everybody raises hell. Take it or leave it. I didn't, never have, never will, raise hell while I am in the army. Why? First and most important, I've got my own conscience to answer to. Next, my parents, and then I am an officer in the U.S. Army. I am damn proud of it and with the rank and position I hold, I wouldn't think of doing anything to bring discredit to my outfit, my para, boots, wings, and patch or the army. That sounds like an idealistic high school kid and there just is no such thing as an idealistic setup in anything or anyplace. But that's it. That's how I feel.

You ask what I read in the Bible. Well, it's like this. I am no authority on the Book, never intend to be, so when I read it it's not necessarily to improve my mind or to learn the Proverbs so I can impress somebody by quoting them, but just for relaxation and atmosphere. So I read wherever the Book happens to fall open, and sometimes it opens at just the right spot.

Now, next and last, you want to know what I dream of. Oh my aching back! Well—there are many kinds of dreams, some this way, some that way. Since I am in the army, I daydream of fights, fighting Jerries, out-maneuvering, out-thinking, out-shooting, and out-fighting them. But they're tense, cruel, hard, and bitter. They consist of about 80% of my dreams, but they pay off. You'd be surprised. Sometimes when you dream over and over a problem, you get the solution, and by gosh, crazy as it may seem in the cold morning light, it usually works. In fact to date, they've always worked.

As for the other 20%—which you're most likely more interested in, relax, sit back in that plush chair instead of on the edge. Well, 10% are about the happiness and pleasure of a nice warm, comfortable home, good chow, and all the pleasures of a kid. The other 10% are of future operations and plans for happiness. Believe me I intend and hope to see the day when I can enjoy life a little bit and relax.

Incidentally, I am now doing two jobs: Bn. Exec., and Bn. Plans and Operations.

Well, kid, it's now 0015, Jan 23rd, another day, so best of luck.

Dick[26]

Dick turned twenty-seven years of age the previous day. Over the prior eight months he had witnessed enough combat to last a lifetime. His ensuing nightmares underscored the cruelties and deprivations withstood in the Bois Jacques. Although Winters commanded his own fears and never believed psychological trauma hindered his abilities, he nonetheless recognized the distinctive hell his outfit experienced. "I'm not sure that anybody who lived through Bastogne hasn't carried with him, in some hidden ways, the scars of war." The invisible wounds never quite fully healed.[27]

There was little rest for the weary. Reacting to Operation Nordwind, the Germans' effort to steer Americans away from the Ardennes, the paratroopers shifted to the banks of the Moder River in the region of France known as Alsace. Snow still blanketed the sloping hillsides. Citizens were seen moving back into their homes and rebuilding their lives. The regiments intermittently paddled back and forth across the river to conduct reconnaissance and obtain prisoners for intelligence. On February 5, the 506th PIR occupied the sector encompassing Haguenau, France, a city of some 20,000 residents only a few miles upriver from the Rhine. That same week, the mountains of snow began to melt—flooding the lowlands and creating considerable logistical problems. The clumps of mud made for scenes even bleaker than those at Bastogne.[28]

Winters (left) stands at the road sign for Hochstett, France, south of Haguenau, in February 1945. In the middle is division photographer Al Krochka, who traded Winters a large batch of photos in exchange for a Luger pistol at war's end.

Thanking DeEtta for a treasured Christmas package, Dick alluded to mediocre conditions in his February 15 letter. "If you read the papers you'll see that 101 has been with the 7th army for awhile and they've been feeding us beans and marching us daily," he wrote. "At the present it takes all the personal discipline I have to write a letter just saying hello. . . . This old war is mighty rough at times, becomes a bit tiring. But if those Russians can keep going, so can I." One week later he added, "Time to daydream, play, or write just doesn't exist. Of that I am firmly convinced. So don't be griping at the mail clerk or me. Hell, I don't even have (enough) time to sleep and eat to keep an ordinary man going." Additionally, he asked DeEtta for sailor undershirts and sweatshirts—items for warmth in the rawness of the season. His satirical disdain for the Navy did not preclude him from desiring its practical uniform components. "All of my things were stolen on the last jump" he complained. "Nice buddies."[29]

Ensnared in a drawn-out standoff along the Moder, Easy Company never had it so good in the combat zone. Indoor accommodations presented a lifestyle more amenable than the standard foxhole. Yet the troops did not grow too comfortable in their comparatively snug environment. The enemy was across the river. Pvt. David Webster ominously observed, "I frowned at the Moder River. Swollen with spring rains and the melting snow, it looked like boiling lead mixed with tar. The bare trees on its near bank seemed to be wet ghosts walking toward me." Webster feared the enemy overrunning his outpost.[30]

This scenario was reversed on the night of February 15 when Winters, under orders from Col. Sink, facilitated a patrol to the opposite bank with the intention of capturing prisoners. Poised on a balcony in Haguenau, Webster nervously awaited his comrades' return. "Silent and tense, the outposts on both sides of the Moder River watched and waited for the first burst of fire," he remembered. Shots rang out and American artillery followed. The Haguenau shoreline was illuminated by machine guns and tracers. The foray was successful in corralling prisoners for interrogation. Sink deemed the patrol a triumph and ordered a subsequent assignment for the following night.[31]

Wishing to avert further danger for his men, Winters secretly refused the order. The regiment had the intelligence it needed. Dick supervised a barrage on enemy positions but sent no man on patrol. He lived comfortably with this act of disobedience the rest of his life. Only days later, the battalion was removed from the line. The men soon returned to Mourmelon for rest and refitting. Few days of combat remained.[32]

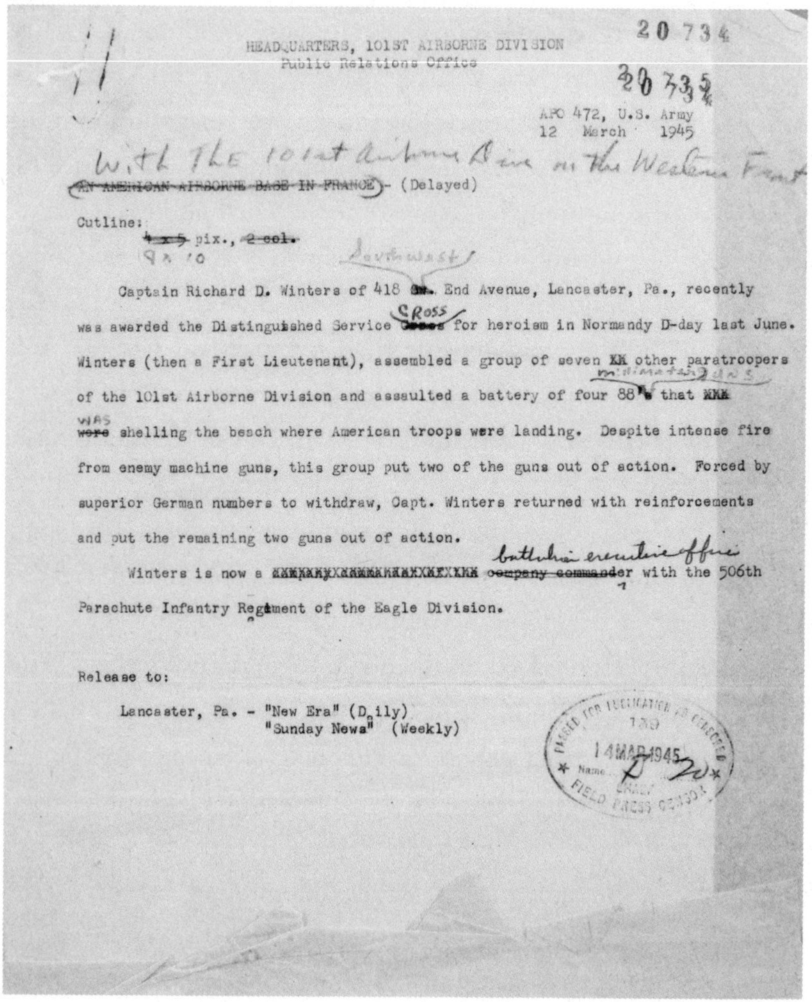

HEADQUARTERS, 101ST AIRBORNE DIVISION
Public Relations Office

20734

20735

APO 472, U.S. Army
12 March 1945

With The 101st Airborne Div on the Western Front ~~AN AMERICAN AIRBORNE BASE IN FRANCE~~ - (Delayed)

Cutline:
~~4 x 5~~ pix., ~~2 col.~~
9 x 10 Southwest

Captain Richard D. Winters of 418 ~~Ch.~~ End Avenue, Lancaster, Pa., recently was awarded the Distinguished Service Cross for heroism in Normandy D-day last June. Winters (then a First Lieutenant), assembled a group of seven ~~XX~~ other paratroopers of the 101st Airborne Division and assaulted a battery of four 88~~'s~~ millimeter guns that ~~XXX~~ was ~~were~~ shelling the beach where American troops were landing. Despite intense fire from enemy machine guns, this group put two of the guns out of action. Forced by superior German numbers to withdraw, Capt. Winters returned with reinforcements and put the remaining two guns out of action.

Winters is now a ~~XXXXXXXXXXXXXXXXXXXXXXXX~~ ~~company commander~~ battalion executive officer with the 506th Parachute Infantry Regiment of the Eagle Division.

Release to:

Lancaster, Pa. - "New Era" (Daily)
"Sunday News" (Weekly)

PASSED FOR PUBLICATION AS CENSORED
14 MAR 1945
FIELD PRESS CENSOR

This March 12, 1945, press release written by 101st Airborne public relations staff cited Winters's Normandy heroics. The statement was dispatched to Lancaster newspapers for publication.

Bn. Commanding Officer

12 March, 1945
France

Dear Wave–

Tonight I am dead tired. I was going to hit the sack early, but I decided to take a little workout. Then after washing up, I decided that I still had enough energy left to at least drop you a line.

You know you've been plenty nice to me, why I can't figure out! But in the past week I've received your swell calendar and then all this real [nice] writing paper and envelopes with stamps. Before I've always had to bum or steal writing material so rather than steal, I just didn't write. That calendar calls for a lot of razzing for I never have any pinups or pictures of any kind in my pocketbook or elsewhere. So, I am getting the well-known berries. But that's O.K.

You may wonder about this latest promotion. Well, I just got it last week. So it looks as if I can prove worthy of the job, if somebody of senior rank doesn't show up to take over, and if my luck holds out, some day I may be a Lt. Colonel, say within the next six months.

It sure was an honor to get the bn. for it means I've come straight up from junior second lt. to commanding officer in the same bn. in a period of 2 ½ years.

As far as the promotion in rank goes, I don't give a damn, but I do like the job and responsibility that go with it.

Just what job does a lt. col. hold in the navy? How many stripes, or whatever they get, does he have? And while I am asking the questions, just what do you mean by asking me, "how do you like being a sounding board?" What I want to know is what are you trying to find out? Explain yourself more in detail.

Had three small fillings put in today. Hope that holds me until the end of the war—which I say will be within the next 100 days. Count them! I am sure I'll sweat each and every one of them out.

Love,
Dick

[P.S. Added in 1996]: I was the only officer during the war (in the 506 Regt.) to go from platoon leader in Normandy to Bn. Commander. Think of it! I was a private in June 1942 and a Bn. Commander in March 1945. And you were my best friend all the while!![33]

On March 8, Winters was at last promoted to major. The pace of life did not slow down for a brass bureaucrat. The division settled into a calmer lifestyle in Mourmelon. Hot food, warm showers, laundry services, and cots under wall tents were niceties not fully savored in months. Only one week after Dick's promotion, Gen. Eisenhower paid tribute to the division with a personal visit. Ike carried with him a special designation from Washington. "Never before has a full division been cited by the War Department, in the name of the President, for gallantry in action," Eisenhower boasted. "This day marks the beginning of a new tradition in the American Army." The paratroopers did not object to the praise. As veteran Don Burgett concluded, "Paratroopers are a special breed....It was the paratroopers who held Bastogne with that certain pride and unbreakable spirit....But Bastogne wasn't the end for us."[34]

On March 15, 1945, Dwight Eisenhower paid homage to the 101st Airborne during a special ceremony at Mourmelon. "Dictatorship cannot produce better soldiers than can aroused democracy," he declared to the troopers. "I know that you will meet every test of the future like you met it at Bastogne."

"Sort of tired tonight" (1945)
should be
"Sort of Bitchy" (1996)

24 March, 1945
France

Dear De–

What kind of stuff are you reading nowadays? From the line of icky stuff you wrote about my picture it sounds like 15¢ worth of pulp magazine. Something that would be called "Ten thrilling love stories" or "True confessions." Anyway don't hand me that kind of stuff. I get to look in the mirror about once a day when I shave and when I'm honest with myself, I just say, "Boy, are you ugly." So to be brief I am just glad I don't have to go around all day looking at myself.

Then you talk about my hair being darker. Hell, no, it's just dirty. I don't get a chance to wash it but a couple times a year. Then there's worry muscles on my forehead. My aching back! I've worry muscles all over my face and the longer this war continues, the deeper they'll grow for I've got over 600 big individual worries myself when I get time to think about my future.

Now we come to the part [in your letter] where my "eyes are keen and seem to follow you wherever you go." This is too much for me, I quit! Hell, that's the way I sleep! Next, my "mouth seems firmer, and my face broader, yet muscular." Naturally, if you'd been beaten around for so long and eaten nothing but K rations, you'd need more than a lipstick to look -----

"When I think of what your eyes have seen, I just can't visualize or imagine that much." Have you read these combat stories in the newspapers and magazines and seen these movies on combat? It makes me shiver too. "Do you jump when somebody slams a door, hit the ground if a car backfires?" Well, that's about all there is to it. Once you've seen one French village, you've seen them all, Holland, Belgium, Alsace-Lorraine, Germany—all the same.

So you met a boy from the 511 [Parachute Infantry Regiment, 11th Airborne Division]? Is that outfit in this man's army? Never heard of them doing anything! Gee, that sure must have been interesting to hear what the lad had to say about what paratroopers must go through. Terrible, I imagine. I'll just bet they run him to death. And if his officers don't work him to death, he'll most likely get killed on a practice jump. Did he tell you about the time he killed three Germans with his bare hands? Or about the time he got a letter from his girl and he was so inspired he went out and killed ten more of those dirty old krauts?

Yes, yes, those poor, poor, tired old krauts, just aching to give up. All you have to do is walk over there and invite them to give up. Why, I imagine he told you how a Yank is better than any three, old, tired krauts. Then there's the one about how they can't shoot worth a damn, can't hit a thing. I know, I've heard them all. To be brief, that's about the same grade as the stuff you handed me in the letter I just went over with you.

Sort of tired tonight. This thing of running a battalion can be rough if you want to make it that way.

On the radio they just announced that the 101st jumped east of the Rhine today. Mighty interesting! Wish they would have told me so I could have gone along.

Well, here's to the end. This letter looks and sounds like I must have been drinking but I am about as sober as a judge. Only just so tired I am too lazy to lift my pen, let alone think.

Well, I'll be seeing you in church—

Dick[35]

The fatigue was apparent in Dick's words. His March 24 letter lacked the typical paratrooper bravado of previous correspondence. Winters was tired. The same was true of his men. He concealed his weariness from them as he always had.

The jump "east of the Rhine today" caused additional agitation in the division's ranks. Dick alluded to Operation Varsity, the largest single-day airborne operation of the war. The endeavor consisted of 16,000 paratroopers from the British 6th Airborne and the US 17th Airborne. Their task was to gain a foothold on the western bank of the Rhine River—laying another brick atop the foundation for the final push into the Third Reich.

The 82nd and 101st Airborne were to be withheld from further action until the anticipated jump into Berlin—a mission that never materialized.

In a twist of fate, Winters's favorite compatriot, Lewis Nixon, participated in the operation as an observer. Leaping into Germany gained him a distinction few men attained. Nixon participated in all three paratrooper combat jumps in Western Europe. He did not boast of the distinction. His C-47 suffered a direct hit, killing all but four on board. "Nix" was one of the lucky survivors who departed the plane immediately prior to the blast. For the beleaguered officer, the tragic episode overshadowed what was otherwise a highly successful operation portending Allied victory.[36]

I have been put in my place!

10 April 1945
Germany

Dear DeEtta–

Received your letter of 30 March this evening in which you received my letter of about 28th of April [March]. I'd been sweating that one out. Guess it just took a long time to get moving.

It's impossible for me to write my true feelings under present conditions. For myself, I like to think things over a couple of days in my subconscious mind, during the hours a person just spends waiting on this and that. But when you're fighting as a front line battalion, there is just no spare time. Your mind is occupied at all times.

[...] Now, look, you talk about meeting somebody like me and falling in love with him. Hell, I am nothing like "Jesus." I am just like a million other guys.

Oh boy, talk about being able to concentrate. I've got people asking me questions about weapons, targets, harassing fire, grazing fire, chow, transportation, base of fire. It never ends. Yet, here I am trying to explain how I feel about love. Love, hell! Does such a thing exist? That is, where you can consider a person's feelings, devotion, and all that stuff. The army necessitates that your thoughts and feelings be hard, cold, to the point, and effective. So how do I know what the score is? All I know is that I am in no position to say I love anything or anybody.

I don't know, I am just ignorant, or to be blunt, not mature. So there's but one thing to do. Wait till the war's over then I'll start out on that subject. I hope to use my head, not the heart, well, not too much.

[...] These folks in Germany haven't been hurting near as much as our papers would like to have us believe. They're quite well off, much better than France, Holland, England, Belgium, or any other country over here. But now that we're playing ball in their backyard, a fellow has some satisfaction in knowing that these people are going to pay for it all. They know it too.

Their large cities are really something to see. Never saw anything like it in England, France, or any place. Some of them are just leveled, not a house worth mentioning in a whole city. Lovely, lovely. After seeing what others have gone through, it does me a lot of good to see them take a bit of medicine.

Before I close, let me say one thing, or rather ask one thing of you. Don't call me a brass hat! Please! If I've hurt your feelings, pardon me, I didn't mean to, but I just didn't want to have anybody standing around waiting for me when I come home. Or have anybody with any ideas. Of those who have worked with me in the army, and there are only a few of them that really know and understand how I feel and think about life in general, guess there's really only one, Lt. Welsh, a good little Irishman. At home there are my folks, and that's it. I don't think I have another soul who knows me. There were two fellows, one's in the army but I lost all respect for him after the way he fought the army for a year so he could stay with his wife. The other is a marine and a hell of a good guy, intends to be a preacher. I understand he's been wounded on Saipan and is to be discharged but I haven't heard from him or seen him for over two years.

Well, it's 0100, 11 April and high time to hit the sack while all's quiet on the western front.

Dick

P.S. What's this Sp (S) 2C stuff—a promotion, demotion, good conduct ribbon, or what?[37]

Winters perceiving himself much like "a million other guys" is revealing of his character and his generation. He admitted years later, "I never felt that this country owed our generation anything. For me, it was an honor to serve my nation. We were at war. The fate of democracy was at stake. I could not have lived with myself had I avoided military service. The current generation owes me nothing." Selflessness should always trump selfishness. Millions of his countrymen agreed. Even the French monument bearing Dick's likeness is not dedicated to him alone. Rather, the statue honors "the leadership abilities of all U. S. Army junior officers of all divisions and corps during the Normandy phase of Operation Overlord."[38]

While Dick brushed off DeEtta's adoration, he simultaneously found satisfaction in the destruction of German cities. His philosophy of an officer remaining "cold" and "to the point" is perhaps best exhibited here. Furthermore, Dick maintained strict discipline by reinstituting arduous exercises. Subordinates felt as if they were repeating basic training. Surprisingly, the conquering GIs felt at home in Germany. Resistance was much fiercer in prior campaigns. The food was good, the beer plentiful, the homes comfortable, and the landscapes stunning. Some Americans were impressed by the German work ethic as the civilian population rebuilt its shattered country. David Webster observed, "In explaining the superficial fondness of the G.I. for the Germans, it might be well to remember the physical comforts which he enjoyed nowhere else in the army but in the land of his enemies." The contentment was indeed one-dimensional. In the coming weeks, the paratroopers discovered the worst of their enemy's ghastly secrets.[39]

Summer Dress: Instead of two undershirts, one is enough.

April 16, 1945
Germany

Good morning-

This is quite unusual for me to have a few spare moments in the A.M. and still more that I do some writing.

Never feel like writing anymore. Don't know why but it's like I must force myself. In fact the only feelings I can arouse are ones of anger and after being mad all day and half the night, I am just plain tired. Mad at what? Just about everything for just about everything is done wrong or it isn't done perfectly. Since nothing but perfect is acceptable, I am mad.

You don't want to have any disagreements until after the war? Fine! For I am not a fighting man and after this war's over, all I want is a blissful state of tranquility and that's all. All I ask of the world is "let me alone."

[...] So the Waves have overnight passes and summer uniforms. Well, that's just fine. We also have changed to summer dress. Instead of wearing two undershirts, one is enough, and to top it off, I even had two baths within three days—the kind you get wet all over at once. That was the first time since January. In between I had about two or three showers.

This Germany, as you can see, is O.K. Nothing but the best. We move into a town, pick the best house, tell the folks, "I'll give you a reasonable time to move—fifteen minutes. Leave the beds, silverware and cooking utensils." At the end of the reasonable length of time, I've a nice C.P. for myself. And if time permits, a good meal, bed and bath. Very nice way to fight a war. Much better than Normandy, Holland or Bastogne, where we lived in foxholes most of the time.

Thanks for sending those quarter sleeve shirts. The way you talk about the size, I am wondering if they'll be big enough for a tent. I weigh between 180-185, but well, we'll see.

Both of us are wishing for the same thing when it comes to the point of this battalion being right in there for this final round of the fight. At the present, I am quite happy with it all. Things are going as they should, both with the outfit and the war. Before long the latter is going to come to an end. I hope the former lives on forever.

You vaguely mention "whatever I think of you." Well, whatever I think of you or what anybody else thinks of you isn't very important at all. It's what you think of yourself.

As ever,
Love,
Dick[40]

Earlier that week the division learned of the death of President Roosevelt. The fact that the man who led the nation through its greatest challenges would not witness final victory seemed harshly unfair. "Roosevelt was more than a fixture in our lives," Dick recalled. "He was the only president most of us could remember. Every American soldier in the U.S. Army held the commander-in-chief in utmost respect." They now had to finish the war without him. "His ideals and hopes for a better world, combined with his pleasing personality," noted David Webster in a letter to his parents on April 14, "could have given the United States a high position in Europe. Now that he is dead, I do not have much confidence in the coming peace."[41]

It's springtime: Waves trip out in shorts.

20 April 1945
Germany

Dear DeEtta–

The story of the paratroopers can never be told as to the full significance of the role they played in this war. They have been proven beyond all doubt to be practicable, which was the only doubt I had in my mind a year ago. But even the ever present threat of our employment is of no little importance in the general picture. And when we do drop, it's been proven that they actually just take off, plain scared. Of course in Normandy that wasn't the case and as a result we had one hell of a good fight. Even when we bump into SS or panzer units on the line, they don't concern us as much as the knowledge that we've got paratroopers to shoot at. It's actually noticeable that the shooting and fierceness of the fight is much sharper against German paratroopers.

So the Waves tripped out in shorts to show the sailors that spring is really here, I mean to work in their gardens. Some people really have it rough. Honestly now, what's a sailor's chance of pulling through this war, that is on a percentage basis. The way it looks to me, if a sailor doesn't drink himself to death, he should have a darn good chance of dying of old age in bed.

I feel it my duty to write your C.O. and inform him of what's going on atop the barracks on these nice sunshiny days, Waves getting tanned. I'll write him a formal note immediately!

Do I drink coffee as yet? Yes, I started when we went to Normandy, stopped when we went back to England, but have started once again. Reason—water situation in Europe is always dangerous, especially with a war on and sewage and water systems being broken and demolished.

At 0400 I would consider it a good time to read something solid, if I were on duty and had nothing to do. But I guess women are a bit different. Seems such a waste of time to me "wasting tender thoughts" on a soldier. For tender thoughts are to me something I took off and left behind in the marshalling area prior to starting this war. There's no room for them. There's little thought about death, so how can one waste thoughts that are simply tender. Death? Yes, I think earnestly about the dead, but there is no time to mourn for them.

Don't call me a "so and so!" That's disrespect to an officer! Unless you want to take an enforced slimming course of thirty days of bread and water, never let that happen again or the long arm of military law will reach out and slap you right where it would do the most good.

April 23 Pardon the delay.

This is pretty far from the type of territory you'd expect to see a Wave, but I feel sure you'd like it for it's beautiful. You'd love this setup. If I owned a home like this, with a small farm attached, I'd go about one more year in the army at my present salary and retire for life.

These Krauts weren't hurting for much during this war, but who would expect them to with France, Poland, and a handful of other countries to supply them with silk stockings, etc. That is, they weren't hurting until we started throwing some punches. You should see this place now, they're really hurting, especially in the large cities. It's something you can't describe for cities that are famous, just don't exist. There is nothing there but a few people wandering around in a lot of rubble. They can imagine how terrible it can be, but they can't appreciate it till they see a city fall around them.

Reading your punishments is like remembering mother's threats as a boy. We aren't troubled with a great deal of court martials, but when we are, the sentence is always rough, five, ten, fifteen years, dishonorable discharge. Something to make a man think. But that's the only way to handle things. You've got to mean business when you talk. Otherwise it's just best to keep quiet.

Look, Squirt, if I want to call you a soldier, wave, or anything I want, I'll do it, see! And all the screaming you do about being a sailor doesn't impress me. Why as a soldier I've seen more of the sea than you ever have or ever will. You're just a land-bound, drydock, saltless salt. I imagine a sailor would think of you, on the same level as I consider an S.O.S. [Services of Supply] (red circle with blue star) boy a soldier. They wear the uniform and draw the pay, but that's it. They just don't know the score. They can't even walk, or act like a soldier.

It looks like June should see the end of the war but when I am true to myself, I realize that it'll be another two years at the best before I get through with the C.B.I. [China, Burma, India theater of war] and home. Sure seems like a long time looking ahead but if a fellow just takes it one day at a time, it's not so bad. So here's to the end with

Love,
Dick[42]

German forces within the Ruhr pocket finally capitulated on April 18, 1945. The collapse served as yet another nail in the coffin of Hitler's regime. Some 325,000 enemy soldiers surrendered to Allied forces. Any celebration on the part of the paratroopers was tempered by the nightmare encountered days later.

On April 27, elements of the 12th Armored Division in the Landsberg am Lech vicinity of Bavaria discovered a crime heinous and unforeseen—a concentration camp. Specifically, the facility was named Kaufering IV, a sizeable sub camp of the even larger and deadlier Dachau concentration camp. Since the previous June, the site's 30,000 prisoners suffered as slaves in the construction of underground *Messerschmitt* hangars. Half the camp population did not walk out of the gates alive. That April, as the Allies approached, many prisoners were relocated to Dachau. Multitudes too weak to walk were shot while others were locked inside barracks thereafter set aflame by SS guards. Troops of the 12th Armored found 500 corpses, many of them mutilated and emaciated, upon their arrival. The 101st Airborne arrived the following day.[43]

Winters was aghast by the scene. "It stops you," he remembered. "You've never seen anything like this. It's a complete shock. It just stumps every feeling of emotion that you have. The horror of it…you could never imagine anything like this." The terror was impossible to rationalize. "The memory of starved, dazed men who dropped their eyes and heads when we looked at them through the chain-link fence, in the same manner that a beaten, mistreated dog would cringe, left a mark on all of us forever." Dick now fully realized the extent of Nazi atrocity. He knew why his and his men's suffering had been worthwhile. "For the first time I understand what this war is all about," he thought. "Now I know why I am here!"[44]

American soldiers encounter the gruesome realities of the Holocaust at Kaufering IV on April 29, 1945. United States Holocaust Memorial Museum photo, courtesy of the National Archives.

Easy Company's Edward Heffron was no less devastated by the gruesome spectacle. "All we could do was look at each other with our mouths open. We couldn't believe what we were seeing. It was bad. Hundreds of prisoners in black-and-white striped uniforms. They were like skeletons. They could barely stand." A miasma of death clung to everything; the stench seemed to suffocate the air itself. Pale bodies were piled as if cordwood, like railroad ties. Eddie Stein, one of Heffron's pals, was trembling with sorrowful anger.

"Babe," he declared, "can you believe what man can do to man?"

Gazing out on the mounds of corpses, Stein bit his lip and muttered, "They're my people."

"I know," Heffron replied. Both men broke down in tears.[45]

Upon learning of the murder factories, David Webster offered a blunt confession to comrade Burton Christenson. He said of the Germans: "I'm glad I fought those people, Chris. I didn't believe in the war till I got to Germany and saw what they were up to with their lagers and their concentration camps. I only killed one Kraut for sure, but knowing what I do now, I'm sorry it wasn't more."

"Those cold-blooded sonsofbitches," was Christenson's curt response.

"Here was Germany," Webster concluded in a homebound letter. "Here was the new order; innocent lives ripped up from their homes and forced to labor for the Master Race." The end of the Reich was near—and the Americans were thankful for that mercy. For untold millions, however, their liberators arrived too late.[46]

Dick made no mention of the camp or its many dead in his letter to DeEtta. The recent memory may have proven too painful even for a battle-hardened veteran to recount.

CHAPTER SEVEN

VICTORY IS OURS

May to July 1945

11 May 1945
Austria

My favorite Wave–

Well, it's high time I drop you a note, for before me I have three beautiful letters from you, April 23, 26, 30, and in the last you mention the possibility of the end of the war before I receive it. Also, today I received three quarter sleeve jerseys—for which I could kiss you. Only thing is that wouldn't be very soldier-like and my dignity would take a big slump. Can't let that happen so let's just say thanks.

This letter of the 30th is a good long letter of advice. Not bad, but it shows you've been reading too many success books or some of that chain story get-ahead stuff. It's all right and I guess right now I need it for I've been really cracking down on the boys since this day called V-E Day. Seems like most people wanted to throw a big drunk. They're really snapping around now.

Well, the war ended about as gloriously as I'd ever hoped. Berchtesgaden was really the heart of Germany, not Berlin, and it was quite an honor to be in on it. Goering, Kesselring, generals by the dozen, and Krauts by the thousands. Never saw anything like it or could imagine it, that was really something. They were backed up right into the mountains and no place to go. Then they threw in the towel and started coming out of the hills. Days before the final surrender all knew it was over. There just wasn't any fighting, thank God.

The country is near as rich or beautiful as along the Rhine but these Alps are really something. They go right out of this world.

What a hell of a mess this whole place is over here though. You have thousands and thousands of allied prisoners of war, millions of displaced persons, who are really slaves, brought here to work from other countries, and now thousands of German soldiers. They all want something. They need help, food, medical care, everything. Ye gods, I look at these people and think how they're lucky to be alive, really, for many have died and others are crippled. Here they are, all wanting to go home, yet when they get there, millions won't have a home, food, or any families. There are soldiers like myself who have been lucky and come through with only a scratch or so and then there's the rear echelon, they just don't know the score. As for our folks back home, you can't talk to them, for they can't imagine. Then come the slackers back home. Brother, I'd just like to have a couple and beat the devil out of them just on general principles.

Now that this war is over in Europe I've been thinking what's the use of sitting around over here for six months or so as occupational troops. So my friend, Capt. Nixon, and I plan to take off for the C.B.I. or at least tomorrow we're going to ask for a transfer to some parachute unit in the C.B.I. or any good infantry unit for it's going to be no good sitting around here. You gotta die sometime, so why not? Besides, I can't stand to see somebody tell me all about how tough it was down there. So we'll have a grass skirt for you, maybe.

As ever
Love,
Dick

In the company I keep, a bath or two doesn't make much difference either way. As a result, odor has no charm. So perhaps "Follow Me" will make a good tail light.[1]

Hitler was dead. On May 8, just over a week after the Führer committed suicide in Berlin, Victory in Europe Day was celebrated worldwide by the Allied powers. Easy Company soldier Don Malarkey, still in Belgium and attempting to reunite with his outfit, was in the town of Verviers when he heard the momentous news of German capitulation. "Belgians. Americans.

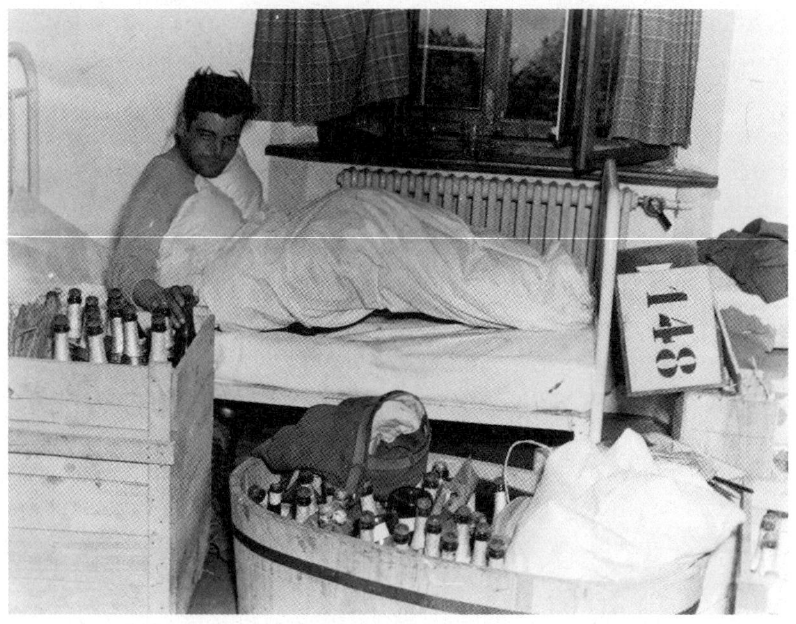

Lewis Nixon recovers from a spirited end to the war in Europe.

Brits. Canadians," he enthused. "All wrapped together in a sort of frenzied celebration born of pain and loss and a million memories we all wanted to forget but knew we never would." His only regret was that he was not with his comrades.[2]

Nearly 500 miles to the east, the survivors of the 506th PIR regaled with lavish supplies of captured food, alcohol, and enemy loot. In the days prior, the outfit streamed down the Autobahn toward Berchtesgaden, the idyllic community near the Austrian border that was a culturally symbolic landmark of the Reich's identity. Contrary to popular belief, the paratroopers were not the first Americans to enter the iconic Bavarian bastion of Nazism. That honor was bestowed upon the 7th Infantry Regiment of the 3rd Infantry Division, one of the most battle-tested units in the US Army. Elements of the 101st Airborne were not far behind. American troops removed the swastika from Hitler's flagpole, raised the stars and stripes, and then lowered them to half-staff in honor of President Roosevelt.[3]

The division marked its arrival in the alpine municipality with an air of jubilation. The men celebrated the impending conclusion of the war but also survival. Winters and Harry Welsh commandeered the luxurious Berchtesgadener Hof Hotel as regimental headquarters and subsequently absconded with a case of fine silverware from the dining hall. Souvenir hunting became sport in this hour of triumph. Dick's efforts of "really cracking down on the boys" to prevent flagrant drunkenness and carousing posed considerable challenges.[4]

GIs appoint themselves makeshift cavalrymen with liberated horses outside the deluxe Berchtesgadener Hof Hotel.

Hovering above Berchtesgaden was the *Kehlsteinhaus* (Eagle's Nest), Hitler's personal mountain retreat presented to him on his fiftieth birthday in 1939. At the nearby Berghof, Hitler's private residence, GIs looked out from the panoramic window offering a stunning view of the Alps. A May 7 *New York Times* article chronicled a correspondent's explorations of the buildings and passageways: "A reporter tried the one [entrance] behind the kitchen and stumbled down 300 steps, made three or four sharp turns in a white cement corridor and finally walked into the main quarters—a bizarre maze of winding brown-carpeted corridors that could have been born only in a madman's dream." Elsewhere the reporter found engraved silverware, fine linens, an elaborate wine cellar, and oil paintings by classical artists. The paratroopers occupied the strangely opulent environment with immense satisfaction. Winters had no compunction in seizing or occupying property for billeting. "Some people wouldn't approve of that," said Winters, "but after what we went through, I had no problems at all; my conscience didn't bother me."[5]

Even as the revelry swelled, many recognized that unfinished work remained. After all, another war against the Axis was still ongoing 6,000 miles away.

The Eagle's Nest: Adolf Hitler's plush mountaintop retreat at the Obersalzberg.

Winters (sitting, third from right) and officers of Easy Company enjoy the sunny splendor of the Alps at the Eagle's Nest.

The spoils of war.

16 May 1945

Dear "De"—

Well I am going to start a letter here and see how it goes one time. You see the three musketeers sit around the table here shooting the bull, so while it rolls on I'll see if I can make any sense out of this. The three are Irishmen—one Capt. Nixon, and Lt. Welsh and last of all the Major. Now Capt. Nixon is the biggest drunk I've ever seen, known, or hope to see. He's worth a small fortune, never'll have to work a lick in his life, but absolutely the most reliable man I've ever known. Welsh is as bull-headed as you'd expect an Irishman to be.

Now what do we talk about? Well this evening it's not bad, old battles, transferring to another outfit in the So. Pacific, talking about snafu officers we know and have known. Then about putting on some flashy review with pigeons being released as the colors pass the reviewing stand, and buglers blasting out from the top of one of these Alps and let the music bounce around in the valleys. Then about the loot, and about this and that and Nixon and myself agree the hell with going home—let's go to the C.B.I. and see how tough the Navy is having it down there. Welsh said he'd like to go along, but he has a little Irish lass back home who's supposed to be waiting for him. So, since love has all this power to make people go crazy, he's had it—poor boy!

The drink tonight is champagne 1928 and it's from our good friend Hermann Goering's place in Berchtesgaden, a fine fellow Hermann. As for myself, I am amusing myself practicing squeezing off shots with my new Luger pistol.

The other day I met a major from a German panzer unit. A true German, and one hell of a good soldier. We talked over tactics, soldiering in general, and were pleased to find that at Bastogne we fought each other tooth and nail. Quite a coincidence. He has been wounded six times so far, but he's one hell of a good soldier. Tomorrow he's going to give me his pistol as a formal surrender between the two of us rather than lay the pistol on a desk in some office someday in the future.

What say you come on over for a little vacation. Now if you like the mountains, you'd love this. You could have any cottage, castle, or home you'd want in this valley or the three others in my sector fifty miles by thirty miles. If you'd want to take an airplane ride, boat ride, automobile, jeep, tank, go horse back riding, [or] mountain climbing all you'd have to do is say the word and your every wish would be my desire. You could have any number of servants you wanted. In fact you wouldn't have to worry about how many you need. I'd just arrange it all, so you wouldn't have to lift a finger. That's the spoils of war, the price of defeat for the loser, and payment for the victor. So it goes. Now let's see how the other half of the world looks, and how good the Japs really are. If they are as dumb as I hope they are, the only thing a fellow has to worry about is malaria. Then I guess there'll be nothing to do but face the home front. That I am afraid will be the one that'll get me, for I won't feel at home among civilized people who won't be able to understand how a soldier thinks and feels. What do you think will be the outcome of soldiers coming home?

Love
Dick[6]

Winters embarked on a thought-provoking roam through the lounges and studies of Germany's most nefarious leaders. The landmarks were deceiving in appearance. The homes and terrain resembled vignettes from ancient folk tales, yet sinister plans were devised on these terraces. *Reichsmarschall* Hermann Göring's lodge was badly damaged by Allied bombing, but his private wine and liquor cellar nearby remained intact. According to his memoirs, Winters discovered the subterranean stockpile while conducting a nonchalant jeep patrol. Cautiously wandering down a stone staircase, Dick was astonished by the sight. "Lord, I had never seen anything like this before," he confessed. "This high room, about fifty feet long and thirty feet wide, contained rack upon rack of liquor, wines, champagne, all the way to the ten-foot-high ceiling." Perhaps 100,000 bottles were shelved there.[7]

Dick was not about to let the spirits be wasted. First seeing to other business, Winters eventually unveiled the cache to Lewis Nixon, who was known to enjoy fine liquor. Dick instructed Nix to take what he pleased and distribute the remainder among the companies. Nixon executed the orders with pleasure. David Webster recalled the moment with similar zeal. In May 1952, the *Saturday Evening Post* published his colorful account of liberating Nazi booze. The article was fittingly entitled, "We Drank Hitler's Champagne."[8]

With 25,000 prisoners charged to his supervision, Dick coordinated the logistical process from Kaprun, Austria, an equally bucolic community some fifty miles south of Berchtesgaden. Initially fearful of Nazi diehards waging guerilla warfare from the mountains, Winters discovered most German soldiers simply wished to go home. When Dick accepted the surrender of a "hell of a good" enemy major, he was pleased to discover the officer's abdicated sidearm had never been discharged. "There was no blood on it," Winters insisted. "That's the way all wars should end—an agreement with no blood on it." Winters retained the pistol as a prized memento the rest of his life. He never fired it.[9]

No censorship.

20 May 1945
Kaprun, Austria

Dear De–

Finally, they've lifted the censorship so this is the first letter since I've been overseas that I can talk about the places I've been and seen and where I am at the present time. It's a good feeling. You almost feel like writing a letter.

Now, when I came to England I landed at Liverpool and went to a little country town in Wiltshire, England, called Aldbourne, near Swindon. We stayed there until we went to Normandy. Landed just on the outskirts of a little town called St. Mere Eglise [*sic*], the hottest place in the world at that time. If you look back in the newspapers they'll tell you quite a bit about American troopers being hung, etc. around there. It's all true. Then we fought on down to the beachheads and our objectives and later on into Carentan.

Before returning to England, I had a week near Cherbourg, and then back to England.

When I went to Holland I hit near Zon, Holland, and the next day went into Eindhoven—I led that one personally. Then I fought east of the town, and then up to Nuenen and Veghel. Then at Uden my company was surrounded and cut off after we'd been in Holland for about four days. Then we went up to Nijmegen and the Island where we sat and fought off counterattacks from the north and east. At that time our strength was low and our front big. It was at this time I had the biggest thrill of the war when I took a squad (12 men) and beat the devil out of a machinegun crew, then brought up two more squads (40 men in all), and attacked two companies of SS troops across 175 yds. of open field and cut them all to pieces. That was the payoff of it all.

Shortly after that I was made Bn. Exec. Officer and we proceeded to sit out a total of 73 days of continuous war, without relief. That was hell on nerves.

Then we went to a camp near Rheims [*sic*], France. On that trip I saw Brussels and all big towns in between. Back from Holland two weeks, all weapons, ammo, and equipment in for inspection and repair, and with the Bn. C.O. in England, we got a 12 hour notice at 2400 on the

17th of December, that we were moving out. We did. The C.O. caught us on the way. Not all men had weapons, we had only a little rifle ammo, some had none, no mortar ammo, and no winter clothes to speak of.

We drove into Bastogne, got off the trucks and into one of the most confused fights I've ever been in, outside of Normandy. That of course was a cold, hungry deal, and then to top it off we attacked and took Noville and Rachamps, when we were half our strength. Then the prospects of a second bulge took form down around Haguenau in Alsace-Lorraine. [S]o what do they do? Zip, down we go and hold that line. By February they shipped us back to Rheims. We left there the start of April and went down to the Ruhr pocket and helped clean that up. That is the most beautiful and rich country I've ever seen, along that Rhine River. While there I saw Cologne and Frankfurt, and they're a mess. Nothing there at all. Then we shipped south again, Stuttgart, Ulm, Munich, Berchtesgaden, and now, Kaprun, Austria, near Bruck, at Zell am See. This is something; it's so quiet. And despite the fact that I have 25,000 Krauts under my charge, there seems like nothing to do, no reason to work.

That's about it, the big picture. I fought [well] with every army on the Western Front but the French 1st [Army]. I fought with them once and that's enough, thank you. What a wild outfit that is.

You know where to come now if you want to find me. I think one of these days I'll run up to Innsbruck and through the Brenner Pass to Italy. And I'd like to see Yugoslavia.

Fraternization, of course, is out around here but what do you think of my little girlfriend here? Cute? [An enclosed postcard showed a German boy and girl sitting in the mountains.] Only trouble is, it looks like I've a little competition and this Dutchman seems to have a lot on the ball. That something that he's got that I don't have is

Love,
Dick[10]

Like a repressed historian eager to set the record straight, Dick offered an overview of his European travels to DeEtta for the first time. Thanks to the curtailing of censorship, he was finally granted the opportunity to openly reflect. In a subsequent letter, he outlined some of his battlefield heroics after learning DeEtta visited the White House. "But don't think you'll ever have to be looking for a place to stand when I get decorated by the President," he warned. "For yours truly that will never happen, I hope." Dick suspected he "came very close to achieving" the Medal of Honor not once, but twice. "In Normandy I was as hot as a baked potato. It scares me when I think back on what I did....But at that time they thought you had to kill an army and we had no setup for writing decorations up," he rationalized.

In Dick's view, his second instance of supreme gallantry occurred in October 1944. "In Holland when I made that bayonet charge," he continued, "if I'd have had a machinegun instead of an M-1, I'd have had the better part of 250 Krauts, I feel sure. As it was I only got two clips (sixteen rounds) of Krauts, but a few shots got more than one. All came out O.K. for I had my small group and machineguns coming up and we cleaned them up, and that's the object anyhow."

Winters then mocked his own reminiscences to DeEtta: "Oh him, sounds like a broken G.I. talking for a few beers." He added, "I don't think I want the Congressional Medal of Honor. For a paratrooper, it costs you about two of those 9 lives we're supposed to have. I feel like I've used all nine already and it's only due to an administrative error that I am still here." For Winters, the fortunes of durability sufficed as the ultimate reward.[11]

Interview with 13th Airborne for transfer.
(They are scheduled for C.B.I.)

26 May 1945
Kaprun, Austria

Dear DeEtta–

So you've found yourself a secluded little spot all your own, so convenient, yet so nice. That always gives me a feeling of satisfaction, to find a place like that myself, one where you're alone with your own thoughts and moods and where no one else can observe or study you. At times, in combat, you become just a bit frustrated when you realize that you can't get away from telephones, noise, questions, decisions, and people in general. If you can just take a walk alone, it usually helps, but in combat it's just too dangerous, so you lose yourself in your work and forget about your feelings.

[...] Tomorrow afternoon I plan to go deer hunting with an old sgt. of mine in Easy Co., one of my favorite soldiers. It isn't the hunt, but I enjoy being out with this boy. We don't have to talk to enjoy each other's company, nor do we have to talk in combat or during battle. A word or two, or wave of the hand, and we know what the other guy's thinking. That makes working just lovely.

Say, by the way, this A.M. I had an interview with Maj. Gen. Chapman, C.O. of the 13th A.B. Division. I wanted to transfer. I figured they were hot and going to the So. Pacific, straight and quick. However, it looks like everybody goes through the States first, so that means I just can't cut any corners on that count. Stuck, damn it! He did say he'd be glad to have me if his outfit left and the 101st was scheduled to stay in the States. So—there I am, no further ahead than before, but a bit wiser for my trouble.

Can't figure you women out. Here you tell me that most women don't want men to know they read. Yet you admit that is just a bluff for all women are very brainy. Very subtle, I call it.

C.B.I. means China, Burma, India. That's where I'd like to go next. Going along, salty?

All is not gold that glitters, or all that glitters is not gold. Either way, the meaning's the same. Don't knock yourself out worrying about being an officer. What difference does it make? If you don't feel it necessary to pad your ego or your self-confidence by becoming an officer, the devil with it. Forget it. Who cares but yourself? Do what you think is right and you're O.K. I find there is about 1 out of 1,000 that has anything that even resembles brains.

[...] I received your second package the other day with the second batch of three quarter sleeve shirts and sweat shirt. All fit just fine. I realize you're not an army pup, but is it possible for you to buy service ribbons, etc? If you can, how's about seeing if you can find a place to get one strip of D.S.C. and Bronze Star, and a second with Purple Heart, pre-Pearl Harbor, and E.T.O, ribbon with an arrowhead on the right hand side and four campaign stars.

D.S.C.	Bronze Star

-Roger?

Purple Heart	Pre-Pearl Harbor	△ ☆☆☆☆

European Theatre of Operation

Also, a presidential citation with one cluster. Can't buy the stuff over here and here I am without any—lost it.

Well, sailor, let's keep those radishes and tomatoes well-watered and free of weeds and maybe I'll decorate you with the blue ribbon for first prize for the best garden and the best suntan. ---- I'll have to get one of those things myself.

As ever,
Love,
Dick[12]

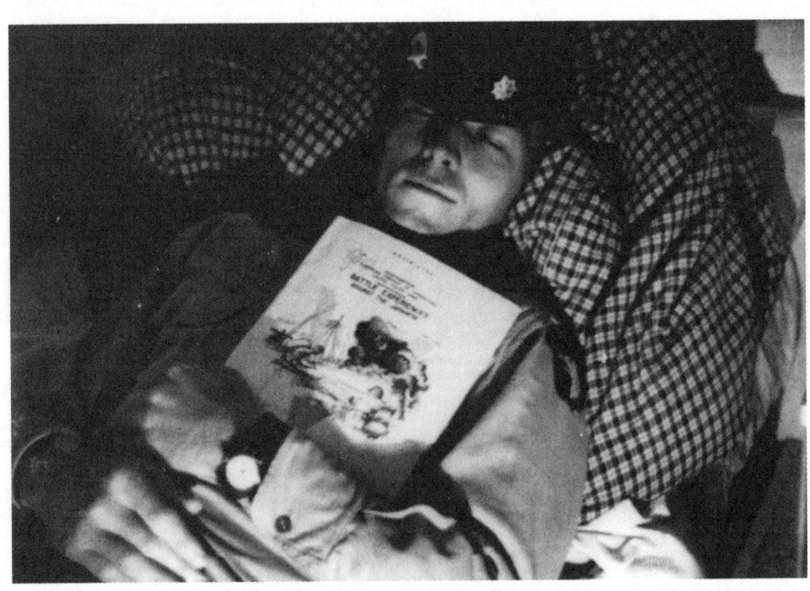

Winters falls asleep in his Kaprun quarters while reading Battle Experiences Against the Japanese.

Dick's attempts to transfer to the 13th Airborne Division and hasten his journey to the Pacific did not conclude in the manner he had hoped. Maj. Gen. Elbridge Chapman's interpretation of Winters's record was that he already had done his share. If the 101st transferred to the Pacific, Dick's men deserved to have him along for the ride. In any case, the 13th Airborne never saw a day of combat.

The "old sergeant" Winters affectionately described was Floyd Talbert. Dick held Talbert in high esteem ever since the early days at Toccoa. The two men "developed a personal relationship that transcended rank. Talbert was athletic and dedicated," Winters recalled. "You knew if your life were on the line, he would come through." Talbert expressed the full extent of their camaraderie when he wrote prior to his death in 1982, "Dick, you are loved and will never be forgotten by any soldier who ever served under you. You are the best friend I ever had."[13]

Friendship was most poignantly exhibited when comrades were in danger. While driving his truck on May 27 near Saalfelden, Sgt. Chuck Grant encountered a drunken Company I private, Floyd W. Craver, by a vehicle he stole. Craver discharged his souvenir Luger at the truck and, when confronted by Grant, the private shot the unarmed sergeant in the forehead. That same day, Craver, (doped on marijuana) murdered a decommissioned German officer (owner of the car) and a British passerby. Capt. Ronald Speirs rushed Grant to a civilian surgeon after being informed by an army doctor there was no hope for the patient. Craver was apprehended not far from the hospital where Grant was ultimately saved. Incensed by the near-death of the beloved and dependable Grant, the men of Company E almost summarily executed the gunman. Winters found the situation tragically ironic. The war was over yet people continued to die.[14]

What we do/what we talk about.

29 May 1945
Kaprun, Austria

Dear DeEtta–

Received your letter of the 21st tonight, which is damn good, and I think I am right on the ball in shooting one right back at you.

Reason: 1) Just plain glad to receive your letter. 2) Received orders tonight that I am now the proud wearer of the Bronze Star. In addition, I am in for another. So, if on filling that request I made of you last week for some ribbons, how's about seeing if you can put a cluster on that Bronze Star? Also, don't forget those four stars and the arrowhead in the E.T.O. ribbon. 3) Received a few pictures from one of the boys this evening which I thought you might want to start a fire with. My gosh, I'm beginning to look like man o' war!

Now, here the boys go again talking about old battle experiences. Doesn't matter what the conversation starts out about, it isn't long until it turns to combat. Funny thing, you'd think the conversations would become boresome, but not to us. We talk the same battles over and over, just like you Waves talk about last night's date, movie, or that so and so officer.

That trip to D.C. you had when you saw "Sing Out, Sweet Land," sounds like a good time. In fact your hitchhiking experiences remind me of old times at Croft.

30 May 1945

Sorry, Salty, but that bull session was just a bit too much, so I had to stop and then hit the sack.

Life isn't too bad the past week. Up about 0700, breakfast, paperwork, inspect guards, kitchens the rest of the A.M. After a little lunch, fool around for a while, and then take a sunbath for a few hours while I read or just lie and think. That's what I really enjoy, just drifting around thinking of nothing in particular. In the evening we play a volleyball game, after which I take a run, some exercises, and then we shoot the bull, maybe try and write a letter or read, but it's really just a lot of foolish talk.

At the present time we're (Nixon and I) ribbing Lt. Welsh about marrying an Irish girl by the name of Kitty Grogan. He hopes to be married inside of four months. We're carefully explaining that some 4F will grab her off before that. If he does manage to get married, we promise to steal the bride for the balance of his leave unless he hires us to protect him from others who may have the same intentions. Price is 1 qt. of scotch for Nixon and 1 qt. of ice cream for myself. He doesn't take us seriously.

Last night one of the officers reached the point where he thought he was a Jap spy. Pretty good show.

Say, those bottles you see on the table belong to the boys, not me. I am still a non-drinker. That stuff comes from old Hermann Goering's place.

Well, my little farmer, it's time to hit the hay so I can get up and make hay while the sun shines. You have the cows milked and breakfast ready—two eggs and toast.

Dick[15]

Nixon and Winters reading and reminiscing in Kaprun, Austria. Winters refrained from the alcohol.

Late-night bull sessions regularly occurred among the men once hostilities ceased. As many had done in their correspondence, they began to make sense of their experiences. The special bond they shared became all the more conspicuous as these conversations of brotherhood unraveled. That *esprit de corps* forged amid the challenges of military life resonated decades later at reunions. Unit cohesion was fundamental in forming these emotional ties. During the war, American airborne units proportionately suffered the lowest psychiatric casualty rates in the nation's armed services. The sense of togetherness instilled in paratroopers from the outset possibly contributed to that outcome.

In the view of war correspondent Sebastian Junger, "If war were purely and absolutely bad in every single aspect and toxic in all its effects, it would probably not happen as often as it does. But in addition to all the destruction and loss of life, war also inspires ancient human virtues of courage, loyalty, and selflessness that can be utterly intoxicating to the people who experience them." Winters similarly recognized those traits in his ranks.[16]

Welsh and Nixon mix the drinks for tonight
(Vodka, Rum, Vermouth).

2 June 1945
Kaprun, Austria

My favorite Wave–

Tonight is a night to remember. I am really on the ball with the pen and paper stuff. After supper I knocked off a lot of administrative work. Then knocked out three letters—Mother, a neighbor who'd just sent a box of candy, and "Mother" Barnes, my English mother. Then a good two mile run, calisthenics, a little wrestling, a good hot bath and now I feel like saying a good night to you before hitting the sack.

It seems to me I've relaxed a bit in [the] past week. Got rid of my two divisions of kraut prisoners. So now our work is almost done as far as getting this, our final area (I hope), in shape. So I've let the men concentrate chiefly on resting. In fact I've taken a few afternoons off myself for mountain climbing and sunning. How lovely it is just to look at those snow-capped mountains, and watch a cloud or two bump into an Alp. Nothing more than my own boys to worry about. They're such nice, quiet lads that they're really no trouble at all.

Enclosed you'll find a picture of Kaprun and White C.P. [Code for the Battalion Command Post]. In reality it's not quite as picturesque as it might appear here. In fact it's quite ordinary.

I've mentioned Capt. Nixon I believe, of Nixon, N.J. [W]ell I've got him writing his first letter since last Nov. to his wife. Quite a guy, he's having one hell of a time getting organized and down to work. Claims he hasn't anything to say to her, just to his dog. He has a baby boy that he's never seen, but he won't talk about his son, it's always his dog. Knowing you, why I know you could spend an enjoyable two or three hours talking about how awful he is—if you knew him. However I'll tell you he's idealistic. I've known him three years and lived and slept aside and fought with him for two. This guy loves one thing right at this stage of life: a bottle of spirits or a fight. He's OK in a fight, but Jesus, outside of that he's absolutely the most undependable man you'd ever want to find.

Since we've been overseas he's only run around with one girl. An English girl and she was anything but beautiful. However she was a good listener and companion. In fact I am not too sure but this guy might end up staying over here in England. Ah yes, things are really snafu—and don't ask me what that means.

Now here we have Welsh & Nixon mixing Vodka, rum & vermouth—oh boy it won't be long now.

Say look, cookie, what the hell is the hold up on this mail? A week and no mail. What is this, Army vs. Navy? Or are you working too hard on your garden? Personally, I don't know.

Love
"Dick"

P.S. This thing all kraut soldiers wear on the left breast.
[Edelweiss flower enclosed][17]

Nixon found comfort in the bottle during his marital strife. Upon return from an extended leave later that month, however, he seemed a new man. "Captain Nixon just got back from his leave in England," Dick reported to DeEtta on July 2. "Believe it or not, he looks better than I've seen him in six months, at least. His eyes are all asparkle [*sic*] and he's not near as bitter. Guess what? I think, in fact, I know, he's going to ask, or tell, his wife to go get a divorce and jump in the lake, and marry his E.T.O. wife." Winters was of the mind that Nixon's first spouse married him solely for his family's millions "and Nix, as a result, lost all faith in women. He hated them all." Nixon's second marriage was no less strained than his first. His third time was a charm. In 1956, he married Grace Umezawa, who was incarcerated alongside 110,000 fellow Japanese Americans when Nixon was overseas. The two enjoyed a fruitful marriage until Nixon's death in 1995.[18]

With the war drawing to a close, romance was on the minds of many. DeEtta may have had ambitions of her own in that regard. In reply to one of her summer letters, Dick responded, "So a couple of army officers tried to pick you and your girlfriend up? Interesting, to say the least." He then offered commentary on new fraternization guidelines his soldiers had to abide by. "The boys can be seen with displaced persons providing they have their arm bands on and are registered. Really messes things up, I should say." Dick thought the order ridiculously degrading and unrealistic for displaced people who wished to interact with GIs. "That's the sort of thing that makes me blow a fuse once in awhile," he howled. "Sometimes I get something accomplished, but generally, like this time, I just make myself heard but nothing happens. It's the sort of thing that makes me believe I don't belong in the army after all."

Winters possessed no talent along the lines of fraternization. "When it comes to combat, I go along beautifully," he explained. "Can understand things and movements, and plans just come naturally. In garrison, I like the soldiering part, but as for social activities, I am a Class A flop." Despite any insecurities about his lack of social skills, he concluded, "Looking forward to another D-Day and you." Enclosed in the envelope was a small leaf of edelweiss, an Alpine mountain flower symbolic of purity and soldier nobility.[19]

Regardless of Dick's imperfections, his next letter to DeEtta underscored the true extent of their warm friendship. The note is one of his most heartfelt and revealing messages.

"You're so damn understanding."

Tuesday evening
19 June 1945
Kaprun, Austria

Dearest De–

What a gal. What a friend. You thank me so beautifully and write such nice letters all because I was thoughtful enough to write you a couple of old stinky, dry lines. Most likely didn't say anything that was interesting. In fact, I'll bet outside of talking about myself, I didn't say a thing. Then in return you write me letters like this.

Well, tonight I am paying you the highest tribute I can think of, being in my present position. I am writing one letter tonight, my first in two weeks, and it's to you. Normally, and any other time, I'd write to my mother, and then another night to you. Maybe it's because of the moon and all the stars that are out tonight.

You know, I am beginning to understand why I like to receive and read your letters so much and why I enjoy your friendship. During the past year I didn't stop to dream about abstract and beautiful thoughts. So writing to you was just like writing to a sister, no more, no less. I didn't feel one way or the other. Now I realize a little why I've enjoyed your line. You're so damn understanding!

When I went overseas you seemed to know and feel homesickness as I did; you felt a change in weather, customs of the English, the pinch of ice cream and candy; and then before D-Day, you felt the tightness of nerves that comes from waiting, which was something I didn't fully realize existed. I'll never forget your one letter saying, "and when you're in a tight spot, remember you've got to come back." So, by gosh, what happened in the biggest and toughest fight I was ever in? I am so pooped I can hardly walk after three nights and four days of no rest, and I am running through an actual hail of bullets, two or three times an hour, and I am not kidding, it was a hail. This one time I am halfway through and a machine gun opens up on me, down I go, and he thinks he has me, I am playing dead, and what do I think, yep, she said I've gotta come through. Here I am today—lucky fellow. For that day's work and several others they recommended me for the Congressional Medal of Honor. I got the D.S.C. instead, but today they've been giving them away compared to some of the deeds and awards I've seen in the past.

Then, damn it, you were so glad when I was promoted and if I was in England, Holland, Bastogne, or Hell, you always understood how I was feeling. Then when I went to Paris on a 48 hr. pass one time, you understood how I felt and what I should have done—just blow my top completely, like everybody else does. And you even told me that's O.K., you deserve a party, enjoy yourself. That burnt me up, I don't know why, perhaps because you understood, and yet you knew damn well my conscience wouldn't let me do it.

Now the war is over, my mother writes and tells me, "don't go to the South Pacific, you've done your part, be smart and come home." She writes that before she even received my letter telling about volunteering. What will she think or say when she does hear? In the same mail you write, you've already heard of my plans and as usual, you understand. Damn it, how can you always be so understanding? That's just what I needed, understanding and sympathy, for I felt pretty bad about disappointing my mother.

But, I am sure she doesn't understand. I am not going down there for the trip or any personal gain. I feel that God has been good enough to let me go through this war. As a result, I am combat wise and in a position to do some good to help a lot of men. I know I can do the job, better than, or as well as, any of the rest. How can I sit back and see others take men out and get them killed because they don't know; they don't have "it." Maybe I'll get hurt or killed for my trouble, but so what if I can make it possible for many others to go home. Their mothers want them too, the same as me. So what else can I do and still hold my own self respect as an officer and a man?

So, once again, thanks.

This isn't what you want to hear or have me write. Actually, I should write all about love, and how sweet you are, and all that stuff. I could if I wanted to. I know all those words from movies and magazines. But that wouldn't be right. I don't feel that way and I am in no position, and

I don't want you to think that way. What I want is for you to get married to some good guy who comes along. There are always a couple around. You need a husband and a family to be really happy. Those ideas about college and getting a degree after you're out of the navy, you're crazy, and you know it. You don't want that any more than you want to make the navy a life's work.

Now it's barely possible that I might come home before the South Pacific, and I am definitely going, for this unit was picked, so I don't even have to transfer. Now, suppose it does. If I have a week, 10 days, 15 days, I most likely wouldn't even think of spending three or four days traveling around to see you or going to N.Y., to see some sights. Hell, no, all I want is home life and no traveling around at all. I don't want to even see a crowd, a pair of O.D. pants, or think about moving. All I could do is drink up some of that home atmosphere. If I had 30 days, I'd most likely get a bit restless and fed up with home and want to pay you a visit.

So you see how it is. I like and enjoy seeing you write, "love, De" and all that stuff, but I don't want you to actually feel that way because it's just going to end up with you being hurt. And goodness knows, you've been hurt enough times before and I don't want to do a thing like that to anybody, and especially a swell egg like yourself. As a matter of fact, I wouldn't even kiss a girl's hand, for as a soldier I don't want any more people than possible to even know me. It's no good. If a soldier lives, O.K., get out of the army and forget it. If he doesn't, O.K. there are just that fewer people [who] feel the toll of war.

But this is getting all very sad and depressed like, which is no good. I just want you to understand the score and stop playing faithful or anything similar. I don't want it. I'd rather see you happily married.

Had a wonderful leave in England. Went straight to Aldbourne and spent seven beautiful days right there. Went to town once to a show. The rest of the time I just puttered around in the garden and cut grass, and slept. Oh boy! The day I was supposed to leave, the plane didn't show up. So I spent the evening in London, the most lonesome night I've had in years. All air corps men, and not a man or soldier in the bunch. I couldn't talk to any of them, they're boys, kids, no depth. Hell, I quit and found a corner in the lounge to myself and read. Nuts!

It's 0100 and time to hit the sack. You understand, I know, my

Love,
Dick[20]

The potentials and complications of romantic notions aside, Winters remained focused on his tasks as a leader. His earnest expressions of duty and commitment emphasized unwavering conviction in the national cause. Dick's willingness to fight in the Pacific displayed his comfort in wielding authority and a wish to prevent the misery of less experienced officers.

Inner strength and steadfastness did not spare him from an emotional farewell to troopers at month's end, however. "[T]omorrow all 85 point men leave and quite a few of the old boys have been dropping in to say goodbye," he wrote to DeEtta. "It's a good thing you weren't around to see that one. You'd think we were a bunch of schoolgirls. If you'd heard some of the things they had to tell me, you'd understand why I want to stick around and see the end of this war out in the front line. They sure appreciate—everything." The feeling was mutual.[21]

"While in the Alps I find a church of my own."

28 June 1945
Kaprun, Austria

Hi Squirt–

What a break. Last night about this time I start writing you a letter. I am going along good about 0015 when in comes the S-1 with a big problem and so I drop the letter. This evening all I can find is the start of page two.

Sort of forgot what I was going to say now but Sunday I did pick up a flower for you. Bet you never saw one like it. It's called elde-something [edelweiss]. It's one of the few flowers to grow in the snow, above the tree line, in the Alps. Patches of these are really beautiful, along with flowers of blue, red, and yellow.

Sunday I did some real mountain climbing, right out of this world. Got a guide and we went up to a mountain lodge, where I send 15 men every five days to learn how to ski and to hunt. These men are on their own, no officers, nobody but a cook, a few servants, and two instructors. They're so far away nobody would think of bothering them so they can really relax. Well, this guide and I went to the lodge and then up and up. I left at 0500 in the A.M. and returned at 2230. I was one tired cookie with all that climbing and my ankle still weak and stiff. So that's where the little flower that is so rare comes from, only I don't know the name offhand.

Oh, yes, I told you on the lost page about my delay en route to the South Pacific. Seems like I'll be here until January, then have Feb. off at home, then assemble at Ft. Bragg. So stand by the anchor. I'd still transfer if it would get me there any quicker, but I am afraid it wouldn't and besides it's almost impossible to transfer.

Had a good sock on the chin today, but I felt it had to come. You see, they've broken up two other parachute divisions and one regiment in this division, so that left a lot of Lt. Col.'s without a job. Col. Sink tried like hell to keep 'em off, but today we got one. So now I am Bn. Exec. again. I don't feel at all chagrined but I am afraid the other officers and men are. But perhaps I shouldn't say that and be more modest.

I've got lots of good pictures now of combat and things and places I've seen. One of my friends fixed me up. All went home, but sometime I'll show them off.

Enclosed you will find a snap of my C.P. on V-E Day at Berchtesgaden.

Nice juicy letters I am receiving nowadays. No, damn it, those shirts you sent are just right. They're not too big. But what are those buttonholes along the bottom for? Do these bellhops hold something up with them, or the shirttail down? Any way at all, it's silly.

You can tell those gals they don't have to worry about their boys getting married overseas. And my dear dumb nitwit, that isn't why they have a non-fraternization policy over here. It goes a little further than that. I don't believe out of 600 men (30% married), that over 10 have been married. All those were to English girls. And in about 6 cases, they drew a lemon, I'd say. Something that should come with a sack where they really wear a hat.

You sound as though it's hot back there. Over here, as I've told you before, the sun is good and warm but the mountain breeze keeps things moving. We always sleep with two blankets.

On Sunday was running around hunting mountain goat on a pair of skis and in a pair of shorts. Lovely! You'd like that ski lodge. It's right out of this world.

While in the mountains I found a church of my own. The aisle is two mountain ranges down which you can see for 10 miles at least. At the end there's just a series of mountain peaks. A storm came up and the dark clouds covered everything but the far end, where the sun shone through on those many peaks. The color was all shades of rose, a light, soft, rose, nothing hard or bright, but just rays of light coming through the clouds. They were the most beautiful stained glass windows I've ever seen, or hope to see. What a wonderful place to pray. What a magnificent church. I'll never forget it.

Well, Skipper, it's precisely 2400 and high time this boy hits the sack. Had a nice workout again this evening and that usually takes the ginger out of me. Starting to get in pretty good shape again, 174. Just ten pounds off my fighting weight and I could make that in three, four days. How's your fighting form? Don't answer that.

Sweet dreams,
Dick[22]

Winters (far left) and comrades enjoy summertime skiing near Kaprun.

"I find myself changing as the weeks go by," Dick observed later that week. "I was really bitter and put out with everybody and everything." The bureaucracy, the prisoners, his unsuccessful transfer, and the shooting of Sgt. Grant exerted considerable strain in these supposed days of peace. Dick escaped high into the mountains to find seclusion, serenity, and even a hint of spiritualism.[23]

He wrote to DeEtta on July 9, "Over the weekend I accomplished something I've always wanted to do, shot myself a nice mountain goat, a bull. That's real sport. Of course, on two occasions, the government almost had to pay my $10,000 [GI Insurance Policy]." While hunting alongside a local guide, Winters slipped in the snow and nearly plummeted to his death. "It cost me one nice, clean-cut front tooth, many bumps and bruises, water on one knee, and a very tired body....Looks like hell now and I can't talk very clearly." Only temporarily fazed by his stumble, Winters still bagged the goat he was stalking. Its horns are on display today at the Hershey-Derry Township Historical Society, not far from Dick's postwar home.[24]

Having averted death's grasp over the course of multiple campaigns, Winters was glad not to have been outdone by an Austrian mountain goat.[25]

CHAPTER EIGHT

TO GO HOME

July 1945 and Onward

"There is a difference between a Distinguished Service Medal and a Distinguished Service Cross."

3 July 1945
Kaprun, Austria

Dear De–

Received those lovely ribbons this evening and they are just that—lovely. They're the best looking ribbons I've seen anybody have, and that includes the generals. However, they have just a few more. One thing though, I am not sure, but I think you got me the Distinguished Service Medal. I am authorized the Distinguished Service Cross. The first is for good work shuffling papers and fountain pens under terrific strain and for long hours. The D.S.C. is for valor in action, you know, for shooting people. If you hit so many ducks, you get the Bronze Star, a few more, the Silver Star, then the D.S.C. Understand? If you'd be good enough to let me know the damage, I'd like to settle up. I mean for those shirts, ribbons, and all the paper, envelopes, etc.

This weather around here has been really something, raining every day for the past two weeks. Ye gods, but I am getting tired of it raining. Most days it just rains all the time, others it teases a fellow fifteen minutes per hour. The only thing that keeps me from going crazy is to ignore the whole thing and go out and run around a bit. In fact like tonight, a two mile run in the rain, followed by a bath, has taken the edge off. Of course people think I am nuts. I might be surprised someday if I found out they're right.

This displaced person problem is easing up quite a bit. We've sent most of them home, so I feel better as far as the local situation is concerned.

Did I tell you, the other day I bought a beautiful pair of binoculars called Zeiss, supposed to be the best, for $75. They're 8x40 if that means anything to you. But you can depend on it, they're good, or I wouldn't buy them over here when I already have a decent pair at home.

Going up to my hideout over the weekend and getting away from that damn telephone and do a little mountain goat hunting. Of course the only trouble is it's about a fifteen mile walk, and then you must get up around 0300 and get out to the hunting ground by 0400–0430. But that's just ideal for a doughboy's holiday.

Well, it's 0035 and I know you'd rather that I get my rest than sit around scribbling like this, but I did want to let you know how much I really appreciated those ribbons and all the trouble you went to in getting them. I take a lot of pride in things like that, being an officer, so thanks a lot.

If there's anything I can get for you over here, say the word. Don't be bashful. Won't promise a thing, but I'll always give it a try.

Sweet dreams and
Love,
Dick

[1996]: After reading my own mean letters of 1945—I have the nerve to call you a brat? I deserve to lose a front tooth![1]

Winters's July 3 letter is ripe with sardonic humor. His tone suggests ease regarding the war's conclusion but aggravation with ongoing military bureaucracy. Blunt specificity about service ribbons is equally revealing. He did not want to be mistaken as an officer who sought safety and comfort behind the lines or a desk.

When veterans returned home, civilians often greeted them with curious inquiries about what each ribbon signified. Innocent illiteracy on the subject of decorations highlighted disconnection between soldiers and civilians. Speaking of his buddies who returned home as the war was ongoing, Marine Eugene Sledge remarked, "[T]he gist of their disillusionment was a feeling of alienation from everyone but their old comrades.... Plenty of people were ready to buy a Marine combat veteran wearing campaign ribbons and battle stars a drink or a beer anytime. But all the good life and luxury didn't seem to take the place of old friendships forged in battle." In the coming months, Winters would be able to relate to that sentiment all too well.[2]

Zielinksi, my orderly, delivering the mail—
"Nine from the Navy today."

8 Aug 1945
Joigny, France

Dear De–

[...] What the hell am I talking about? Can you tell me?

One reason I haven't been writing for the past few weeks is that I traveled up and down the continent exactly three times inside of two weeks. Need I say I was bored, tired, and sore, you know where. Had to take a large convoy of trucks to Paris for redeployment to the Pacific. It was a mess. Everybody turned in their worst trucks and tires. No tools to change tires, and for drivers, the 8 balls. I worked my head off keeping that mob together and at the same time, I drove them right into the ground. By the time I returned those boys to Austria, they knew just what an officer in the paratroops was like, dominating as hell! You see, they all were from outside of the division.

Col. Sink was quite pleased with the job though, and let me have a couple days to rest up and then let me come up in a special chartered plane. The regiment moved for France by rail the day after I returned.

Joigny is 80 miles S.E. of Paris. Like any other France town, it's hot, dirty, and, being French, I can't say anything good about it. I am prejudiced.

Quarters here are terrible for the men, crowded, dirty. Latrine facilities actually don't exist. This 13th A.B. just dug holes, but our inheritance finds no more space for holes, so I am stealing lumber and equipment to build a "honey bucket" latrine. Ever hear of one before? No? Well someday I'll explain in detail. Washing for the men—two little faucets about 100 yards from their quarters, and that's all. Damn, they lived just like pigs. Nobody gave a damn, evidently. [Have] started building washstands and getting a gadget to have hot water to wash and shave under cover from the rain. This camp was a concentration camp before the liberation and the 13th A.B. was content to live like that for seven months.

My quarters are O.K. I got out and scrounged myself a lovely private billet. Clean as a pin, modern, and even on the beautiful side. Even have a private bathtub which is something that just was invented over here in the late thirties—mine's modern.

Chow in France is good. However, it's so warm that you can't eat much. It's not actually hot, but it's the change from the Alps that we're not just used to yet.

Water is a problem. Never drink it in France, or very little, if you do, for it'll gnaw the ____ right out of a fellow.

Women—ye gods, have never seen such hair do's in all my life. Fancy as hell, and all shades. You've seen red, yellow, black, I know, but did you ever see green and blue? For makeup they must use something like milk, it's chalky white anyway. The normal thing is to see a mother all slicked up, really sharp, dragging a little kid along who hasn't had its face washed for several days. Most likely she hasn't either, but the kid looks the worse for lack of makeup. I've never seen the men say this is too much for them but after Paris most of them are sick of women, for the time being at least. That place tops anything yet.

That thesis of yours on love is really good. Tell me more. It's something like being told the facts of life. But don't think I am going to be an easy prey to a bit of "fluff." There's one time I am going to have to use my head and not my heart. I've thought it over and I am getting set to look the herd over.

The idea of yours about marrying more of a friend than a lover is "solid." That's the stuff that makes "solid citizens." But couldn't [you] just throw in a little love into this thing? As it stands, the whole thing sounds sorta bare, barren, and too business-like to be much fun. Sounds more like the result of a business transaction brought about because it's the custom of the race, the human race.

So you don't have to bother with 4Fer's with all the sailors and marines next door. Maybe I am a victim of propaganda, but what's the difference between a sailor and a 4F? The marine doughboy, he's O.K., the rest I can't understand.

Well I have so many letters here from you that I feel as though I can't help but be spoiled. Received over two weeks mail at one time and there were "nine from the 'Navy'" my orderly told me. Can't answer them all at once, so I'll try again tomorrow.

Look inside the envelope again. See anything? Well, you should, for in each corner there's lots of

Love,
Dick

P.S. Booklet picked up on trip to Italy.[3]

Joigny, an ancient city on the banks of the Yonne River, was a final place of European residency for Winters. Located outside the commune, the American camp was lackluster in appearance and facilities. Dick immediately set forth to tidy the installation previously used as a forced-labor camp by the Nazis. In these postwar days, boredom was the new enemy. Winters did his utmost maintaining discipline and keeping men out of trouble—difficult tasks considering the levels of fraternization and inebriation. Dick largely turned a blind eye to the issue of carousing with civilians unless a serious breach of behavior occurred. Playing babysitter for soldiers without a war to fight was not his cup of tea.[4]

Two days prior to Dick composing his August 8 letter, a fifteen kiloton bomb ravaged Hiroshima, Japan. The nuclear age came to life with frightful capacity. Three days later the city of Nagasaki met a similar fate. Winters caustically expressed doubts over the use of the powerful mega weapons. Americans in all theaters of the war likely echoed the sentiments of Omar Bradley in a letter to Eisenhower: "It certainly didn't take long for the Japs to make up their minds after we started hitting them with atomic bombs." If anything *was* certain, Dick was no longer bound for Japan. His parents were glad.[5]

V-J Day–the war is over!

11 August 1945
Joigny, France

Dear De–

Here of late I am having an awful time getting around to writing letters. I finished my second letter home in five weeks this afternoon and last night I managed to write a decent letter to Mother Barnes. So this will bring me up to date for the time being.

Well, your prediction of my coming through the Pacific wars turned out to be correct, once for a change. It seems as though that atomic bomb carries as much punch as a regiment of paratroopers. It's almost inhuman to employ either on the human race. You think I am kidding? Well, just ask these French frogs. They're scared to death of these boys, despite the fact that we make an honest attempt to keep them in line. Sometimes I wonder how it's going to be the first time we turn them loose in the States. It's going to be a ticklish proposition. Maybe they'll be nice and sociable and happy and drunk. If they're disappointed and put out by the fact that things aren't as they expected, oh my ---

The only trouble is, they're so full of fun. Then there's this non-fraternization policy which means, of course, that all German, Austrian, Hungarian, and Russian women are out of bounds. That leaves Poles, Ruskies and French foreign laborers, and it's quite a problem to tell the difference between the nationalities. So I just say, no messing around at all. That covers it altogether, as far as I am concerned. However, I am army-wise enough to know that what goes on behind my back is more than just a little. But what I don't know doesn't hurt me, and as far as I am concerned the results are 100% O.K., that is on the surface. I ask for 100%, get maybe 40%, but to all appearances on the outside, it's as I wished.

After about three months of being chief around here, these people are sorta snapping to when they see me come. I am not exactly a grizzly bear, but if something is [not] right, somebody hears about it pronto.

The army has finally seen its way clear to give me seven days leave. I'd turned down a few offers to leave while at Mourmelon, France while we were resting. The war was still on and you never know when they'll call on an outfit. But now it's done, so they're fulfilling my request to visit my "second home" in England. It's the first break I've had in the way of a rest since England. It's the first break I've had in the way of a rest since Normandy. I did have a 48 hr. pass to Paris in Dec., but that's like running through a reception center. It's all army and, as a result, a series of lines to stand in and buck. This should be good, to fly to England, spend one night in London, see some shows, buy some clothes I need, then to Aldbourne, Wiltshire, by the second night.

Since I left there last fall, when we went to Holland, Mr. Barnes has died, leaving only Mother Barnes and her store. But I know she's saved my room and bed for me, just as I left it, and there'll be a cup of tea. Then next Sunday, I think, is Children's Sunday. Last year I left before we had this program. Here's hoping I make it this year. I've a lot of friends who will be taking part. Sometime you must visit Aldbourne. It's really what you'd hope to find in the way of an English village. There are many things I don't like about the British, their army, etc., but they also have some real people. Hope to hell you can read all this jumble of ----

Say, on your next trip to D.C., how's about picking up the D.S.C. and Bronze Star on a pin—like that last one that was the D.S.M. They sure look good. Just to be sure, I'll send this page of ribbons you sent some time ago. Did I tell you that Belgium has awarded us the *Fourragère* over Palm (a rope about the left shoulder)?

[...] Well, it's 2030 and if I don't get out and take a run now, it'll be too dark and then I'll have to sweat my ankle out on every little stone and rut. This habit of mine to run, creates no end of curiosity among the civilians. They do about everything but cheer as you go by.

It shouldn't be long now till they start letting all you pretty little Waves go home and do what you've been doing all this time on Uncle Sammy's payroll—nothing. That is, of course, unless you're going to be foolish enough to volunteer for that duty on the islands. In my opinion, that's a very foolish thing for a girl to do and they would most likely give me a stiff reprimand if they knew I'd said a thing like that or this. But if you use your pretty little head, you'll soon understand why they send WACS to Berlin or overseas in the first place. The biggest reason is to be social companions for our soldiers. The navy, I imagine, has the same problems on the islands. As I said before, time to close with

Love,
Dick[6]

The glow of victory faded. With Japan's final submission, Dick's main preoccupation was to reach home. He wrote on September 2, "Well, now that the war's all over, about which I couldn't really get excited, for one could see it coming sure as hell for the last two months, I am ready to get the hell out of the army." The wind was knocked out of his sails. His enthusiasm diminished. "In the paratroops, the money looks good," he added. "That's the end of it though, for it's a big party after that with a man growing lazy, both mentally and physically and going to hell fast. They can have it all, I'll dig ditches first." Dick strongly contemplated the next chapter of his life. The ever-faithful comrade Lewis Nixon presented at least one option—gainful employment at the Nixon Nitration Works in New Jersey. "I don't count on a thing until I have it," Dick confessed, "but it sounds good."[7]

Capt. Nixon left for home.
I'm as lonesome as a lovesick swab
who married a Wave on an eight hour pass.

16 Sept. 1945
Joigny, France

Dear De–

Glad to note in your 4 Sept. letter that you've been treating the soldiers to that southern style hospitality. They'll appreciate it, I know.

So you're wearing civies and having parades and inspections. My, my, leaves me speechless–with envy.

Do you know what this new ----- regimental C.O. has gone and done? Declared me essential. Why? Well you know all those nice things one can say at a time like that. Me, with 100 points as of V-E Day, and about the only officer in the regiment who has enough points to get out, and who doesn't want any part of the army, stuck until the division goes home. Which won't be this year. Boy, do you smell smoke? Don't worry, it's just me.

Capt. Nixon left this week, which makes everything just dandy. I am about as lonesome as a lovesick swab who married a Wave on an eight hour pass.

But, my fair and beautiful one, don't think I am stopped. This guy's really going to see a lot of me and it's going to be quite a battle of wits. Haven't started working yet for I've been so mad and burnt up that I'd lose my head. Waiting until I cool off and can rationalize and think on my feet, instead of just seeing red, before I start.

Going to make another jump this week, which will be the first in a year. One year ago today, we hit Holland on the nose and tried to hold open 180 miles of road so the British 2nd Army could make an end run. But they stopped for tea too often and didn't put enough (what do you Americans call it?) umph [into it]. Really not looking for an extra thrill nowadays but this will break the monotony of things around here. Gee, but it's boring. Quite a few of the men are going to refuse to jump on this one. Claim the chance isn't worth the money. Personally, I'd jump for $10 a go, and for $100 I'll land on my head. During the war if a man would refuse, it was S.O.P. (standard operating procedure)—the guardhouse, no pay, and at least six months. My, my, how things change. Now, they just say, not today, thank you. Oh well, I don't hold anything against them nowadays, if they're old combat men.

[...] You know, I am just as glad as anyone the war is over, but when I think back to what I was doing a year ago today, and tomorrow, and for the next 73 days, I wish I could relive some of those thrills and glows of satisfaction that fill a man when he's out-maneuvered, out-fought, and out-guessed Jerry. Great sport. Then there's the one like the Lt. I had in my company. I'd told him a hundred times in training, don't walk around out in front like that, you'll get it sure as hell. Tomorrow A.M., one year ago, I walked up front with him, showed him just how I wanted his platoon to cross this open field—½ mile—to the suburbs of Eindhoven. Compree? Ya. And he took off, but he didn't think, which was why most people get it. As I walked two hundred yards behind him, I remarked to some of the men, "He's going to get it." He did, about seconds later, right through the neck. Went down like he'd been hit with a baseball bat. Made one of my better decisions right then and there. I took over the platoon and pushed them forward to the town and sent back for another Lt. to replace him. Ended up I had to be with the lead platoon until we had the town. By pushing on we saved a lot more men and the medics were able to save that guy's life, although they thought he was dead for half an hour. Three cheers for me! But not too loud, please.

Another thing, I'll never spend another night like the one a year ago tonight. I was wet, through and through. And, naturally, being a paratrooper, I didn't have a change of clothes along. No blanket, nothing. And it was cold as a son-of-a-gun. Things were all snafued, walking around in the black of night, not knowing where you are exactly, where anybody else is, and houses burning, people crying (civilians), shaking your hand, and every bush a prospective enemy. Oh boy, I think I'll quit, hit the sack, and forget it all.

Better hold off on reserving those two seats at the theatre until I have a little heart to heart talk with some of my friends around here.

It isn't much fun, being good, but you better be good anyway. Why? Because, remember, you're a Wave, and all Waves are good kids. It helps the boys overseas to think that, at least there are a few decent women left in this world. But it is discouraging to the soldier to think that the Navy got 'em all.

Ah yes, such are the breaks of life. The poor doughboy never was appreciated by anybody but his mother.

Enclosed you will find a miniature major's leaf that I picked up in London. Don't know what good it could be to a Wave, but maybe sometime it'll be useful in holding something up, or something down, or even both at the same time.

Love,
Dick

P.S. Maybe one pin won't do the job, so if you need another for the other side, you can use the 506th P.I. regimental insignia with no fear, for a paratrooper never let anyone down.[8]

Nixon was gone and Dick was largely left to his own thoughts. Hardly any Toccoa men still stood at his side. The state of isolation and emptiness intensified by the day. Prior letters indicate the meditative mood Dick was in as his venerated chums journeyed Stateside. Other than basketball, softball, and running, daydreaming was about all there was to do during those lonely days in Joigny. Prior to his final exercise jump, Dick could not help but recall the grave circumstances of Lt. Bob Brewer, the tall and heedless officer shot through the neck during Market-Garden. The lesson Winters found in the anecdote was one of adherence. Those men who absorbed the advice of trustworthy commanders possessed greater potential as leaders and survivors. Brewer neglected this key precept and nearly paid for the lapse with his life.[9]

Long awaited news arrived late in September. Dick at last received orders to depart for America. Initially, he was at a loss for words. Surprise evolved into excitement, followed by unrest. His letter of September 26 highlighted his cabin fever. "Everything is set to go," he enthused. "Now if I can get that damn navy on the ball, I'll be home by the end of Oct. Yep, did it again. Saw the weak spot and using my sixth sense (had to, I lost my other five), I attacked and captured the objective: one trip home." Winters was one step closer to Lancaster.[10]

Your letters are always good for two pages of—
Giving me Hell!

29 Sept. 1945
Joigny, France

Dear De-

Well, this is my last Sat. night with the 506. I've spent quite a few just like I am spending this one, writing letters to you. Tonight they have a party, dance, and clambake. I've attended two parties. They held one in Mourmelon when they served supper at the party and I had to go.[...]The big problem, it seems, is to get nice girls for the dances. It's recognized, of course, that we can't get all nice girls, so the minimum is no lower than what's allowed at the E.M.'s (enlisted man's) parties. Ahem! That's a hard question to decide when an officer drags some new lady into the club. But, personally, I don't give a damn what they do or don't do.

As it stands, I'll be leaving 5 Oct., next Fri. Just where I go is evidently undecided as yet. Some say the E.M.'s to Reims and the 75th Div., and the officers to Marseille. I doubt that, for they should realize

we can handle them with tact, just bang 'em on the ear with my swagger stick, or ball bat, if one's handy.

[...] Nixon, N.J.? Beats me. Haven't the slightest idea. My dad doesn't think much of it, I am afraid. Would like me to stick around home. But, I've got other ideas, even if it hurts. I've seen too many boys stay home and they're always just old Dick, or Bill. Go away and you're an expert. I can see his point though. He'd like me to be around home same as I'd like to be around home. I'd be nice and comfortable but not good for me in the long run. I'd be a single man, tied down like a married man with six kids and an $18 a week job.

Got a couple of pictures from home this week, the first in just about a year. Damn, but the folks look good. My mother is more beautiful than ever. Her hair is just pure white now. Dad is plump as ever. And my sister, Ann! Wow! She's going to be some gal. About 5'7", I guess, and slim and neat as a destroyer. Gosh, I almost feel cheated in not being able to see her in the flesh instead of in a picture. Such a change from the pigtails I last saw her wearing. Hope I am home for her 15th birthday on Dec. 1st. I've got to get acquainted with that young lady. Now she seems to be somebody I met a long time ago, just casually. So we're going skating together, hunting, fishing, to shows, and on walks, and next summer I think I'd like to take her for a little trip, camping on the way. I'd teach her to camp. I am taking two nice bedding rolls home, and show her the country. Ah yes, I can dream, can't I?

I hope your 26 points are enough to get you out when you wish to. Haven't heard you talk much about getting out, staying in, or what you're going to do. Seems as if you're always talking about somebody else or what you did on some bike ride, or giving me hell, that's always good for two pages. Boy, you're the only person who ever gives me the devil. My mother, dad, Mrs. Barnes are always soothing. You're telling me what a bum I am, and I am this and that. But enough of that. Let's hear just what your plans are besides buying clothes that cover as little as possible with the maximum of dignity.

Love,
Dick[11]

Dick's farewell to the 506th Parachute Infantry Regiment was bittersweet. The unit was his home for three years. The relationships he formed were of lasting importance. Although the days of living, marching, and eating with stout paratroopers were done, profound memories remained. In that respect, he was never far removed from his brothers in arms. But his moment for departure was at hand. Though unabashedly proud of his service, Winters had been deprived years of family memories as a result of the war. His little sister, Ann, had grown from a little girl into a young lady. The notion of lost time aggrieved him. He heartily welcomed the occasion to rectify the issue. As eager as he was to rekindle family ties, his waiting was not yet over.

Welsh has the answer for battling boredom:
Get drunk and then get in a fight.

21 Oct. 1945
Camp Pittsburgh, France

Dear DeEtta-

Two weeks ago I figured "well this is the end of letter writing for I am on my way." But I haven't gone as far as I'd hoped and I am so fed up with these insipid looking sad sacks around here with their cheap talk about combat that I just gotta talk to somebody.

I am located exactly the same spot I was last March with 2nd Bn. 506th. My job is 2nd Bn. Exec. Off. of the 290th Inf., 75th Inf. Div. A.P.O. 451, c/o P.M. N.Y. So far I've found out chiefly what a wonderful job they did in combat. Their first action was in the Ardennes, Xmas Day, 1944. Oh yes, I remember that day myself and the best wishes for a merry Xmas sent by all.

Two weeks almost I've been here and not a sign of moving out. Nobody seems to have moved for over two weeks now. Those strikers sure tied things up just fine. I'd hoped to do some hunting this year but the way it looks, I won't get home until Dec. and so I'll have to wait for another Nov. to roll around.

Boy, this waiting is killing me. Take a good run every day, always get up early in the A.M., but gee, I still feel like tearing things apart just to do something. You know a person must be careful nowadays and not maim people. For some reason nobody seems to understand such action.

> [...] My buddy, Lt. Welsh, and I have been palling around here and talking over our plans when we get home. He has the outlet of getting drunk to pass time. During one of these spells he told one of the jokers off the other night. Being a good friend I smoothed things over by sending Welsh off and explaining that the kid was just a bit "off," too many mortar shells and artillery shells. Just feeling the reaction since the war's been over. That fixed things up and has been a good joke between Welsh and myself.
>
> This cracking up at this stage is actual. Every once in awhile somebody loses a nut too many and they have been taken away. Usually they were the good men in combat that went all the way through doing a hell of a good job. I feel the reactions of combat affecting myself in many ways off and on, most people do, if they are capable of recognizing it and admit it.
>
> Well, it's fried chicken tonight and to miss a meal around here means but one thing—you'll have to live to the next meal on
>
> Love,
> Dick[12]

In October 1945, Dick transferred to the 75th Infantry Division's 290th Regiment at Camp Pittsburgh at Marseille. The massive base was a bustling mobilization center playing host to prisoners of war, replacements, and troops eagerly awaiting tickets home. The tent community was known as a "City Camp," one of many temporary installations named after American metropolitan areas to evoke a sense of home. At Camp Pittsburgh, however, Winters felt nothing but frustration. His anticipated journey to the United States was perpetually delayed. He was less than enthused with his new position in a standard infantry regiment. Few of his fellow officers were as fit or experienced. "What little contact I had with these officers was reserved for them telling me how the 75th Infantry Division had won the war," he groaned. He confessed to DeEtta on October 23, "[W]ith 108 points over here I am about as rare as a man in a Wave barracks."[13]

Men "cracking up" added to the unsettling nature of transition. Although many veterans had postwar plans and embraced fresh opportunities, others remained psychologically scarred and withdrawn. Two years after war's end, half the patients in Veterans Affairs hospitals possessed what is now defined as post-traumatic stress disorder. According to historian Thomas Childers, GI homecomings could be as troubled as they were celebratory. "With few psychiatrists to treat them and a cultural ethos that hardly encouraged open discussion of emotional problems," Childers claims, "many veterans simply suffered in private—often with devastating consequences for them and their families." Given this historical context, Winters's correspondence with DeEtta takes on increased importance. Unlike many in uniform, Winters *did* discuss his wartime experiences—both during the conflict and well beyond. Equally significant, his pen pal was "damn understanding." The letters were indeed a saving grace.[14]

For Winters, writing both during and after the war was undoubtedly therapeutic. Author Brad Graham suggests this process offered "inner peace" and opportunities for Winters to set the record straight. "But serenity means more than mere survival," Graham continues. "It is the ability to feel and function, to get on with living, even in darker times, even when challenged by the unexpected." Winter was, in fact, prepared to move on with life.[15]

1 Nov. 1945
Marseilles, France

Dear DeEtta-

Pull up the anchor! I've hit the staging area and hope to sail about the 5th and no later than the tenth. So by the time you get this I'll be on the high seas and from then on I'll be in the arms of the navy.

They gave me this battalion about a week or so ago when the C.O. was transferred because he didn't have enough points. It sure is funny watching these low point officers trying to make a boat.

Went through some new and interesting country on the way down here which took over two days by train. Not much rest on a trip like that for the French have a habit of stopping the train and walking off to see a friend or to have a drink. Besides keeping 1,150 G.I. monkeys from jumping off the train to kiss girls riding on the top of cars, you must watch the engineers, figure chow stops, etc. It certainly keeps a fellow from becoming despondent from thinking of going home.

This area is a sight—tents on top of a hill so hard that you must use iron stakes in order to pitch a tent. It's just like solid rock, in fact that's what it is, with a wind that suddenly picks a tent off 16 sleeping men to leave them at the mercy of the elements.

Took a jeep and ran into Marseilles this afternoon and spent a couple hours looking the town over. The port is mighty big and in fair shape but the Krauts sank a lot of boats and blasted a lot of piers and warehouses before leaving. As for the town—it's rough and tough and ugly, a typical port town.

Well, I'll say this is the last of this operation.

Nov. 2, 1945
Same place

Poop for today: I sail on the *Wooster Victory* and dock at Hampton Roads, Va. Supposed to sail about 4. Nov. and separate at Indiantown Gap.

Love,
Dick[16]

Unlike many previous operations in France, the liberation of Marseille in August 1944 was largely achieved by the French themselves. The Americans, initially assisting in a subsidiary role, soon boasted a growing influence in the seaside city. According to historian Hilary Footitt, "In Allied planning, Marseille had been positioned as the southern port urgently required for the delivery of men and supplies for the rest of the campaign." Like Cherbourg, Marseille was bound to be a major military port. There, Americans constructed one of the largest installations in Europe—the Continental Base Section. It was from this location Maj. Dick Winters departed France on November 4. The ship transporting him, SS *Wooster Victory*, was one of 500 such cargo ships used to ferry men and supplies in the latter stages of the war. The vessel was subsequently used to usher immigrants to the United States. Less than four weeks after his departure, Winters was officially separated from the Army at Fort Indiantown Gap, Pennsylvania. His parents picked him up within an hour of his homecoming telephone call.[17]

Returning to Lancaster seemed a dream. Dick intended to show his appreciation to his community and his nation. Always the civic-minded individual, he set forth to the local IRS office shortly after his arrival. Winters wished to pay his taxes. The tax official offered to waive the return, but Dick insisted. He contributed as an officer and now he planned to contribute as a civilian.[18]

26 Nov 1945
Lancaster, PA
Home!!

Dear DeEtta–

Arrived home Sat. night as Mr. R.D.W. Never had a chance to even read your letters that dated from 4 Oct. to 17 Oct. waiting for me, with neighbors and relatives keeping me occupied all day.

Perhaps by now you too have joined the ranks as a Pvc., with the rank of Miss. In one way I hope so, but I'd like to see you as a "Wavy Wave" before you change uniforms.

That picture you sent that was taken in Sept. with your summer uniform is nothing short of pin-up grade triple A.

Look, how about doing the S-3 (plans and training) work on this operation of arranging date, place, time, and atmosphere, so that I can introduce this stranger, Mr. Winters. So far my only plans are to go deer hunting for about 30 Nov. to Dec. 3, 4, 5. Outside of that, I am just visiting neighbors and friends of the family.

Till 22 Jan. I am on terminal leave and it'll be just about that long till I am out of uniform. Civilian clothes are rough and I am advised to wait until about 10 Jan. when some new ones are expected.

Things seem to be very nice back here. So clean, nice, everything's so nice. Lots of food, heat. Now that's something, heat. Everyplace you go, it's warm. All homes and rooms are heated. I'd almost forgotten how nice it was to be warm and comfortable in the wintertime.

Well, enough of this, I want to get this letter off pronto and go buy myself all the darn chocolate I can eat for a couple of weeks. This diet of milk, ice cream, and eggs is just wonderful.

Love,
Dick[19]

Dick never took indoor heating or a warm meal for granted again. He slowly transitioned back into life on South West End Avenue. As autumn grew colder, he recalled his experiences of a year earlier. In Belgium, he endured freezing temperatures with only a few layers of wool. Those days were past. On the eve of the one-year anniversary of the Battle of the Bulge, Dick penned a final letter to DeEtta.

From being a hero to being a heel.
CHISTMAS CARD

Dec. 15, 1945

"WITH ALL GOOD WISHES FOR CHRISTMAS AND THE NEW YEAR"

Don't forget your fair feathered friends on Xmas, especially your "Dickie Bird."

Received your letter after "farewell to arms," and was glad to know my feelings were in tune with yours. In fact today, (Fri.), I still feel like a heel, a dishrag, or in other words, limp, and just like a Wave teddy bear.

Thanks and goodbyes and all the other chit chat is just so much extra wasted time and effort when you know the party of the second part is in harmony with you on all feelings, be what they may.

Mother gave me hell for not bringing home a picture of us together. That's the first thing she asked me. A good scout, my mother.

Dad has this record of "People Will Say We're in Love." Reminds me of a couple I once knew, so there's that tricky smile on my lips and a wee bit of twinkle in my eye as I listen.

May you and all your family have a happy reunion on this Xmas. And if any number thereof want to know if you're O.K., just tell them you're my "Ace in the Hole."

Love,
Dick[20]

"The war changed me," Dick earnestly confessed. "I returned to the States bitter, a different man than the young man who had enlisted in the army in 1941. I was hardened when I returned. First impressions were more important than they had previously been." Coping with mental exhaustion, Dick formed different perspectives on life and society. He feared an emotional gulf between himself and family, who could not relate to the conditions of battle. Sharing memories could be difficult. There was little inclination to associate with men his age who did not serve. He harshly judged them for not stepping forward in times of national emergency.

All the while, Winters felt profound concern regarding his abilities to readapt to civilian life. One day when Dick was walking the streets of Lancaster, a boy passing by ran a stick across a picket fence, creating a *zip* sound reminiscent of a machine gun burst. "I picked myself up out of the gutter," Winters admitted. In his mind, Dick was still fighting the war. "This takes time and it's never easy," he concluded of his transition. "You live this every day."[21]

After some time to decompress, Winters eventually accepted the promised position of personnel manager at the Nixon Nitration Works in New Jersey. The job was not without its irritations, including the overseeing of layoffs and contending with Lewis Nixon's woes of alcoholism.

While waiting for his commuter train one day in 1948, Dick met the attractive Ethel Estoppey. He sheepishly asked for a date and, after considerable investigation on her part, she accepted. Within months the couple was married.

By 1951, the husband and wife were raising a son when the army called on Dick's services once more. Experienced officers were required for leadership roles in the escalating Korean War and, in January 1952, Winters reassumed the rank of major—this time with the reactivated 9th Infantry Division. After serving in a series of thankless positions, Winters applied to Ranger School at his old stomping grounds of Fort Benning. Although Dick was a decade older than most soldiers at his side, he had little difficulty in matching their pace or outwitting them. He appreciated a good challenge. Transferred to Fort Lawton, Washington, deployment to Korea seemed inevitable. To Dick's great surprise, however, he was offered an out that September. A superior attempted to convince the battle-tested major to remain, but to no avail. One war was enough.

In the ensuing years, Winters and family moved throughout New Jersey and Pennsylvania as the father worked various factory, laboratory, and agricultural jobs. In 1960, a home on Winters's bucolic farmland was completed. He at last had the peaceful retreat he long desired. Eight years later, he embarked on an entrepreneurial venture in which he sold Hershey food by-products to regional farmers as animal feed. The enterprise was lucrative and Winters eventually purchased a second house in Hershey. As he aged, Dick further contemplated his war experiences. In the process he cataloged a vast archive of military records and personal reminiscences pertaining to Easy Company. He actively did so at reunions, lectures, and via letter writing.

Dick's extensive collection and networking among World War II veterans fostered a friendship with historical writer Stephen Ambrose, who thereafter pledged to bring Easy Company's story to life as a compelling narrative. The 1992 non-fiction book *Band of Brothers* was the culmination of Ambrose's interviews with Winters and comrades. Dick traveled to West Point and a range of other institutions to share his tales of leadership. In a fortunate twist of fate, his storytelling reunited him with a dear old friend.[22]

Winters and DeEtta Almon met only once immediately following the war. They thereafter fell out of touch. In 1947, she attained her bachelor of science degree with honors in business administration from the University of Tennessee. She then gained supervisory roles at S. H. Kress and Montgomery Ward in Asheville before accepting a position at Miller-Motte College in Wilmington, North Carolina. DeEtta wedded army veteran Johnnie Spurgeon Robbins and the couple had two daughters. Johnnie passed away in 1995.[23]

The success of *Band of Brothers* reintroduced DeEtta to Dick's story. The book let forth a flood of wartime memories. She vowed to relocate her dutiful pen pal of fifty years prior. With the help of a daughter, she achieved her aim. They were reconnected via a heartfelt phone conversation in December 1995. DeEtta offered an upbeat conclusion to their lengthy chat. "Dick," she said, "I saved all the letters you sent me. I have them here. Would you like them back?"[24]

"My God, yes," was the reply. "I'd like that." Winters recognized such materials as "the key to your memories and telling your story."[25]

Upon receipt of the decades-old correspondence, Dick and Ethel embarked on a mission of reading, transcribing, and photocopying the pages of his past. Reproduced volumes with notations were assembled. Winters described his association with DeEtta as "platonic" and had no reservations in freely discussing the relationship with Ethel. The Winterses ventured to Wilmington in May 1996 to gift DeEtta copies of the letters for her birthday. One can only imagine the joy they felt in meeting each other once more. The pen pals revived their association and actively maintained it until her passing on February 20, 2001, at age eighty-eight. She was a true friend.[26]

DeEtta did not live to see the global prestige her old swain received as a result of HBO's *Band of Brothers*. The miniseries, in which Winters is the spine of the script, hurled Dick into the international spotlight. He served as a special guest at the Emmys, was heralded by President George W. Bush, nominated for the Medal of Honor, and coauthored his memoirs. Fan mail deluged his home. He did his utmost to respond to all the warm gestures but eventually changed his phone number and used a post office box. Dick was honored and overwhelmed by reaction to the film. By the time he was bestowed an honorary doctorate from his alma mater at Franklin & Marshall College in 2009, Winters was out of steam. The officer, once so vigorously fit, was now in his nineties and physically failing. He receded further from public life and soon moved into a senior home near Hershey. There, on January 2, 2011, Dick Winters passed away. He was three weeks shy of his ninety-third birthday.

On the following March 19, hundreds of guests poured into the stately Hershey Theatre for a televised memorial service. Outside, *Band of Brothers* producer Tom Hanks was greeted by media. "That visage," Hanks recalled of Winters's iron gaze, "could pierce a tank. He was a complicated, magnificent human being." Inside, the major was eulogized by those closest to him, including Bob Hoffman—one of Dick's dearest friends. For as notable as Winters's wartime exploits were, Hoffman believes Dick's greatest contribution was to be a catalyst for changing perceptions of the American veteran. In the post-9/11 age, Winters symbolized the dignified brand of leadership newer generations sought and simulated. There was no finer tribute.[27]

In his twilight years, Dick was asked by an interviewer to offer advice to young Americans. His emotions swelled.

"I have one message to all," he reflected. "Hang tough."

"Do your best every day," Dick urged. "You don't have to know all the answers. No way. Don't expect that of yourself. Just do your best. Satisfy yourself so at the end of the day, you can look in the mirror after you've brushed your teeth, and say honestly to yourself, *Today I did my best.* If you do that...everything is going to be okay." His parting words remain abiding lessons from a life well-lived.[28]

BIBLIOGRAPHY OF HISTORIES AND MEMOIRS

Information pertaining to primary sources including letters, military documents, newspaper articles, and interviews can be found in the Endnotes.

Alexander, Larry. *Biggest Brother: The Life of Major Dick Winters, the Man Who Led the Band of Brothers*. New York: Berkley Caliber, 2005.

——. *In the Footsteps of the Band of Brothers: A Return to Easy Company's Battlefields with Sergeant Forrest Guth*. New York: Berkley Caliber, 2010.

Ambrose, Stephen E. *Band of Brothers: E Company, 506th Regiment, 101st Airborne from Normandy to Hitler's Eagle's Nest*. New York: Simon & Schuster, 2002.

Antal, John. *Hell's Highway: The True Story of the 101st Airborne Division during Operation Market Garden, September 17–25, 1944*. Minneapolis: Zenith Press, 2008.

Atkinson, Rick. *The Guns at Last Light: The War in Western Europe, 1944–1945*. New York: Henry Holt, 2013.

Bando, Mark. *Avenging Eagles: Forbidden Tales of the 101st Airborne Division in World War 2*. Mark Brando Publishing, 2006.

——. *101st Airborne: The Screaming Eagles in World War II*. Beverly, MA: Voyageur Press, 2011.

Berry, Jerald W. and Richard Blackburn. *In the Company of Heroes: The Memoirs of Captain Richard M. Blackburn Company A, 1st Battalion, 121st Infantry Regiment—WWII*. Bloomington: Xlibris Corporation, 2013.

Birdwell, Michael E. *Celluloid Soldiers: Warner Bros.'s Campaign Against Nazism*. New York: New York University Press, 2000.

Boroughs, Zig. *The 508th Connection*. Bloomington: Xlibris Corporation, 2013.

Brotherton, Marcus. *A Company of Heroes: Personal Memories about the Real Band of Brothers and the Legacy They Left Us*. New York: Berkley Caliber, 2011.

——. *Shifty's War: The Authorized Biography of Sergeant Darrell "Shifty" Powers, the Legendary Sharpshooter from the Band of Brothers*. New York: Berkley Caliber, 2012.

——. *We Who Are Alive and Remain: Untold Stories from the Band of Brothers*. New York: Penguin Press, 2009.

Brubaker, Jack. *Remembering Lancaster County: Stories from Pennsylvania Dutch Country*. Charleston: The History Press, 2011 [Google Books].

Burgett, Donald R. *Currahee! A Young Paratrooper's Terrifying Eyewitness Account of the Normandy Invasion in WWII*. New York: Ballantine Books, 1967.

——. *Seven Roads to Hell: A Screaming Eagle at Bastogne*. Novato, CA: Presidio Press, 1999.

Chapman, Reid and Deborah Miles. *Asheville and Western North Carolina in World War II*. Charleston: Arcadia Publishing, 2006.

Childers, Thomas. *Soldier from the War Returning: The Greatest Generation's Troubled Homecoming from World War II*. New York: Mariner Books, 2009.

Clark, James. R. *American Soldier at 13 Years Old: WWII*. Bloomington, IN: Trafford Publishing, 2006.

Collins, W. L. George. *Into Fields of Fire: The Story of the 438th Troop Carrier Group during World War II*. Bloomington, IN: Xlibris Corporation, 2004.

Compton, Lynn "Buck" and Marcus Brotherton. *Call of Duty: My Life Before, During, and After the Band of Brothers*. New York: Berkley Caliber, 2008.

Congdon, Don. *Combat: European Theatre, World War II*. Auckland, New Zealand: Pickle Partners Publishing, 2016.

Conn, Stetson, Rose C. Engelman, and Byron Fairchild. *Guarding the United States and Its Outposts*. Washington, DC: US Government Printing Office, 1964.

Cooke, Alistair. *The American Home Front, 1941–1942*. New York: Grove/Atlantic, 2007.

Davis, Anita Price. *North Carolina and World War II: A Documentary Portrait*. Jefferson, NC: McFarland, 2014.

——, and James M. Walker. *Spartanburg County in World War II*. Charleston: Arcadia Publishing, 2004.

Dedijer, Stevan. *My Life of Curiosity and Insights: A Chronicle of the 20th Century*. Lund, Sweden: Nordic Academic Press, 2010.

Dehays, Antonin. *Sainte-Mère-Église: An American Sanctuary—1944–1948*. Bayeux, France: Orep Editions, 2015.

DePastino, Todd. *Bill Mauldin: A Life up Front*. New York: W. W. Norton, 2008.

Deschodt, Christophe, and Laurent Rouger. *D-Day Paratroopers: The Americans*. Paris: Histoire & Collections, 2004.

de Trez, Michel. *At the Point of No Return: A Pictorial History of the American Paratroopers in the Invasion of Normandy*. D-Day Publishing, 2008.

———. *Orange Is the Color of the Day: A Pictorial History of the American Airborne Forces in the Invasion of Holland*. D-Day Publishing, 2008.

Einhorn, Dalton. *From Toccoa to the Eagle's Nest: Discoveries in the Bootsteps of the Band of Brothers*. Charleston, SC: BookSurge Publishing, 2009.

Eisenhower, Dwight D. *Crusade in Europe*. Baltimore: Johns Hopkins University Press, 1997.

Footitt, Hilary. *War and Liberation in France: Living with the Liberators*. New York: Springer, 2004.

Fussell, Paul. *Wartime: Understanding and Behavior in the Second World War*. New York: Oxford University Press, 1989.

Gardner, Ian. *Airborne: The Combat Story of Ed Shames of Easy Company*. Oxford, UK: Osprey Publishing, 2015.

———. *Deliver Us from Darkness: The Untold Story of Third Battalion, 506th Parachute Infantry Regiment during Market Garden*. Oxford, UK: Osprey Publishing, 2012.

———. *No Victory in Valhalla: The Untold Story of Third Battalion, 506th Parachute Infantry Regiment from Bastogne to Berchtesgaden*. Oxford, UK: Osprey Publishing, 2014.

———. *Sent by the Iron Sky: The Legacy of an American Parachute Battalion in World War II*. Oxford, UK: Osprey Publishing, 2019.

———. *Tonight We Die as Men: The Untold Story of Third Battalion, 506th Parachute Infantry Regiment from Toccoa to D-Day*. Oxford, UK: Osprey Publishing, 2009.

Guarnere, William and Edward Heffron. *Brothers in Battle, Best of Friends*. New York: Penguin Press, 2008.

Guptill Manning, Molly. *When Books Went to War: The Stories that Helped Us Win World War II*. Boston: Mariner Books, 2014.

Hambucken, Denis. *American Soldier of World War II: A Visual Reference*. Woodstock, VT: The Countryman Press, 2013.

Jolivet, Caroline. *A French GI at Omaha Beach*. Barnsley, UK: Pen and Sword Military, 2018.

Junger, Sebastian. *Tribe: On Homecoming and Belonging*. New York: Twelve, 2016.

Kay, Alan F. *Militarist, Millionaire, Peacenik: Memoir of a Serial Entrepreneur*. New York: Cosimo, Inc., 2008.

Kennedy, David M. *The American People in World War II*. Oxford, UK: Oxford University Press, 1999.

Kennett, Lee. *G.I.: The American Soldier in World War II*. Norman, OK: University of Oklahoma Press, 1997.

Kingseed, Cole C. *Conversations with Major Dick Winters: Life Lessons from the Commander of the Band of Brothers*. New York: Berkley Caliber, 2014.

Klokner, James B. *Individual Gear and Personal Items of the GI in Europe—1942–1945: From Pro-Kits to Pin-Ups!* Atglen, PA: Schiffer Military History, 2005.

Koskimaki, George. *Hell's Highway: A Chronicle of the 101st Airborne Division in the Holland Campaign, September–November 1944*. Philadelphia: Casemate Publishers, 2013.

Lancaster High School. *The Vidette* (Yearbook). Lancaster, PA: June 1937.

Lewis, Brenda Ralph. *Women at War: The Women of World War II—At Home, at work, on the Front Line*. Pleasantville, NY: Reader's Digest, 2002.

Lewis, Jon E. *Voices from D-Day: Eyewitness Accounts from the Battle for Normandy*. New York: MJF Books, 2014.

Leone, Tim. *The Hershey Bears: Sweet Seasons*. Charleston, SC: Arcadia Publishing, 2003.

MacKenzie, Fred. *The Men of Bastogne*. New York: David McKay Company, Inc., 1968.

Maddox, Robert James. *Hiroshima in History: The Myths of Revisionism*. Columbia, MO: University of Missouri Press, 2007.

Magellas, James. *All the Way to Berlin: A Paratrooper at War in Europe*. New York: Ballantine Books, 2003.

Malarkey, Don and Bob Welch. *Easy Company Soldier: The Legendary Battles of a Sergeant from World War II's "Band of Brothers."* New York: St. Martin's Publishing Group, 2008.

Mauldin, Bill. *The Brass Ring: A Sort of Memoir*. New York: W. W. Norton, 1972.

McManus, John C. *The Americans at D-Day: The American Experience at the Normandy Invasion*. New York: Forge, 2005.

———. *American Courage, American Carnage: 7th Infantry Chronicles: The 7th Infantry Regiment's Combat Experience, 1812 through World War II*. New York: Forge Books, 2009.

———. *September Hope: The American Side of a Bridge Too Far.* New York: Berkley Caliber, 2012.

McNab, Chris. *Pearl Harbor to Tokyo Bay: Pacific War Combat Missions—First-hand Accounts of Air, Land, and Sea Operations.* New York: Metro Books, 2016.

Morgan, Martin K. A. *Down to Earth: The 507th Parachute Infantry Regiment in Normandy.* Atglen, PA: Schiffer Publishing, 2004.

Shirley, Craig. *December 1941: 31 Days that Changed America and Saved the World.* Nashville: Thomas Nelson, 2011.

Nordyke, Phil. *Four Stars of Valor: The Combat History of the 505th Parachute Infantry Regiment in World War II.* Beverly, MA: Voyageur Press, 2010.

Northern Neck Chapter of the Military Officers Association of America. *Recollections: World War II Memoirs of Twenty-Eight Who Served.* Bloomington, IN: Xlibris Corporation, 2008.

Powers, Jake. *Easy Company: The 506th Parachute Infantry Regiment in Photographs.* Guildford, UK: Genesis Publications, 2008.

Pyle, Ernie and David Nichols. *Ernie's War: The Best of Ernie Pyle's World War II Dispatches.* New York: Simon & Schuster, 1987.

Rapport, Leonard and Arthur Northwood, Jr. *Rendezvous With Destiny: A History of the 101st Airborne Division.* Auckland, New Zealand: Pickle Partners Publishing, 2015.

Richman, Irwin. *The Pennsylvania Dutch Country.* Charleston, SC: Arcadia Publishing, 2004.

Reid, John. *Movies Magnificent: 150 Must-See Cinema Classics—Volume 11 of Hollywood Classics.* Morrisville, NC: Lulu Publishing, 2005.

Ryan, James Gilbert and Leonard C. Schlup. *Historical Dictionary of the 1940s.* New York: M. E. Sharpe, 2006.

Saunders, Tim. *Hell's Highway: US 101st Airborne & Guards Armoured Division.* South Yorkshire, UK: Pen & Sword Books, 2001.

Schrijvers, Peter. *Those Who Hold Bastogne: The True Story of the Soldiers and Civilians who Fought in the Biggest Battle of the Bulge.* New Haven, CT: Yale University Press, 2014.

Sheeran, James J. *No Surrender: A World War II Memoir.* New York: Berkley Caliber, 2011.

Sledge, Eugene B. *With the Old Breed: At Peleliu and Okinawa.* New York: Ballantine Books, 2007.

Sparrow, James T. *Warfare State: World War II Americans and the Age of Big Government*. Oxford, UK: Oxford University Press, 2011.

Speranza, Vincent J. *Nuts! A 101st Airborne Division Machine Gunner at Bastogne*. Atlanta: Deeds Publishing, 2014.

Stelpflug, Peggy A. and Richard Hyatt. *Home of the Infantry: The History of Fort Benning*. Atlanta: Mercer University Press, 2007.

Tollison, Courtney L. *World War II and Upcountry South Carolina: We Just Did Everything We Could*. Charleston: The History Press, 2009.

Trollinger, Susan L. *Selling the Amish: The Tourism of Nostalgia*. Baltimore: Johns Hopkins University Press, 2012.

Turkel, Studs. *The Good War: An Oral History of World War II*. New York: MJF Books, 1984.

Webster, David Kenyon. *Parachute Infantry: An American Paratrooper's Memoir of D-Day and the Fall of the Third Reich*. New York: Bantam Dell, 2002.

Weintraub, Stanley. *11 Days in December: Christmas at the Bulge, 1944*. New York: Free Press, 2006.

Whidden, Guy C., Julia Ann Whidden, and K. Bradley Whidden. *Between the Lines and Beyond: Letters of a 101st Airborne Paratrooper*. Self-published, 2009.

Willbanks, James H. *Generals of the Army: Marshall, MacArthur, Eisenhower, Arnold, Bradley*. Lexington, KY: University Press of Kentucky, 2013.

Willis, Jeffrey R. *Spartanburg, South Carolina*. Charleston, SC: Arcadia Publishing, 1999.

Willmott, H. P., Charles Messenger, and Robin Cross. *World War II*. New York: Dorling Kindersley, 2009.

Wilson, Stephen L. *Advising Chiang's Army: An American Soldier's World War II Experience in China*. Minneapolis: Hillcrest Publishing Group, 2016.

Winters, Richard D. and Cole C. Kingseed. *Beyond Band of Brothers: The War Memoirs of Major Dick Winters*. New York: Berkley Caliber, 2006.

United States Army. *A Camera Trip through Camp Croft, Spartanburg, South Carolina: A Picture Book of the Camp and Its Activities*. Spartanburg: United States Army, 1943.

Yellin, Emily. *Our Mothers' War: American Women at Home and at the Front during World War II*. New York: Simon and Schuster, 2010.

PHOTO COLLECTIONS AND CREDITS

Unless otherwise noted, all historical photos are from the Major Dick Winters Collection at the Gettysburg Museum of History. Every effort has been undertaken to credit original photographers where possible. Artifact photos were taken by Dan Jenkins.

ENDNOTES

A Note from the Editors

Sources marked GMOH denote items from the collections of the Gettysburg Museum of History, typically correspondence featured in the bound volume entitled Letters to DeEtta.

1 Liesl Bradner, "*Band of Brothers* Actors Are a Successful, Tight Unit," *Los Angeles Times*, September 8, 2011.
2 Ibid.
3 Andrew Collins interview with Jared Frederick, January 3, 2020.
4 Alexander, *Biggest Brother*, 282.
5 Graham, 284.
6 Bradford Freeman quoted in AP news report by John Leicester and Raf Casert entitled, "Chasing Demons: 75 Years on, D-Day Haunts, Drives Its Vets," June 3, 2019, as provided by WJLA ABC 7 News, www.wjla.com.

Introduction to the Letters

1 Dick Winters introduction in *Letters to DeEtta*, excerpts hereafter labeled as "Winters Letters," GMOH.

Chapter One

1 Winters quote on social awkwardness from Winters to Almon, Winters Letters, June 5, 1945, GMOH; Winters and Kingseed, 5.
2 Winters and Kingseed, 6; Richman, 50.
3 Kingseed, 101.
4 *The Vidette*, 46; Alexander, *Biggest Brother*, 26; Winters and Kingseed, 6.
5 Alexander, *Biggest Brother*, 26–27.
6 Winters and Kingseed, 6–7; Alexander, *Biggest Brother*, 28–29.
7 Richard D. Winters Draft Card, National Archives and Records Administration. Electronic Army Serial Number Merged File, 1938–1946 [Archival Database]; ARC: 1263923. World War II Army Enlistment Records; Records of the National Archives and Records Administration, Record Group 64; National Archives at College Park. College Park, Maryland; Alexander, *Biggest Brother*, 29.
8 Winters and Kingseed, 6–7.
9 1940 Census: Lancaster, Lancaster, Pennsylvania; Roll: m-t0627-03530; Page: 7A; Enumeration District: 36–57; National Archives and Records Administration. Electronic Army Serial Number Merged File, 1938–1946 [Archival Database]; ARC: 1263923. World War II Army

Enlistment Records; Records of the National Archives and Records Administration, Record Group 64; National Archives at College Park. College Park, Maryland.

10 1940 Census; Census Place: Asheville, Buncombe, North Carolina; Roll: m-t0627-02878; Page: 9A; Enumeration District: 11-31; Alexander, *Biggest Brother*, 30–31.

11 Winters to Almon, Winters Letters, November 27, 1941, GMOH.

12 Alexander, *Biggest Brother*, 31.

13 Davis and Walker, 115–122.

14 Tollison, Information on Camp Croft gathered from the chapters "The Totality of War" and "The Army in the Upcountry" in the digital version of *World War II and Upcountry South Carolina.*

15 Winters to Almon, Winters Letters, December 2, 1941, GMOH.

16 "Caskeys Plan 64th Wedding Anniversary." *Asheville Citizen-Times*, Asheville, NC. September 15, 1955, p. 22; Alexander, *Biggest Brother*, 32.

17 Winters to Almon, Winters Letters, December 9, 1941, GMOH.

18 "Reports Presented at Defense Club Meeting," *Asheville Citizen-Times*, December 9, 1941, p. 19.

19 Winters and Kingseed, 7–8; Alexander, *Biggest Brother*, 31–32.

20 Willis, 124–126; Jolivet, Chapter 2 [digital version]; Davis, 41–42.

21 Winters to Almon, Winters Letters, December 16, 1941, GMOH.

22 Winters to Almon, Winters Letters, December 18, 1941, GMOH.

23 An excellent summation of charge-of-quarters duties can be found in Eugene J. Small's account found in *Recollections*, written by the Northern Neck Chapter of the Military Officers Association of America, 112–113.

24 Winters to Almon, Winters Letters, December 21, 1941, GMOH.

25 Winters to Almon, Winters Letters, December 22, 1941, GMOH.

26 Clark, 52–55.

27 Winters to Almon, Winters Letters, December 22, 1941, GMOH.

28 Winters to Almon, Winters Letters, December 24, 1941, GMOH.

29 Nelson, 447–452.

30 Winters to Almon, Winters Letters, December 28, 1941, GMOH.

31 Kingseed, 83–87.

32 Kennett, 78. Kennett offers a detailed description of antipathy toward draft dodgers.

33 Kingseed, 128.

Chapter Two

1 Winters to Almon, Winters Letters, January 6, 1942, GMOH.

2 Birdwell, 129.

3 Winters to Almon, Winters Letters, January 7, 1942, GMOH.

4 Berry, 114–115.

5 Berry, 114–115; Kingseed, 55.

6 Boroughs, 9.

7 Winters to Almon, Winters Letters, January 10, 1942, GMOH.

8 Winters to Almon, Winters Letters, January 13, 1942, GMOH.

9 Leone, 11.

10 *A Camera Trip through Camp Croft*, 2.

11 Blackburn and Berry, 128–129.

12 Ibid.

13 Winters to Almon, Winters Letters, January 22, 1942, GMOH.

14 Stelpflug and Hyatt, 139–140.
15 Winters to Almon, Winters Letters, February 10, 1942, GMOH.
16 Trollinger, 26–27.
17 Brubaker, digital version of Chapter 5: Lancaster at War.
18 Winters to Almon, Winters Letters, March 2, 1942, GMOH.
19 Kingseed, 200.
20 Winters to Almon, Winters Letters, March 8, 1942, GMOH.
21 Dedijer, 125.
22 Hambucken, 40–41.
23 Winters to Almon, Winters Letters, March 29, 1942, GMOH.
24 Willbanks, 186; Wilson, 12.
25 Winters to Almon, Winters Letters, April 8, 1943, GMOH.
26 Winters and Kingseed, 11–13.
27 Franklin D. Roosevelt Library & Museum Collection: Grace Tully Archive, Series: Grace Tully Papers Box 7; Folder—Logs of the President's Trips: Inspection Tour, April 13–29, 1943, p. 8–10.
28 Winters and Kingseed, 12.
29 Winters to Almon, Winters Letters, May 10, 1942, GMOH.
30 Whidden, 75, 136.
31 Malarkey and Welch, 33–34; Winters to Almon, Winters Letters, May 24, 1943, GMOH.
32 Winters to Almon, Winters Letters, May 31, 1942, GMOH.
33 Capt. Charles Askins Jr., "Sports Afield," *El Paso Herald Post*, January 1, 1942, p. 14.
34 Winters and Kingseed, 12.
35 Winters to Almon, Winters Letters, June 23, 1943, GMOH.
36 "Tresta Trenta Dies, Plant Manager," *Lancaster New Era*, February 21, 1985, p. 11.
37 Winters to Almon, Winters Letters, June 30, 1942, GMOH.
38 Winters and Kingseed, 12–14.
39 Winters to Almon, Winters Letters, August 31, 1942, GMOH.
40 Gardner, *Sent by the Iron Sky*, 14.
41 Guarnere and Heffron, 15–18.
42 Winters to Almon, Winters Letters, September 24, 1942, GMOH.
43 "Hit the Silk!" *Sunday News* (Lancaster, PA), October 4, 1942, p. 11, 19.
44 Ambrose, 19.
45 Gardner, *Sent by the Iron Sky*, 18; Brotherton, *A Company of Heroes*, 154.
46 Winters to Almon, Winters Letters, December 16, 1942, GMOH.
47 Gardner, *Sent by the Iron Sky*, 18, 53–54.
48 Winters to Almon, Winters Letters, January 15, 1943, GMOH.

Chapter Three

1 Winters to Almon, Winters Letters, February 7, 1943, GMOH.
2 Gardner, *Airborne*, 24.
3 Alexander, *In the Footsteps of the Band of Brothers*, 32–33.
4 Winters to Almon, Winters Letters, March 28, 1943, GMOH.
5 Winters to Almon, Winters Letters, April 15, 1943, GMOH.
6 Winters and Kingseed, 27.
7 Pyle and Nichols, 194; Hanson W. Baldwin, "Our Army Leadership: Elimination of Unfit Is Held to Be Necessary Before Invasion of Europe," *New York Times*, March 20, 1944, p. 6.

8 Winters to Almon, Winters Letters, July 3, 1943, GMOH.
9 Winters to Almon, Winters Letters, August 2, 1943, GMOH.
10 Webster, 1–2.
11 Burgett, *Currahee*, 62, 72.
12 Alexander, *Biggest Brother*, 55.
13 Ibid, 58–59.
14 Winters to Almon, Winters Letters, December 11, 1943, GMOH.
15 Alexander, *Biggest Brother*, 58–59.
16 Winters to Almon, Winters Letters, February 10, 1944, GMOH.
17 "Cpl. Elmer R. (Sonny) Lovil Writes Parents from England," *Carthage Panola Watchman*, March 23, 1944, 1; Winters to Almon, Winters Letters, February 29, 1944, GMOH.
18 Allan M. Morrison, "Britain Goes about Its Business Calmly, Come Hell or Invasion," *Stars and Stripes*, May 16, 1944, p. 2
19 Winters, 52–53.
20 Malarkey and Welch, 74.
21 Winters to Almon, Winters Letters, March 20, 1944, GMOH.
22 Brenda Ralph Lewis, 15, 73.
23 Ibid.
24 Nordyke, 105; Mauldin, 198.
25 Winters to Almon, Winters Letters, April 14, 1944, GMOH.
26 "Churchill Visits U. S. Air-Borne Troops," *North Adams Transcript*, March 25, 1944, p. 1; Phillip H. Bucknell, "Churchill, Eisenhower Watch Sky Show by Airborne Yanks," *Stars and Stripes*, March 25, 1944, p. 1.
27 "Churchill Sees Major Test Near," *Lowell Sun*, March 25, 1944, p. 1.
28 DeWitt Mackenzie, "The War Today," *East Liverpool Review*, June 2, 1944, p. 1.
29 "General Says Losses Won't Be Heavy," *Zanesville Signal*, April 7, 1944, p. 2.
30 Ibid.
31 "Descriptive Letter from Emile Dumas," *Concord Enterprise*, March 2, 1944, p. 4.
32 Winters to Almon, Winters Letters, April 23, 1944, GMOH.
33 "Secret Is Kept Until D-Day By U. S. Soldiers," *Ogden Standard Examiner*, June 29, 1944, p. 3. "Shadow of D-Day," *Hanover Evening Sun*, April 15, 1944, p. 8. Republished from the *New York Times*.
34 Winters to Almon, Winters Letters, May 6, 1944, GMOH.
35 One can find a splendid overview of the ill-fated paratrooper landings in Sicily in the article entitled "Friendly Fire's Deadliest Day" by Robert F. Dorr at www.americainwwii.com.
36 Winters to Almon, Winters Letters, May 6, 1944, GMOH.
37 Ibid.
38 Winters to Almon, Winters Letters, May 16, 1944, GMOH.
39 Winters to Almon, Winters Letters, May 21, 1944, GMOH.
40 Marriage information on Ronald Speirs was found on www.ronaldspeirs.com.
41 "Invasion Preparation Fills Sky With Paratroopers," *Gettysburg Times*, May 10, 1944, p. 4.
42 "Eisenhower Inspects Air, Ground Units," *Bradford Era*, May 20, 1944, p. 12.
43 Jon E. Lewis, 19.
44 McManus, *The Americans at D-Day*, 57–59.
45 "The War Today," *Hanover Evening Sun*, April 26, 1944, p. 7; "What is D-Day," *Fitchburg Sentinel*, June 8, 1944, p. 6
46 Eisenhower, 246.

Chapter Four

1 Winters to Almon, Winters Letters, June 2, 1944, GMOH.
2 Ambrose, 63.
3 Descodt and Rouger, 42–43, 63–67.
4 Ambrose, 66–67.
5 Ibid, 64.
6 Compton and Brotherton, 11.
7 Gardner, *Sent by the Iron Sky*, 45.
8 Winters offered this commentary in the prologue of the *Band of Brothers* episode "Day of Days."
9 Ambrose, 66.
10 Ibid.
11 Sgt. Saul Levitt, "Airborne Action," *Yank*, August 18, 1944, p. 6; Collins, 78–79, 87–89.
12 "A Tribute to Maj. Dick Winters: Part V." Pennsylvania State Representative John D. Payne conducted hours of filmed interviews with Winters as part of a legislative report. These videos are available in five segments on the congressman's YouTube channel. Each episode is typically entitled, "A Tribute to Maj. Dick Winters…."
13 Winters, "D-Day Diary," June 22, 1944, GMOH. The authors have been unable to determine the identity of the soldier described as "Suarnen." No name as such is listed in the Easy Company roster immediately prior to D-Day. The GI—whose name might be spelled incorrectly in Winters's diary—may have been a combatant from another company or regiment.
14 Bando, *101st Airborne*, 50.
15 Alexander, *Biggest Brother*, 8.
16 Winters and Wynn are interviewed on this topic in the HBO documentary *We Stand Alone Together*.
17 Bando, 101st *Airborne*, 24.
18 Kingseed, 11–12.
19 "Rep. Payne's Legislative Report: A Reflection of Maj. Winters: Part II."
20 Winters to Almon, Winters Letters, August 6, 1944, GMOH.
21 Wes Gallagher, "Airborne Assaults Spread Confusion behind Nazi Lines," *Centralia Evening Sentinel*, June 7, 1944, p. 1.
22 Winters to Almon, Winters Letters, June 17, 1944, GMOH.
23 Gardner, *Sent by the Iron Sky*, 66–74.
24 Graham, 273.
25 Jack Foster, "Rough on Paratroopers at Carentan," *Stars and Stripes*, June 17, 1944, p. 2.
26 Winters to Almon, Winters Letters, June 23, 1944, GMOH.
27 "Wounded At Carentan, Commended For Bravery," *Lancaster New Era*, June 27, 1944, p. 12.
28 Winters to Almon, Winters Letters, July 2, 1944, GMOH.
29 Sgt. Dewitt Gilpin, "D-Day +365," *Yank*, July 6, 1945, 3–5.
30 Ibid.
31 Ibid.
32 Ibid.
33 Ralph Harwood, "Beyond the Beach Men Learn Fast," *Stars and Stripes*, June 22, 1944, p. 3.
34 Winters to Almon, Winters Letters, July 15, 1944, GMOH.
35 Webster, 57–59.
36 Winters to Almon, Winters Letters, July 27, 1944, GMOH.
37 Winters to Almon, Winters Letters, August 6, 1944, GMOH.
38 Robert Bunnelle, "Buzz Bombs Stir Blacker Hatred for Hitler, Nazis," *Lowell Sun*, July 8, 1944, p. 1.

39 Winters to Almon, Winters Letters, August 7, 1944, GMOH.
40 Winters to Almon, Winters Letters, September 29, 1945, GMOH.
41 Kingseed, 77–78.
42 Winters to Almon, Winters Letters, August 19, 1944, GMOH.
43 Ambrose, 102.
44 Don Whitehead, "Fight Around Carentan One Of Most Bitter in France," *Joplin Globe*, June 17, 1944, p. 1; John A. Moroso, III, "Changes Hands Four Times," *Joplin Globe*, June 17, 1944, p. 1.
45 Ibid.
46 Winters to Almon, Winters Letters, August 26, 1944, GMOH.
47 Winters and Kingseed, 112–115.
48 Ibid.
49 Winters prologue commentary from the *Band of Brothers* episode "The Breaking Point."

Chapter Five

1 Ambrose, 106; McManus, *September Hope*, 1–5.
2 McManus, *September Hope*, 1–5.
3 Winters and Kingseed, 117–123.
4 Ibid.
5 Winters to Almon, Winters Letters, September 10, 1944, GMOH.
6 Brotherton, *Shifty's War*, 2.
7 Winters Files, 1992, GMOH.
8 Ibid.
9 Koskimaki, *Hell's Highway*, Chapter 11 [digital version].
10 "Rep. Payne's Legislative Report: A Reflection of Maj. Winters: Part II."
11 Winters Files, Holland Papers, 12, GMOH.
12 Ibid.
13 Ibid.
14 Alexander, *In the Footsteps of the Band of Brothers*, 176.
15 Winters Files, Holland Papers, GMOH.
16 Ibid.
17 Ibid.
18 Ibid.
19 Ibid.
20 Ibid.
21 Winters After Action Report, October 17, 1944, GMOH.
22 Winters Files, Holland Papers, GMOH.
23 Ibid.
24 "A Tribute to Major Winters: Part III." Readers may find this segment of Rep. Payne's Winters video interview particularly moving and revealing.
25 Winters Files, Holland Papers, GMOH.
26 Winters and Kingseed, 147.
27 Winters Files, Holland Papers, 33, GMOH.
28 Heyliger to Winters, November 7, 1944, GMOH.
29 Winters Files, Holland Papers, 34, GMOH.
30 Ibid.
31 Winters Files, Holland Papers, 36, GMOH.
32 Winters to Almon, Winters Letters, November 14, 1944, GMOH.

33 Fussell, 48–50.
34 Webster, 172.
35 "The Old Sergeants' Corner," *Stars and Stripes*, June 8, 1944, p. 6; Winters's quote about "trinkets" is from the HBO documentary *We Stand Alone Together*.
36 Gardner, *Deliver Us from Darkness*, 223.
37 Fussell, 281–282.
38 "A Tribute to Maj. Dick Winters: Part IV."

Chapter Six

1 Winters to Almon, Winters Letters, December 13, 1944, GMOH.
2 Willmott, Messenger, and Cross, 233–235.
3 Weintraub, 42–45; Winters, "Bastogne 1944," Winters Files, GMOH.
4 Weintraub, 45–46.
5 "A Tribute to Major Winters: Part III."
6 Weintraub, 61–62.
7 Gardner, *No Victory in Valhalla*, 124–126; Weintraub, 96–100.
8 Speranza, 46.
9 MacKenzie, 175–177.
10 Gardner, *No Victory in Valhalla*, 126–129.
11 Weintraub, 135.
12 Winters to Almon, Winters Letters, January 6, 1945, GMOH.
13 Malarkey, 193–195; Winters's quote on wounds and death is from the HBO documentary *We Stand Alone Together*.
14 Winters and Kingseed, 167–170.
15 Ibid, 172.
16 Ibid, 178–179.
17 Ibid, 173–174; Winters's quote on the cold and conditions of Bastogne is from "A Tribute to Major Winters: Part III."
18 Willmott, Messenger, and Cross, 234; Schrijvers, 199–200.
19 Alexander, *Biggest Brother*, 152.
20 Ibid, 155; Gardner, *Sent by the Iron Sky*, 180.
21 Bando, *101st Airborne*, 169, 199.
22 Alexander, *Biggest Brother*, 157–159.
23 Willmott, Messenger, and Cross, 235.
24 101st Airborne Division Collection, GMOH.
25 "A Tribute to Major Winters: Part III."
26 Winters to Almon, Winters Letters, January 22, 1945, GMOH.
27 Winters and Kingseed, 173.
28 101st Airborne Division Files, February 1945 After Action Report, GMOH.
29 Winters to Almon, Winters Letters, February 15, 1945, GMOH; Winters to Almon, Winters Letters, February 21, 1945, GMOH.
30 Ambrose, 225–229; Webster, 196, 222.
31 Webster, 250.
32 Winters and Kingseed, 200.
33 Winters to Almon, Winters Letters, March 12, 1945, GMOH.
34 Rapport and Northwood, back matter under "Distinguished Unit Citations;" Burgett, *Seven Roads to Hell*, 223.
35 Winters to Almon, Winters Letters, March 24, 1945, GMOH.

36 Ambrose, 244–245.
37 Winters to Almon, Winters Letters, April 10, 1945, GMOH.
38 Kingseed, 203; Description of the Winters monument quoted from the PR Newswire article entitled, "Richard Winters Leadership Monument Dedication Date Announced," June 7, 2011, www.prnewswire.com.
39 Ambrose, 249–251.
40 Winters to Almon, Winters Letters, April 16, 1945, GMOH.
41 Winters and Kingseed, 213.
42 Winters to Almon, Winters Letters, April 20, 1945, GMOH.
43 Information on the Kaufering concentration camp was obtained via the website of the United States Holocaust Memorial Museum. Learn more by reading the article entitled, "Kaufering" at www.encyclopedia.ushmm.org.
44 "A Tribute to Maj. Dick Winters: Part IV;" Winters and Kingseed, 214–215.
45 Guarnere and Heffron, 203–204.
46 Webster, 376, 435–436.

Chapter Seven

1 Winters to Almon, Winters Letters, May 11, 1945, GMOH.
2 Malarkey and Welch, 212–213.
3 McManus, *American Courage, American Carnage,* 526–531.
4 Ambrose, 266.
5 "U.S. Flag Flies at Berchtesgaden," *New York Times,* May 7, 1945, p. 5; "A Tribute to Maj. Dick Winters: Part IV."
6 Winters to Almon, Winters Letters, May 16, 1945, GMOH.
7 Winters and Kingseed, 220.
8 Ibid.
9 Ibid, 234; Winters's quote on the pistol is featured in *We Stand Alone Together.*
10 Winters to Almon, Winters Letters, May 20, 1945, GMOH.
11 Winters to Almon, Winters Letters, July 2, 1945, GMOH.
12 Winters to Almon, Winters Letters, May 26, 1945, GMOH.
13 Winters and Kingseed, 32, 273.
14 Judge Advocate General Department. Board Review, Holdings Opinions and Reviews, volume 62, Washington, DC, 1946. Digitized on the Library of Congress database, www.loc.gov.
15 Winters to Almon, Winters Letters, May 29–30, 1945, GMOH.
16 Junger, 85, 77.
17 Winters to Almon, Winters Letters, June 2, 1945, GMOH.
18 Winters to Almon, Winters Letters, July 2, 1945, GMOH; additional information on Grace Hideko Umezawa Nixon was found on www.findagrave.com.
19 Winters to Almon, Winters Letters, June 5, 1945, GMOH.
20 Winters to Almon, Winters Letters, June 19, 1945, GMOH.
21 Winters to Almon, Winters Letters, June 27, 1945, GMOH.
22 Winters to Almon, Winters Letters, June 28, 1945, GMOH.
23 Winters to Almon, Winters Letters, June 30, 1945, GMOH.
24 Winters to Almon, Winters Letters, July 9, 1945, GMOH, Alexander, *Biggest Brother,* 212.
25 Winters and Kingseed, 237–239.

Chapter Eight

1 Winters to Almon, Winters Letters, July 3, 1945, GMOH.
2 Sledge, 266.
3 Winters to Almon, Winters Letters, August 8, 1945, GMOH.
4 Winters and Kingseed, 246–247.
5 Maddox, 19.
6 Winters to Almon, Winters Letters, August 11, 1945, GMOH.
7 Winters to Almon, Winters Letters, September 2, 1945, GMOH.
8 Winters to Almon, Winters Letters, September 16, 1945, GMOH.
9 Winters and Kingseed, 253, 290.
10 Winters to Almon, Winters Letters, September 26, 1945, GMOH.
11 Winters to Almon, Winters Letters, September 29, 1945, GMOH.
12 Winters to Almon, Winters Letters, October 21, 1945, GMOH.
13 Winters and Kingseed, 253; Winters to Almon, Winters Letters, October 23, 1945, GMOH.
14 Childers, 8–9, 86.
15 Graham, 286.
16 Winters to Almon, Winters Letters, November 1, 1945, GMOH.
17 Footitt, 104; Winters and Kingseed, 254.
18 Winters and Kingseed, 255.
19 Winters to Almon, Winters Letters, November 26, 1945, GMOH.
20 Winters to Almon, Winters Letters, December 15, 1945, GMOH.
21 Kingseed, 171; Alexander, *Biggest Brother,* 217; "A Tribute to Maj. Dick Winters: Part IV."
22 Alexander, *Biggest Brother,* 215–250.
23 "B.S. Degree Awarded to Miss DeEtta Almon," *Asheville Citizen-Times,* June 23, 1947, p. 7; "Annie DeEtta Almon Robbins," *Asheville Citizen-Times,* February 22, 2001, p. 14.
24 Alexander, *Biggest Brother,* 251.
25 Ibid; "A Tribute to Maj. Dick Winters: Part V."
26 Alexander, *Biggest Brother,* 251.
27 John Luciew, "Maj. Dick Winters Honored by Tom Hanks and Others at a Quiet, but Moving Public Memorial Service," *Harrisburg Patriot News,* March 20, 2011, www.pennlive.com; Colonel Cole Kingseed, "Major Dick Winters: Genuine Legend, Genuine Man," *America in WWII,* June 2011, p. 36–43.
28 "A Tribute to Maj. Dick Winters: Part V."

INDEX

I

J

K

L

M

N

O

P

R

W

Y

Z